DATE DUE

Toward
a New Society

TWAYNE'S
AMERICAN THOUGHT
AND CULTURE SERIES

Lewis Perry, General Editor

TOWARD A NEW SOCIETY

American Thought and Culture, 1800–1830

JEAN V. MATTHEWS

Twayne Publishers • Boston
A Division of G. K. Hall & Co.

The epigraph at the head of chapter two is from the translation
by George Lawrence of Alexis de Tocqueville, *Democracy in
America*, ed. J. P. Meyer and Max Lerner (New York: Harper
and Row, 1966), 270–71. The epigraph at the head of chapter 5
is from George Wilson Pierson's translation of "Quinze Jours au
Désert" in *Tocqueville in America* (Garden City, N.Y.: Doubleday,
1959), 191–92.

Copyediting supervised by Barbara Sutton.
Book design and production by Janet Z. Reynolds.
Typeset in 10/12 Janson by Compset, Inc., Beverly, Massachusetts.

First published 1990.
10 9 8 7 6 5 4 3 2 1 (hc)
10 9 8 7 6 5 4 3 2 1 (pb)

Library of Congress Cataloging-in-Publication Data

Matthews, Jean V., 1937–
Toward a new society : American thought and culture, 1800–1830 /
Jean V. Matthews.
p.   cm. — (Twayne's American thought and culture series)
Includes bibliographical references and index.
ISBN 0-8057-9052-7. — ISBN 0-8057-9057-8 (pb)
1. United States—Civilization—1783–1865. 2. United States—
Intellectual life—1783–1865. I. Title. II. Series.
E164.M38 1990
973.5—dc20   90-42715

Contents

FOREWORD
PREFACE
ACKNOWLEDGMENTS

v

Foreword

The American Thought and Culture Series surveys intellectual and cultural life in America from the sixteenth century to the present. The time is auspicious for such a broad survey because scholars have carried out so much pathbreaking work in this field in recent years. The volumes reflect that scholarship, as well as valuable earlier studies. The authors also present the results of their own research and offer original interpretations. The goal is to bring together books that are readable and well informed and that stand on their own as introductions to significant periods in American thought and culture. There is no attempt to establish a single interpretation of all of America's past; the diversity, conflict, and change that are features of the American experience would frustrate any such attempt. What the authors can do, however, is to explore issues of critical importance in each period and those of recurrent or lasting importance.

Today the culture and intellectual life of the United States are subjects of heated debate. While prominent figures summon citizens back to an endangered common culture, some critics dismiss the very idea of culture—let alone American culture—as elitist and arbitrary. The questions asked in these volumes have direct relevance to that debate, which concerns history but too often proceeds in ignorance of it. How did leading intellectuals view their relation to America, and how did their compatriots regard them? Did Americans believe that theirs was a distinctive culture? Did they participate in international movements? What were the links and tensions between high culture and popular culture? While discussing influential works, creative individuals, and major institutions, the books in this series place intellectual and cultural history in the larger context of American society.

The opening decades of the nineteenth century are less familiar than other periods of American intellectual history. They are easy to skip over as minds rush from exciting decades of revolution and nation building to the turbulence of Jacksonian politics, social reform, and sectional conflict. In this volume Jean Matthews shows just how much is missed in such a leap, for she demonstrates that a crucial transformation occurred in these decades. She gives careful attention to a wide range of topics in the history of science, religion, philosophy, medicine, law, art, and literature. But throughout she makes us aware of the breakdown of long-cherished attitudes toward nature, history, and political order. She traces the emergence of new outlooks on race and gender, specialized expertise and individual imagination, religious emotion, and sexual morality. The great changes that took place in so many fields of endeavor can be identified in different ways: from classicism to romanticism, from amateurism to professionalism, from republicanism to democracy. Their cumulative effect, however, was profound. Professor Matthews helps us to see why some people saw in these changes the demise of all the glories of the enlightened past and why others celebrated the dawn of a new era of human achievement.

LEWIS PERRY
Series Editor

Preface

From the perspective of intellectual and cultural history it has been tempting to regard the years between 1800 and 1830 as part of the fallow period between the *Federalist Papers* and Emerson. In the last fifteen years or so, however, the recovery and exploration of republicanism as an ideology, indeed as a worldview, has focused more historical attention on the early years of the nineteenth century. We can now see this as the crucial period when the republican mind-set crumbled under the impact of social change and was eventually overwhelmed by what later came to be called liberal individualism. At the same time, the secularism and rationalism of the Enlightenment was faltering before the triumphant resurgence of evangelical Christianity and burgeoning romantic ideas of selfhood and personality. In the realm of science, the fixed order of nature was giving way to a more dynamic model of growth and change. In literature the classic adherence to universal models of excellence was being challenged by romantic assertions of personal and national individuality and genius. Important and essentially antithetical systems of thought—republicanism versus liberalism, Enlightenment versus romanticism, secularism versus evangelical Christianity—shared the arena of American intellectual life, sometimes antagonistically and sometimes with curious accommodations. Both republicanism and liberalism could share the potent rhetoric of liberty, equality and virtue.

Because the nation was still so new, it was a period in which practically every activity carried the subtext of debate about the nature of the republic. The Revolution had been led by relatively young men; many of its leaders lived well into the nineteenth century and often reacted with bewilderment and sometimes profound disillusionment to the new world emerging from what they had wrought. People of the post-Revolutionary generation felt themselves in the rather uncomfortable situation of having to uphold the glorious republican framework to which they had fallen heirs and at the same time having to set the direction for the development of the nation's character within that framework. The last two chapters of this book concentrate on the 1820s, when there was a decided quickening of the pace of change together with a new cultural creativity. By the end of that decade, the United States had emerged into a recognizably modern liberal social and intellectual order. Yet the older republican paradigm remained as a substructure to American thinking, reemerging in various ways throughout the nineteenth and even into the twentieth centuries.

This period is conveniently bracketed by the presidencies of Jefferson and Jackson. It would be hard to think of two more dissimilar men than these two slave-holding representatives of democracy: Jefferson, the philosophe in office, the most interesting and elusive of America's presidents, and Jackson, the "Man on Horseback," the epitome of will rather than mind. Both have rightly been seen as representative of an era, and no one can miss the sense of overwhelming change as we move from the age of Jefferson to the age of Jackson. Yet Jacksonianism was implicit in Jeffersonianism; its attitudes toward government, expansion, and race followed the direction set at the beginning of the century.

If Americans of this period did not produce many classic works, they did think about serious problems—in particular, about the nature of the relationship between the health of the republic and the personal and social character of the individuals composing it, about the problem of racial differences and race relations, and about the sustenance of high culture in a democracy. Their thinking on these subjects was seldom original and sometimes pernicious, but the issues, and the terms in which they addressed them, have remained important to the present day.

Acknowledgments

I thank Lewis Perry, Steven Mintz, and Fred Matthews for their insightful readings and invaluable advice at various stages of this manuscript. I thank the University of Western Ontario for giving me the leave that enabled me to write and the following libraries for allowing me full access: the University of California at Berkeley, Stanford University, and San Francisco State University. My appreciation goes also to my Americanist colleagues at Western, particularly those associated with the Centre for American Studies and the *Canadian Review of American Studies*, whose conversation over the years has enriched my understanding of American culture: David Flaherty, Roger Hall, Robert Hohner, Geoffrey Rans, Ernest Redekop, Craig Simpson and Ian Steele.

Part One

The Republic

one

The Republic and the Problem of Virtue

Government is necessary to preserve the public peace, and protect the persons and property of individuals: but our social happiness must chiefly depend upon other causes; upon simplicity and purity of manners; upon the education that we give our children; upon a steady adherence to the customs and institutions of our ancestors; upon the general diffusion of knowledge, and the prevalence of piety and benevolent affections among the people.

—Massachusetts Governor Caleb Strong, 1806

"The history of our country is the history of liberty," declared the poet Joel Barlow in 1807. Yet, he added ominously, "In my opinion, the loss of liberty in this country is not an impossible event." Barlow spoke for many of his contemporaries in believing that the unique American experiment in republican government was fragile and might at any time be subverted. The first fifteen years of the nineteenth century were haunted by a nagging anxiety that the republic that had emerged from the struggles and sacrifices of the Revolution might not survive the unforeseen social and economic changes that revolution had unleashed.[1]

Between 1780 and 1820 the population grew from 2.8 million to 9.6 million, and in 1810 half the white males were under sixteen. People were on the move. Americans were pushing westward to take up new land at a rate unthought of before the Revolution. By 1821 nine new states contained a quarter of the entire American population. The great majority of migrants to the West were young, and many of them moved and then moved again.

3

With such a propensity to leave home, it is not surprising that by the 1820s Americans should have a flourishing popular culture of nostalgia, with such songs as Samuel Woodworth's "Old Oaken Bucket" ("How dear to this heart are the scenes of my childhood") and John Howard Payne's "Home Sweet Home" (written appropriately enough when the author was in Paris), which bequeathed an enduring cliché to the English language: "Be it ever so humble, there's no place like home."[2]

Although the United States remained overwhelmingly rural, it was a society increasingly penetrated by commerce. Cities were still quite small, but they were vital nuclei of trade and innovation. Between 1793 and about 1807 there was a surge of economic growth associated with a boom in foreign trade. The invention of the cotton gin created a dynamic new cash crop for the South, and cotton exports soared after 1800. Internal trade grew along with external as an expanding transport network, plus expanding means of credit, fueled the development of a market economy that drew in more and more of the population. On a small scale Americans were producing a great variety of manufactured goods, sometimes with important technical innovations. Eli Whitney, for example, was manufacturing rifles with interchangeable parts by 1800. Thousands of ordinary people were finding unprecedented opportunities to make money, buy consumer goods, and rise in the world. European visitors were struck by the restlessness, ambition for social mobility, and general spirit of enterprise that pervaded the new nation. Old ties to community and deference to established elites broke down as people felt their own power to move, to rise, and to assert their own judgment. As people from all social classes responded to the new opportunities for the individual "pursuit of happiness," they seemed to be creating a society that few had expected and many could not wholeheartedly endorse.[3]

Republicanism in a New Age

The problem was that this new society elicited patterns of behavior seemingly at odds with the republican ideology that had carried Americans through the Revolution. Republicanism was more than a form of government designed to secure liberty and political equality to its (male) citizens; it was a worldview entailing theories of economy, history, morals, and manners and a vocabulary with which to talk about and comprehend the meaning of economic and political life. Incorporating the experience of the classical republics of the ancient world, the political philosophy of Machiavelli, and the writings of the eighteenth-century English country opposition to the centralizing and modernizing policies of the British Crown, republicanism was compendious enough for different groups to find ideas that met their particular needs and for bitter political enemies to insist plausibly that they alone were its true defenders.

Most, however, shared the fundamental republican assumption of a crucial connection between the maintenance of republican liberty and the moral character of society, the virtue of the citizens. *Virtue* was a key term in the republican vocabulary; it meant essentially the willingness of citizens to subordinate their private desires and convenience to the public good. This public virtue in turn rested on certain private virtues: prudence, integrity, simplicity, moderation in life-style and expenditure, qualities most likely to be found among the middling and independent property-owning ranks of society. But virtue was always liable to be undermined by "corruption," which occurs when the human appetites of ambition and avarice escape restraint, and people pursue wealth, glory, personal ease, and gratification without regard for any greater good. Because the human appetite for self-aggrandizement was always in tension with a reasoned adherence to the public weal, the republic was always in peril, and never more so than when peace and prosperity brought increased wealth and a general relaxation of vigilance. As an interpretive mode, republicanism was always suspicious and anxious in the face of change.[4]

Americans did have other clusters of ideas and values available to them when thinking about liberty and the good society. The moral values associated with Protestant Christianity and the English common law association of liberty with the defense of individual property rights were both deeply rooted in American culture. Moreover, a newer ideology of liberalism had emerged in late eighteenth-century England from attempts to understand the developing world of international commerce and early industrialization. In the liberal model the market rather than the polity is the primary social system and the self-actualizing individual rather than the community of citizens the major actor. Liberal ideology assumed that there was no inherent antagonism between the individual drive for success and communal well-being. Setting free the creative energy of individuals would naturally produce a prosperous order in which all would benefit. Liberalism therefore was much more positive about open-ended change, growth, and expansion.

There has been a lively debate among historians about the extent to which liberalism displaced republicanism as the dominant American ideology by the early nineteenth century. Some historians see the Jeffersonian Republicans as they saw themselves: as bearers of republican values into the new century. Others have maintained that with the creation of the Constitution or at least by the 1790s, the dominant patterns of American thinking were closer to the liberalism of Adam Smith than to traditional republicanism. The historians' debate reflects the ideological confusion of the early republic itself in which individuals and groups moved in and out of different philosophical and explanatory modes as they adjusted to the dizzying speed of social change.[5]

Even while they grasped the new opportunities, Americans anxiously struggled to reconcile the republican values and ideology of the Revolutionary heritage with the new society and to devise ways to shore up republican virtue against the erosion of change. Three areas of change were particularly problematic in terms of the republican paradigm: the expansion of equality in the new republic, the expansion of the American people across space, and the expansion of the market economy.

The Problem of Equality

The extent to which the republican value of equality was transforming the political culture of the young republic became clear in the extraordinarily bitter election of 1800. Both the victorious Republicans and the defeated Federalists interpreted the result as a revolution. The Federalists denounced the Jeffersonians as Jacobins primed to translate all the excesses of the contemporary French Revolution to America. Jefferson saw his triumph as a revolution in the older meaning of that word—as a "return to first principles." He was convinced that the Federalists were bent on transforming the republic into a monarchy, supported, in corrupt British-style, by an oligarchy of wealthy magnates tied to the government through the cash nexus of the public debt. Emphasizing the egalitarian aspects of republican ideology, the Jeffersonian Republicans tapped a seething reservoir of localist fear of centralized power and popular resentment of entrenched privilege and aristocracy.[6]

The new regime determined to wrench the republic back to the basic principles of the Revolution. Jefferson's inaugural address called for "a wise and frugal government, which shall restrain men from injuring one another, which shall leave them otherwise free to regulate their own pursuits of industry and improvement, and which shall not take from the mouth of labor the bread it has earned." This seemingly classic statement of laissez-faire liberalism in fact stemmed from basic republican premises. Limited government maximized the independence of the autonomous self-reliant citizen and minimized opportunities for oppression and corruption. The new regime slashed military appropriations, drastically reduced the number of federal employees, repealed all internal taxes, and determined to pay off the national debt within eighteen years. To Jefferson the debt was always the epitome of corruption. "The principle of spending money to be paid by posterity, under the name of funding," he wrote in 1816, "is but swindling futurity on a large scale." That this was an overwhelmingly popular approach to government was shown by Jefferson's easy reelection in 1804 and the continued inability of the Federalists to regain power.[7]

Jefferson's victory also heralded a permanent transformation of political culture. In learning how to organize a party and to mobilize an electorate in the 1790s, the Republicans had unleashed the democratic potential of the

American political system. "Public opinion," the attitudes of the mass of voters rather than the judgments of small elites, assumed a new importance. Continued competition for votes transformed the rhetoric of politics. Expectations of a disinterested political discourse were rudely shattered as the language of reasoned argument seemed to be giving way to empty bombast and cynical cant. The Federalist Rufus King bitterly deplored the abuse of words in the new democratic rhetoric: "liberty, love of country, Federalism, Republicanism, Democracy, Jacobin, glory, Philosophy and Honor are words in the mouth of everyone," he wrote, "and without any precision used by any one."

The virulence of party conflict sundered communities, disrupted friendships, and even led to fisticuffs and duels. Parties had no legitimate place in traditional republicanism since they seemed to transform politics into mere cynical contests for power rather than disinterested action for the common good, and many older members of the political elite never became reconciled to their existence. But in the early 1800s party conflict stimulated popular interest and voter turnout to new highs. The intensity of popular interest in politics made the possession of the vote seem a natural right of white males, independent of traditional property qualifications. In the first decades of the nineteenth century, new states entered the Union with universal white male suffrage, and the older states steadily chipped away at voting restrictions.[8]

The whole tone of American life was being democratized in this period. As president, Jefferson deliberately reversed the previous administration's trend toward monarchical formality. He adopted a studied simplicity: walking to his inauguration, riding unattended about Washington, receiving foreign dignitaries in his slippers, and flouting protocol at official functions. All this was part of a conscious effort to fix a standard of manners at the nation's capital that would emphasize republican aversion to pomp and commitment to the equality of all citizens. "There is no 'Court of the U.S.' since the 4th of March 1801," he wrote in an anonymous newspaper article. "No precedence . . . of anyone over another, exists in right or practice, at dinners, assemblies, or any other occasions."[9]

The idea of "no precedence . . . of anyone over another" gets to the heart of what equality was to mean in nineteenth-century America. While some nervous conservatives continued to fear that a democratic electorate would use its power to equalize property, in fact ordinary Americans showed no interest in economic leveling. But they were increasingly demanding equality of esteem and refusing to accept anyone as their betters. Foreign visitors were struck by the egalitarian tone of American society, its belligerent disregard of conventional social distinctions, even a blithe oblivion to the idea that there might be any. Terms like *gentleman* and *lady* were becoming less socially precise and might be claimed by anyone. Although their wealth was not challenged, upper-class Americans felt their situation more precarious because the mass of the people no longer implicitly accepted their claims to superiority.[10]

The striking change in dress in the early nineteenth century is symbolic of the way in which formal distinctions between gentry and others were being minimized. The powdered wig of the upper classes had practically disappeared by 1800, and the long hair tied in a queue that replaced it was virtually gone by 1820. By the beginning of the century the knee breeches and silk stockings of the gentry were being replaced by the French revolutionary style of pantaloons, which increasingly became the style for men of all classes. Men's clothes were started on their career of progressive simplification and sobriety, which lasted to the 1960s. Women's dress followed a different pattern. After a marked turn toward a simplicity, indeed a skimpiness, which many moralists found sexually provocative, by the 1820s women's dress was swinging back toward an ever increasing elaboration and amplitude. While millions of Americans continued to wear homespun, the increasing availability of factory-made cloth helped to blur the distinction, in the towns at least, between the clothing of the gentry and other people.[11]

Equality was unfolding in ways the Revolutionary generation had not foreseen. They had assumed that the success of the republican experiment depended on the active leadership of the "best" people. Indeed, one way in which the people at large could demonstrate their virtue was to recognize superior excellence and then defer to it. Even Jefferson, who hated privileged orders, linked the success of republican government to the leadership of a "natural aristocracy" of superior talents as opposed to privileged birth or wealth. In 1813 Jefferson resumed his friendship with his old colleague and rival, John Adams. In a wide-ranging correspondence the two ex-presidents discussed the developments of their time and the problems of government. "May we not even say," Jefferson mused to Adams, "that that form of government is the best which provides the most effectually for a pure selection of these natural *aristoi* into the offices of government?" To many of the traditional leadership class, it seemed that this was exactly what the American system was failing to do.[12]

The old politics of deference were increasingly challenged, and the people could no longer be relied upon routinely to vote their betters into office or to defer to the leadership of the well educated. Gentry leaders felt themselves elbowed aside by a new breed of politicians, "new men," from obscure backgrounds who showed no intention of adopting gentry manners and culture. Unable to cope with the new democratic politics, many old Federalist leaders dropped out of public life altogether and cultivated an aristocratic disdain for the vulgar hurly-burly of politics. Others realized that they would have to court popular favor and study public opinion, but few mastered the new style. The fact that they tried, however, indicates how sweeping was the triumph of democratic modes and assumptions. Republicans naturally had more reason than Federalists to believe with the optimistic Jefferson that "in general" the people "will elect the really good and wise." Many Republicans openly accepted the label "Democrat," realizing that much of the electorate was coming to see democracy as respect for the rights of the people. Even some Republicans, however, were disturbed by what appeared to be a popular preference for mediocrity. "Our state legislature does not contain one individual of superior talents," complained the architect Benjamin Latrobe about Pennsylvania. "The fact is, that superior talents actually excite distrust."[13]

The committed Jeffersonian Hugh Henry Brackenridge expressed similar disillusionment. After graduating from the College of New Jersey, he set up his law office in the frontier town of Pittsburgh. Here he found himself embattled and isolated—a representative of cultural standards that the people mistrusted or ridiculed. After one term in the state legislature, he was voted out in favor of an uneducated weaver. His experiences and his ruminations on democracy are embodied in a long, rambling novel, *Modern Chivalry*. Its central figure, Captain Farrago, a modern Don Quixote, is a well-meaning gentleman of the old school endeavoring to maintain virtue on the frontier, but his efforts are continually undermined by the escapades of his Irish servant, Teague O'Regan. O'Regan is conspicuously lacking in virtue of any kind, but this does not prevent him from being elected to public office. The novel was written over several years—part 1 published in the 1790s, the whole book not until 1815—and the tone grows sharper as the book progresses. At one point a candidate for office is accused of having been seen with a book in his hand. "I am innocent of letters as the child unborn," Brackenridge has him exclaim. "I am free from the sin of learning, or any wicked art."[14]

The Problem of the West

The question of the compatibility of democracy and excellence seemed particularly sharp in the new western settlements. Reports of western squalor, ignorance, and violence—the rumored sport of eye gouging was particularly horrifying—deeply disturbed many eastern gentry and revived all the old colonial fears of relapse into savagery in the New World. Was civilization moving west, they wondered, or unraveling at the edges?

The president of Yale University, Timothy Dwight, expressed a typical conservative reaction to the constant dispersion of the American population. A dominant force in New England orthodox circles and fiercely anti-Jeffersonian, he was also a man still attached to many Enlightenment ideas, an innovative educator, and interested in science. As a young man he had been a poet and a leading member of the bright young group of writers known as the Hartford Wits, but his most effective writing is his four post-humously published volumes *Travels in New England and New York* (1821–22), covering his trips through the region in the Yale vacations between 1795 and 1816. These rambling surveys take in politics, agriculture, scenery, social conditions, and interesting local stories. Above all, they are a celebration of the civilization of New England, with its neat farmhouses and compact villages with their white steepled churches, a civilization based on stability and moderation. Communities of this kind needed time to grow and mature, and they needed their children to remain and sustain them. Rootedness enmeshed individuals in the bonds of community so that they were always aware of something outside and greater than themselves. Loosed from this discipline in the sparsely settled areas of the West, it was too easy for men to revert to savagery, especially since, Dwight was convinced, the frontier was peopled by the dropouts of "regular society," who were unwilling to pay the price of civilization in terms of laws and taxes.[15]

The Problem of Wealth

The aggressive egotism Dwight feared would be let loose on the frontier was also apparent closer to home as people scrambled to take advantage of new economic opportunities. Material prosperity was accompanied by a pervasive anxiety about the materialism of American society and the commercialization of values. Public speeches and private letters resound with denunciations of what seemed to be a national mania for money making, and particularly for getting rich through speculation. To many of the older generation especially, this was profoundly disillusioning. Speculation that produced quick fortunes without any corresponding service or real product devalued sober industry as a means to prosperity and divorced the economy from moral values. A republic dedicated to money making was surely not what the Revolution had been fought for.

Among the disillusioned was Benjamin Rush, Philadelphia's most famous medical man and a signer of the Declaration of Independence. Although a Jeffersonian in politics, he maintained a long correspondence of mutual lament with John Adams in which the two old gentlemen deplored the state of the country, the lack of public spirit, and the pervasiveness of money. "I sometimes wish I could erase my name from the Declaration of Independence," wrote Rush in one particularly bitter letter of 1803. He recalled an eighty-one-year-old patient, who "of course, . . . knew America in her youthful and innocent days," saying that Americans worshiped only one God, the "God Dollars." "Were I permitted to coin a word suggested by my patient's remark, I would say we were a 'bedollared nation.' In walking our streets I have often been struck with the principal subjects of conversation of our citizens. Seldom have I heard a dozen words of which '*Dollar, discount, and a good Spec*' did not compose a part. . . . Not only our streets but our parlors are constantly vocal with the language of a broker's office, and even at our convivial dinners 'Dollars' are a standing dish upon which all feed with rapacity and gluttony."[16]

No doubt there was a certain sour grapes in much of the gentry's denunciation of money grubbing—the disdain of those who had made it for the man on the make. But there was also a genuine concern that a reckless preoccupation with private gain could not lead to the public good. The southern lawyer William Wirt linked the passion "*to grow rich*," which he said was everywhere in Virginia, with that state's striking degree of public squalor. "Virginia exhibits no great public improvements"; in spite of its wealth, "roads and highways are frequently impassable, sometimes frightful." Preoccupied with private gain, Virginians were so niggardly in sparing money for public expenditures that they doled out miserably inadequate salaries to public officials and the professors at the College of William and Mary and would not undertake a public education system, "that best basis of the social and political equality which they profess to love."[17]

The relationship of republicanism to prosperity was complex. Sheer economic growth and the maximization of profits were not given values to be pursued for their own sake without considerations of moral and social repercussions, and "luxury" and "avarice" were assumed to be the great enemies of virtue. At the same time, liberty certainly had an economic component. A republic was supposed to ensure the well-being of the masses of the people, secure the rights of property, and prevent the wealth of the nation from being engrossed by a few, as in the corrupt Old World. From the 1790s on the cornucopia was a recurring motif in republican iconography, connecting the republic with the enjoyment of plenty. Benjamin Franklin, in his Poor Richard maxims and his own life, had offered an ethic of individual striving and wealth seeking that was still tied to considerations of moderation, social utility, and civic responsibility. Yet this was a precarious balance. John Adams summed up the republican dilemma in an ironic question to Jefferson: "Will you tell me how to prevent riches from becoming the effects of temperance and industry? Will you tell me how to prevent riches from producing luxury? Will you tell me how to prevent luxury from becoming effeminacy, intoxication, extravagance, Vice and folly?"[18]

The Problem of a Virtuous Economy

The task of achieving a "virtuous" political economy, one that would produce material well-being but at the same time nurture, not corrupt, the moral character of the people, was at the heart of the republican problem. It was generally agreed that agriculture was the most natural and inherently virtuous of all economic activities, for it promoted independence, sound judgment, and application. It was the republic's good fortune that most of the population were independent yeoman farmers. Jefferson did not scruple over much in 1803 in stretching executive power to acquire the huge Louisiana Purchase, doubling the territory of the United States. The vast new land was the geographical counterpart to the political Revolution of 1800; it would ensure the perpetuation of his particular vision of the republic by securing to popular virtue its necessary economic base. In opening huge areas of land to cultivation by independent farmers, the purchase would postpone for many generations the time when population would outgrow the availability of land and force the development of a "European" economy in which most people were dependent and impoverished wage earners. For Jefferson too, liberty seems to have been closely bound up with the idea of physical breathing space. A spread-out farming community needed only minimal government; a dispersed people did not press upon one another and generate the tensions that might require strict policing and regulation. The low density of population, which to Dwight seemed to undermine virtue, was to Jefferson one way of preserving it. Jefferson was convinced that "men are disposed to live honestly, if the means of doing so are open to them." Given that assumption, the bounty of the land could be counted on to provide the conditions for a virtuous citizenry. Under public pressure, successive Republican administrations progressively reduced the price at which public lands were sold, transforming them from a source of public revenue to an economic resource to be distributed as widely as possible in private hands.[19]

The extent to which commerce, manufacturing, and banking could be assimilated into the republican moral vision was more problematic, and these questions were debated as much within the ruling Republican party as they were between Republicans and Federalists. Commerce was always a problem for republicans, for trade brought luxury, and the merchant was reputed to love money more than country. Nevertheless, commerce was necessary to dispose of the agricultural surplus produced by American farmers and procure in return those trappings of civilized life that could not be produced at home. Regarded as an adjunct to agriculture, commerce could be seen to serve a republican function. Given the bounty of the soil and the availability of land, it was too easy for American farmers to settle for a mere subsistence and sink into semicivilized torpor. The incentives to effort held out by the market would rouse them to the energy of character necessary to republican citizens. Securing access to international markets for American agriculture, and by extension the protection of American commercial rights in general, became a major plank of Republican foreign policy.[20]

With Europe engulfed in the Napoleonic wars, this policy led to inevitable conflict with Britain, which constantly blocked American neutral trading rights. Determined to avoid war, which would bring the large military establishments, heavy taxation, and swollen centralized government he so feared, Jefferson revived a technique used successfully during the Revolutionary struggle and embargoed all commerce with Europe. To work, the embargo required sustained self-sacrifice—that is, virtue—on the part of the American people. To Jefferson's chagrin, the embargo was widely evaded: smuggling boomed, the federal government was drawn into unprecedented interference in the lives of citizens, the Federalist party got a new lease of life, and there was even some talk of secession in New England, the area hardest hit. Economic sacrifice, as one Republican sadly informed Jefferson, did not appear "adapted either to the nature of our government or the genius and character of our people." In the face of such widespread opposition, the embargo was first modified and then repealed in 1809, and war eventually came during James Madison's presidency in 1812.[21]

The embargo and then the war diverted a good deal of mercantile capital into manufacturing, raising the question of how far government policy should encourage this development. Jefferson's suspicions about manufacturing are well known and were shared by probably the majority of Republicans. Large-scale manufacturing in factories raised fundamental questions about concentrations of capital, which would drive small craftsmen under, and about the moral effect on the factory work force. It was impossible for dependent, regimented factory workers, without skill or autonomy, to be republican citizens. Certain stereotyped images of Europe operated vividly in the American consciousness. One was the image of the French Jacobin Terror; another was the image of the English factory system and its degraded workers. However, rising entrepreneurial groups beginning to develop large-scale manufactures were important in the Republican ranks and were arguing that the degradations of the English factory system were specific to England, not to industrialization as such. In an 1810 report on manufactures, Secretary of the Treasury Albert Gallatin argued not only for a protective tariff but federal loans to supply needed capital for industrial development. This suggestion met no support in Congress, but hostility toward manufacturing was certainly lessening. The argument that eventually brought even Jefferson around to accepting some degree of protection for fledgling industry was that development of a modest manufacturing sector would at last make the United States truly independent of Britain. By 1809 Jefferson was admitting that "an equilibrium of agriculture, manufactures, and commerce, is certainly become essential to our independence." Republicans were working toward an economic ethic that conflated a virtuous economy with one that was nationally independent and that accepted all kinds of productive and useful activities as "virtuous," irrespective of their tendency toward concentration of economic power and their impact on human personality.[22]

Resistance

Banking was the most difficult economic activity to assimilate to republican norms. Gallatin, who had a sophisticated grasp of the financial necessities of a modern economy, persuaded Jefferson not to abolish Hamilton's Bank of the United States outright, but Congress did not renew the charter when it came due in 1811. Widespread demand for credit nevertheless produced a tremendous banking boom at the state level. The twenty-nine state banks of 1800 had become over three hundred by 1819. The growth of banking triggered basic republican fears of corruption and oligarchies of wealth. An aristocracy growing out of banking, warned John Adams in 1810, "will be as fatal as the feudal barons, if unchecked in time."[23]

The danger to the republic of corruption by a financial aristocracy was worked out most systematically in the writings of John Taylor of Caroline, a wealthy Virginia planter and one of a group of "Old Republicans" who feared the pragmatic adjustments being made by the dominant moderates in the party. Taylor devoted much of his leisure to a doom-laden running commentary on the evils of the modern political economy. His most important works were *Arator* (1813) and *An Inquiry into the Principles and Policy of the Government of the United States* (1814). Like Jefferson, Taylor valued republican liberty, believed that agriculture was the foundation of the good society, and feared corruption. Corruption, he felt, could hardly be avoided when the economy developed "artificial" sources of wealth dependent on special grants of privilege or support from the government, like banks, or industries fostered by high tariffs. Along with large armies and government bureaucracies supported by taxes, all these were ways of taking money from one set of people to give to another.

Just as patriots during the Revolution had described the British government as reducing them to slavery, Taylor, a substantial slaveholder, talked of banking and stock jobbing as "in substance . . . a mode of selling freemen." In fact, he felt that this was a worse system of exploitation than black slavery since the planter had at least a self-serving interest in the well-being of his slaves. Taylor argued passionately against government intervention in the economy, not on grounds of economic efficiency but because he was convinced that every government intervention would lead to corruption and "unearned" and oppressive concentrations of economic power. He did not think that Jefferson had been able to reverse the insidious slide begun with Hamilton, and he opposed the Bank of the United States, a protective tariff, and the War of 1812 as all "artificial," and thus unjust, supports to particular economic interests. Taylor believed that virtue was an attribute of the polity rather than of individuals. Once the governing principles allowed concentration of power in the central government and the entrenchment of special privilege, political liberty and equality could not survive. In spite of Taylor's extraordinarily convoluted style, his writings were influential among fellow southerners right up to the Civil War; they identified and analyzed the enemy and provided a way of turning the tables on the slavery issue.[24]

Resistance to the social and moral implications of a developing capitalist market economy also came from the independent craftsmen and skilled artisans in the nation's cities. Artisans carried a good deal of political clout, and urban political rhetoric seldom failed to extol the "noble mechanic" as the backbone of the republic. Artisans saw themselves as the epitome of the republican citizen: independent, useful, and uncorrupted by poverty or excessive wealth. No Fourth of July procession or public celebration was complete without elaborate floats organized by the different crafts demonstrating both their prowess and their centrality and usefulness to the republic.

Mechanics' assumptions about how the economy should work placed a high value on independence, but the economic basis of independence was becoming harder to maintain as an expanding domestic and international market exposed the trades to increased competition. As self-employed craftsmen found it more difficult to make ends meet, as masters cut wages and tried to increase the efficiency of their work force, artisans felt the shadow of the factory looming. They sensed not only a threat to their livelihood but a threat to their status as independent men and to a way of life based on tradition and control of their own time.[25]

Artisan self-respect entailed a certain contempt for the marginal and unskilled. Organized artisan groups, for example, blocked attempts by patrician leaders in New York City to set up government-sponsored workshops for the poor. But within rather narrow limits, artisans retained a strongly corporate vision of a republic of mutually reinforcing rights and duties. Journeymen carpenters on strike in 1809–10 declared, "By the social contract every class in society ought to be entitled to benefit in proportion to its qualifications. Among the duties which individuals owe to society are single men to marry and married men to educate their children. Among the duties which society owes individuals is to grant them just compensation not only for current expenses of livelihood, but to the formation of a fund for the support of that time of life when nature requires a cessation of work." Their claims for decent wages rested on the moral obligation of society to maintain the dignity of its most useful members.[26]

Acceptance

While artisans fought for collective control over the trades by maintaining a uniform schedule of prices for work and restricting entry, other Americans were articulating a vision of society as the free marketplace of competing individuals. At the 1806 and 1809 trials of striking cordwainers in Philadelphia and New York for the old common law crime of criminal conspiracy, the prosecution arguments revealed an acceptance of the idea of labor as a commodity, the market as the natural regulator of prices, and an implicit definition of the public interest as the interest of consumers. In trying to restrict hiring in their shops, the cordwainers had violated the rights of other workers, for freedom meant being able to sell one's labor without restriction. By seeking to keep prices artificially high, they were conspiring against the public interest. In both cases, the strikers were convicted, although the penalties imposed were low. Public support was largely confined to other craftsmen; even Republican radicals found it hard to accept a trade union outlook, involving coercive action by self-interested groups to control the marketplace. Nor were artisans themselves entirely immune from the lure of a free market. New York bakers consistently fought the traditional assize of bread, by which the city authorities regulated the weight and price of loaves, as an unwarranted interference in their right to make whatever profit the market would bear.[27]

Some people were coming to see the essence of liberty in the freedom of the market. In an 1810 book, the Jeffersonian lawyer Charles J. Ingersoll asserted baldly that "the lien of this 'mighty continental nation' is commercial liberty; not mere political liberty, but positive freedom." By positive freedom he meant not the "mere" popular role in government but the economic, social, and psychological space provided for individual self-expansion. "The circumstances of no taxes, no military, no ranks, remove every sensation of restraint. Each individual feels himself rising in his fortunes; and the nation, rising with the concentration of all this elasticity, rejoices in its growing greatness." This was a particularly buoyant celebration of a world of expanding opportunities and one that took for granted a natural harmony between individual ambition and public well-being. This assumption would become increasingly widespread in the years ahead. By 1815 Hezekiah Niles, the young editor of the influential *Niles Weekly Register*, was writing approvingly of "the almost universal ambition to get forward" as part of the dynamic of social progress.[28]

Watershed: The War of 1812

Many of the doubts about the viability of the republican experiment came to a head in the years leading up to the War of 1812. Younger republican leaders like John C. Calhoun, Henry Clay of Kentucky, Ingersoll, and Niles did not share the fears of the older generation about the social and political impact of war. For them war with England was a way to reassert virtue in American life. War would answer the question whether commercial expansion was compatible with republican virtue, whether a profit-and-loss-calculating people were still capable of making personal and economic sacrifices for a nobler end.[29]

The war proved a watershed in many ways. The final peace settlement left most of the issues between Britain and the United States unresolved, but all was redeemed by the decisive victory of Andrew Jackson over a British force at New Orleans in 1815. By not losing the war, the United States had demonstrated that a republic could vindicate its rights against a stronger power, and Americans experienced a great surge of national pride and self-confidence. In spite of strains, the Union had not fallen apart, and the fears that the United States could not survive as a nation began to fade. Fittingly, it was during this war that Francis Scott Key wrote the poem, "The Star-Spangled Banner." The words were soon set to music and became widely popular, though the song did not become the official national anthem until the twentieth century.

The national self-confidence spilled over into a more aggressive drive among younger Republican leaders for the economic development of the continent, with fewer inhibitions about means and fewer fears about effects. By 1815 many younger Republicans were rallying behind Henry Clay's comprehensive plan for economic development involving a national bank, a protective tariff to foster the fledgling American industries, and a scheme of internal communications linking the West to the East. Congress chartered the Second Bank of the United States in 1816 and passed a protective tariff, but these actions did not reflect a wholesale abandonment of traditional fears in the country at large. President Madison vetoed the internal improvements bill not only because he doubted its constitutionality but because he knew there was no popular consensus on the national promotion of economic development. The overwhelmingly negative public reaction in 1816 when congressmen voted themselves higher salaries, and two-thirds of the House of Representatives were replaced in the fall elections, indicated the extent to which popular suspicion of central government and especially government spending and "corruption" still survived.[30]

Educating for Virtue

Political economy provided the context for much of the thinking about virtue in the early republic. But Americans leaders knew that there was a psychological dimension to virtue—qualities of mind and heart that needed active encouragement. Indeed, the more that social and economic conditions opened up temptations and opportunities for nonvirtuous behavior, the more necessary the internalization of virtuous norms became. Gallatin noted with satisfaction that the War of 1812 had "renewed and reinstated the national feelings which the Revolution had given and which were daily lessened." The conflict had given the American people "more general objects of attachment with which their pride and political opinions are connected. They are more American; they feel and act more like a nation." National pride is not the same as virtue, but it has some of the same effects. As Gallatin noted, it provided "objects of attachment." Americans increasingly valued individual initiative and enterprise, but they continued to fear egotism and the fragmenting potential of individualism; they admired energy but dreaded the disruption of order through lack of restraint. The individual needed to be attached to the community and made aware of its moral claims; in the absence of standing armies and police forces, people had to restrain themselves from acting out wilder impulses. The problem of attachment was a task for education in its widest sense; the problem of restraint required instilling a respect for law.[31]

All revolutions are concerned with education since the rising generation must be socialized into the new ideology. From the 1780s on, there was much discussion in the United States about the necessity for popular education, couched in the republican language of virtue and corruption. Joel Barlow, in a typical plea, pointed out that "every citizen is a voter," and without the good judgment that comes from education, "he becomes both an object and an instrument of corruption." Barlow coupled "public instruction" with the construction of roads, bridges, and canals as essentially similar moral enterprises and equally deserving of public effort. Jefferson did the same in 1807 in suggesting to Congress that once the public debt was paid off, customs duties on luxuries might be applied to "the great purposes of public education, roads, rivers, canals, and . . . other objects of public improvement." All these internal improvements would create bonds of attachment to the nation: schools by socializing the young into republican norms and roads and canals, as Secretary of the Treasury Albert Gallatin explained in his great 1810 report on the subject, by creating a network of interwoven economic interests. In a deeper sense, they were all elements of virtue because they required citizens to transcend their immediate interests and, extending their concern across time and space, act in concert for the benefit of posterity.[32]

Although Jefferson was undoubtedly sincere in his concern for education, the embargo killed off any possibility of retiring the national debt, and for him, the debt, the epitome of the canker of corruption at the heart of public life, was always the first priority. At the state level all the many earnest calls for public education produced in fact remarkably little. Since taxation was associated with oppression, there was chronic unwillingness on the part of the state legislatures to tax for public purposes. In the new western states in particular, liberty for many people clearly meant having moved beyond the reach of communal claims of this kind. It was not until the 1820s, with a growing fear of the poor and particularly an urban poor, that effective efforts to create public education systems were set in motion.[33]

For many people, including Jefferson, a more important concern than mass schooling was a proper republican education for the nation's leaders. Many plans were floated for a national university that would draw together elite young men from all over the nation, creating a national governing class with the common bonds of education and youthful friendship. Washington had suggested an institution of this kind, and Barlow drew up an elaborate plan for Jefferson. It was presented several times to Congress but always foundered on questions of constitutionality and the persistent localism of most Republicans.[34]

Jefferson in fact was less interested in a national university than in his own plans for a state University of Virginia, a project into which he threw himself passionately in the last ten years or so of his life. He designed the campus, recruited the faculty, and drew up the curriculum. The new university was to be entirely secular in its orientation and free of that clerical control that Jefferson was convinced restricted freedom of thought in existing institutions of higher education. The curriculum excluded the teaching of divinity and metaphysics and was more heavily weighted toward the sciences than in most other contemporary colleges. The University of Virginia was intended, according to James Madison, to be "a nursery of Republican patriots as well as genuine scholars." Jefferson was determined to get the best available scholars for most of the academic departments, even if that meant hiring foreigners, but he insisted that the professors of moral philosophy and of law must be Americans—and men of the right principles. "This institution," he wrote, "will be based on the illimitable freedom of the human mind. For here we are not afraid to follow truth wherever it may lead." But since the true principles of republican government had already been ascertained, any deviation could only be in the direction of corruption. In the law department, which would include the teaching of government, the branch "in which heresies may be taught," Jefferson selected the first professor with great care and drew up a list of approved texts.[35]

The entire environment is educative one way or another, and ideally republican citizens would be hedged around with symbols to nudge their flickering attachment to virtue into activity. Jefferson, who was passionately interested in architecture, fully realized the symbolic importance to the new nation of its first public buildings since they must express the image of the young republic to itself. Largely through Jefferson's influence, the neoclassical style was not only chosen for the Capitol in Washington but became standard for public buildings across the country. Whether Roman or Greek revival, neoclassicism was a complete break with the architecture of the colonial past and not particularly functional. Its object was symbolic and didactic: to provide a constant echo of ancient Greece and Rome, designed to awaken a feeling that the raw young nation was the heir to past greatness and liberty. The neoclassical style both evoked the memory of past republics and in its own dignity embodied republican simplicity and gravitas. Architects soon began to extend the style to private uses, particularly banking. The first Greek revival building in America was Benjamin Latrobe's Bank of Pennsylvania of 1801, and his disciple William Strickland built a splendid Greek temple for the Second Bank of the United States in 1824. This daring synthesis of finance with the visual symbol of republican virtue was in itself emblematic of the tensions in American republicanism.[36]

Although American leaders never mobilized the arts in support of the republic to the same extent as the revolutionary government of France, they were certainly aware of the importance of iconography. In a rare act of artistic patronage, Congress commissioned John Trumbull to decorate the rotunda of the Capitol with paintings. The choice of subject was a delicate business for a building that had symbolic as well as practical significance. Trumbull decided on actual historical rather than allegorical subjects: the signing of the Declaration of Independence, the British surrenders at Yorktown and at Saratoga, and the resignation of George Washington. The paintings were not Trumbull's best work; in addition, there were difficulties in finding a suitable style for a public art that had to bear the weight of both the historically specific and the universal. John Randolph complained of the *Declaration of Independence*, with its life-sized, accurate portraits of forty or so eighteenth-century gentlemen in knee breeches, that he had never seen a painting with so many legs. But if documentary realism produced problems, so in fact did classical symbolism.

When Jefferson recommended the famous Italian sculptor, Canova, to make a statue of Washington for the state capitol at Raleigh, North Carolina, he suggested that the costume be Roman, since "our boots and regimentals would have a very puny effect." However, when the statue was installed in 1821 it was much criticized: Americans might like to praise Washington's Roman virtue, but they wanted his statues to look American. Davy Crockett liked the realistic Washington statue in Richmond, "where they have him in the old blue and buff. He belonged to his country—heart, soul and body, and I don't want any other country to have any part of him—not even his clothes." The American Horatio Greenough's 1833 statue of Washington in a toga provoked embarrassed ridicule, an indication of the limits of classicism as a reference system in a Christian and increasingly democratic country.[37]

Educated men of the founding generation were steeped in the literature and history of Greece and Rome, but in the new century there were continuing laments about the decline in classical learning and lack of public respect for it in America. Defenders of a classical education trumpeted its political value. "Mankind are too apt to lose sight of all that is heroic, magnanimous and public spirited," mourned the *New England Quarterly Magazine* in 1802. "Left to ourselves, we are apt to sink into effeminacy and apathy." An education in the classics was one way to keep men up to the mark, for "the best ages of Rome afford the purest models of virtue that are anywhere to be met with." In fact, college faculties and other educated men mounted such a successful defense that the classics remained the heart of the university curriculum, at least in the older colleges. No doubt this had much to do with trying to maintain some distinction between those with a genteel education and those without, but the assertion that classical studies were a school for virtue provided a thoroughly republican justification for continuing to study Latin and Greek.[38]

The Revolution itself was a natural source of symbols and examples of virtue, so it was important to keep the memory of the epic struggle vividly alive. When Mercy Otis Warren wrote her *History of the American Revolution* (1805), it was to recall a lapsed younger generation to virtue through reminding them of the principles of their fathers. A member of a prominent patriot family, she had been involved with the Revolution from the beginning and had known its principal actors. Like so many others of her generation, she was profoundly alarmed by what seemed the self-seeking egotism of the 1790s, and her *History* is written in the republican language of the continuous human battle between virtue and avarice. In this battle, memory is a vital adjunct of virtue. The Declaration of Independence, she advised, "ought to be frequently read by the rising youth of the American states, as a palladium of which they should never lose sight, so long as they wish to continue a free and independent people."[39]

A number of biographies held up Revolutionary heroes as models of self-lessness and public spirit. One of the most successful was William Wirt's 1817 biography of Patrick Henry, which supplied the lack of written records of his famous speeches with the author's own eloquence. The greatest hero of all was George Washington, and immediately after his death, the process of mythmaking began. Federalists in particular found in the image of the first president an ideal of the order and moderation they wished so desperately to fasten on the young republic. The numerous writings and orations devoted to commemorating Washington as the Father of His Country emphasized his firmness of resolve, his sober judgment and disinterestedness, and, above all, perfect command over his passions. John Marshall, the chief justice, produced a massive five-volume life and times of Washington in which the hero was not actually born until volume 2. Jefferson was convinced the work was Federalist propaganda and was dismayed that the history of the Revolution was being written by the wrong people. Yet he need not have worried; most people found Marshall's *Washington* unreadable. It was a work almost entirely about the public man, with no attempt to reach out to a broader popular audience.[40]

The work that created the popular image of Washington until the end of the century was the constantly revised little book by the opportunist "Parson" Weems, which came out in 1800 and quickly became a fabulous best-seller, running into numerous editions. Mason Locke Weems was a Maryland Anglican clergyman who spent most of his life as an itinerant book seller, promoter, agent, and writer of popular books and tracts. He proposed a popular biography of Washington to the Philadelphia publisher Mathew Carey right after the president's death: "Millions are gaping to read something about him. . . . We may sell it with great rapidity for 25 or 37 Cents and it wd not cost 10." Writing in a lively style with a good deal of conversation, Weems aimed to humanize Washington and devoted the first three chapters to his childhood and youth, although the cherry tree incident did not appear until the 1806 edition. The work was designed for young people, and the qualities Weems emphasized were the bourgeois virtues of honesty and, above all, industry. Weems showed how Washington's capacity for hard work enabled him to rise from modest circumstances to wealth and from obscurity to fame, and, moreover, kept him healthy and away from vice. The image here is not so much of republican virtue as of the good boy who works hard and rises in the world. In Weems's *Life of Washington* republican and liberal character ideals flow easily into one another.[41]

In spite of the widespread veneration of Washington, in 1810 a petition was deploring the fact that eleven years after his death there was still no national memorial to him, an omission that might "be justly viewed as indications of the decay of that public virtue which is the only solid and natural foundation of a free government." Visible, tangible memorials became more important as the Revolution receded further from living memory. At the dedication of the Bunker Hill monument in 1825, Daniel Webster, the rising young lawyer and orator of the day, pointed out that "human beings are composed not of reason only, but of imagination also, and sentiment." "Our object," he declaimed, "is, by this edifice, to show our own deep sense of the value and importance of the achievement of our ancestors; and, by presenting this work of gratitude to the eye, to keep alive similar sentiments, and to foster a constant regard for the principles of the Revolution." The education of the heart through an appeal to "imagination and sentiment" would link individuals emotionally to a community stretching to the past and to the future and remind them that there was something beyond their own will.[42]

Webster overestimated the available fund of imagination and sentiment, however. The Bunker Hill monument stalled for lack of money and was not completed until 1843; like other similar projects, it ran up against a stubborn popular conviction that monuments were part of European monarchical culture and that money should be used for more obviously "useful" ends. The celebration of the Fourth of July as a national festival of remembrance, on the other hand, became widespread after 1800. The Fourth offered an opportunity for much bombast and self-congratulation, but it also provided a formal occasion for thinking about the state of the republic and was thus, at least theoretically, an occasion for virtue.

The Importance of the Law

The concern for education in its widest sense linked virtue to an enlargement of the individual's sympathies and attachments. Those who feared the anarchic potential of a democratic people, however, increasingly coupled virtue with the idea of restraint, of which the most potent expression and symbol was the law. While the legislative system expressed the communal power of the people, the law expressed their consent to self-restraint and preserved the rights of individuals against the encroachments of others. If administered by a learned judiciary and bar, the law also exemplified that leadership by the "best," which the political system was apparently jettisoning. From this bastion, the wise and good might still exercise authority in society. In the last decade of his life, Brackenridge published a compilation of law reports because he believed that the law had a profoundly educative function. Understanding its principles would direct "the democracy to move in the groove of our noble constitution."[43]

This was an important period for the law in America. The practical implications of state and national constitutions had to be worked out, and a rapidly developing and modernizing economy demanded new legal rules. Between 1783 and 1820 the number of lawyers grew four times as fast as the general population. Law training was still generally haphazard and informal and bar regulations not rigorously enforced. The general fluidity of the profession made it a natural avenue of social mobility for ambitious young men and basic training for a career in public life. As William Wirt pointed out, "The bar in America is the road to honour." To sustain the claim of lawyers to be the natural aristocracy who should lead the republic, leaders of the profession insisted that a lawyer must be a well-educated gentleman. Young lawyers were constantly exhorted to read widely in philosophy, classics, and history. When David Hoffman, the law lecturer at the University of Maryland, published a *Course of Legal Studies* in 1817, he included in it Cicero, Seneca, Xenophon, and Aristotle, as well as the Bible. Jefferson prescribed a similarly comprehensive program of studies for aspiring young lawyers.[44]

The claim to leadership, however, had to be asserted in the face of considerable popular hostility toward the legal profession. In hard times this distrust of lawyers as tricky men who obscured the ends of simple justice merged with hatred of the courts for collecting debts and foreclosing mortgages into a truculent attitude toward the law in general. The English common law came under constant attack after the Revolution as foreign, feudal, and full of unnecessary technicalities and obscurities. A common complaint was that the common law was judge-made law and thus outside the will of the people. At the state level there were often bitter battles. Should the common law be replaced by a simple, easily understood code? Should judges be elected and thus be made more responsive to the people? Radicals felt that the Revolution of 1800 was not complete until the legal system was as republican as the rest of the political system. Moderate Republicans, as well as Federalists, on the other hand, were not averse to putting a brake upon popular majorities and the popular will, and in the law, and particularly in an independent judiciary, they saw a way to do it. In state after state, moderate Republicans allied with Federalists to fend off attacks on the courts and the common law.[45]

Leaders of the bar denounced proposals for codification as the product of "abstract theorizing" and defended the interpretive function of the judiciary. Modern life was too complicated for every man to be his own lawyer; the law would always need its priesthood of professional interpreters. Gradually an impressive body of American legal literature was being built up, which made threats of codification less likely to succeed. By 1821 there were some 150 volumes of reports of state courts and the Supreme Court, creating a body of authoritative, and American, common law. Between 1826 and 1830 Chancellor Kent of New York brought out his *Commentaries on American Law*, and Justice Joseph Story followed with a number of magisterial legal works. This scholarly activity added to the prestige of the American legal profession and the self-confidence of its practitioners. When Alexis de Tocqueville visited the United States in the early 1830s, he concluded that lawyers were the nearest group America had to an aristocracy, and because of their instinctive attachment to order, they functioned as a brake upon the excesses of democracy.[46]

The most important such barrier was the growing authority of the Supreme Court under Chief Justice John Marshall. Marshall was forty-six when he was appointed chief justice by John Adams in 1801, and he remained in that position until 1835, a period of extraordinary dominance in which many of the basic legal principles of the Constitution were laid down. When he took office, the Supreme Court was of little account, and the new Republican government expressed considerable hostility toward the federal judiciary. Relations between Jefferson and Marshall always remained extremely tense. Though a Virginian, Marshall was also a Federalist, and he had developed strongly nationalist principles during active service in the Revolution. Those principles now came into play to restrain actions by state governments and state courts that seemed to threaten the security of property and the conditions for orderly economic development.[47]

Marshall was not a particularly learned judge in a technical sense; it was their generalizing sweep rather than their legal precision that gave his decisions their power. He used the force of his personality to produce a consensus among his colleagues so that the Court could deliver a single opinion, which he usually wrote himself. Court decisions thus acquired an olympian, impersonal authority. By 1835 Marshall had made a strong claim for the Supreme Court, rather than the states or Congress, as the supreme interpreter of the Constitution. He had elevated a hitherto weak and ill-defined Supreme Court into a powerful and autonomous branch of government that could act as a restraint on the actions of the political branches of the system, particularly at the state level. In the course of his long tenure on the bench, Marshall successfully asserted the right of the Supreme Court to review the constitutionality of acts of Congress, to invalidate the acts of state legislatures and the decisions of state courts, to define the limits of state and national sovereignty where the two clashed, and to protect certain areas of private rights against government infringement. Marshall's colleague, Justice Story, celebrated judicial review as the power to "stay the arm of legislative, executive, or popular oppression."

Tocqueville was struck by the way in which legal habits of thought had permeated American political culture. Increasingly, questions about the development of the economy or about race would be referred to judicial rather than political decision making. As many Americans continued to ponder the fundamental problem of what keeps society viable, the law loomed ever larger as a kind of embodied virtue that would supply whatever was lacking in individuals. "Let reverence for the laws," implored Abraham Lincoln in 1837, "become the political religion of the nation."[48]

two

Christianizing the Republic

The religious atmosphere of the country was the first thing that struck me on arrival in the United States. . . . For the Americans the ideas of Christianity and liberty are so completely mingled that it is almost impossible to get them to conceive of the one without the other.

—Alexis de Tocqueville, *Democracy in America*, 1835

The Revolution had been led by men of what Henry May has called the "Moderate Enlightenment." Distinguished as much by intellectual style as by content, the Moderate Enlightenment assumed that the universe is orderly and can be understood by rational inquiry. Essentially secular in outlook, it held that humanity was destined to happiness and that people should use their intelligence to mold both the material world and human institutions to serve human well-being. An interest in scientific inquiry, medical developments, and useful gadgets, improvements in the science of agriculture and in the science of government, characterized this mode of thinking. De-emphasizing the traditional Christian focus on sin and redemption, the Moderate Enlightenment fostered a certain openness to new, even unorthodox, ideas and a distaste for religious "enthusiasm."[1]

In the new republic this kind of outlook was put on the defensive and eventually virtually submerged by one of the most startling developments of the early nineteenth century: the surge to cultural dominance of evangelical Christianity. This was the period in which the United States began its career as the most religious of Western nations. In this process the whole cultural tone of the United States was transformed as republican virtue became conflated with religious piety. The message from the churches for the next half-century was that the virtue necessary to the republic could be sustained only by religious faith. Only Christian benevolence was strong enough to overcome individual selfishness and tie the individual to the community; only Christianity was strong enough to produce the inner check, the necessary internalization of self-restraint. But in superseding the Enlightenment, the new religiosity also subsumed and assimilated some of it. The practical aspects of Enlightened thinking, for example, proved quite compatible with experiential piety. In addition, religion accommodated itself to—and tamed—both republicanism and democracy. The fact that egalitarianism and evangelical religion rose together defused the radical potential of the one and the reactionary potential of the other. By 1820, in the words of Gordon Wood, "the republican citizen had become a Christian democrat."[2]

The Campaign against Infidelity

At the dawn of the new century, however, the triumph of religion could hardly be foreseen, and many of the clergy were plunged in gloom. They saw an ominous declension in religious observance and an even more ominous increase of drunkenness, disorder, and vice. The nation's colleges were rife with student rebellion that culminated in 1802 with riots at Williams College, William and Mary, Yale, and Princeton. Although the unrest was mainly a revolt against excessively close and paternal discipline, professors were quick to see it as rising from the insidious influence of French Revolutionary radicalism and free-thinking on religion. From New England to Georgia, ministers deplored the lack of Sunday observance, the meager number of new converts, a general coldness or indifference. In Virginia visitors commented on the number of church buildings that had been allowed to fall into decay, and the young William Ellery Channing, tutoring in a wealthy Richmond household, lamented that "infidelity is very general among the higher classes." Even in New England, however, if we are to believe the orthodox clergy, the situation was not much better. Surveying the state of the nation in 1801, Yale President Timothy Dwight denounced the creeping corruption of American life through the infection of foreign "infidelity," by which he meant a whole range of opinion from deism through radical European beliefs about human perfectibility to outright atheism; indeed, he was convinced that the first led inevitably to the last. *Infidelity* provided a code word to encapsulate what the orthodox saw as a fatal drift toward secularization.[3]

Orthodox clergy were obsessed with the threat of deism, which they perceived as especially likely to corrupt college youth and the lower orders.

After the publication of Tom Paine's *Age of Reason* (1794–95), an attack on organized Christianity and priestcraft, thirty-five American replies were quickly produced. The book eventually ruined Paine's reputation, but it went into eight American editions between 1794 and 1796 and had a brief vogue, particularly among young men, as something daring. A number of other radical and anticlerical European books were published in the United States in these years, some deistical clubs were formed, and one or two newspapers were established briefly. The deist newspaper of the itinerant preacher Elihu Palmer, the *Temple of Reason*, attracted some support among artisans who already had a strong tradition of anticlericalism.

Many upper-class men of the Revolutionary generation, particularly in the South, were certainly deists in the sense of distrusting the clergy and not believing in the divine inspiration of much of the Bible or in miracles. Many men who later became pillars of evangelical orthodoxy looked back on the colleges of their youth at the turn of the century as rife with ridicule of religion and fascination with the works of foreign ideologues such as Voltaire and the English radical William Godwin. The increased visibility of deism from the mid-1790s coincided with the growth in internal disorder, vitriolic partisan politics, and the threat of war with England. It was easy to assume that it was "detestable deism," in the words of a North Carolina Presbyterian, "that has disadjusted and disorganized society." At the same time the Revolution in France, originally hailed in the United States as an echo of their own struggle, began to turn toward atheism and radical terror. At this point the New England clergy began to fear for the church and to see in the French Revolution a terrible portent. "You must take your side," Dwight exhorted his congregation. "Will you make marriage the mockery of a register's office? . . . Will you enthrone a Goddess of Reason before the table of Christ?"[4]

The clergy were professionally sensitive to signs of religious laxity; in addition, as republicans they were always on the alert for corruption, anticipating that the fragile experiment in free government might be sapped from within by vicious individuals and declining virtue among the people. In 1798 the well-known geographer and Congregational minister Jedidiah Morse had announced with much fanfare the discovery of a secret European organization of philosophes, with American agents, dedicated to overthrowing all the established governments and religions in the world. Although Morse could not actually prove the existence of branches of the Bavarian Illuminati in America, large numbers of the clergy were quick to accept the idea of a widespread plot. It heightened their general sense of crisis and reinforced a growing suspicion of European radical thinkers. On the conviction that both Christianity and the republic were in jeopardy, Dwight, Morse, and their colleagues roused the clergy to re-Christianize America.[5]

The New England orthodox clergy, almost to a man Federalist in politics, were particularly exercised over the presidential election of 1800. Jefferson, who was notoriously indifferent to conventional Christianity, was denounced from the pulpit as well as in the Federalist press as an irreligious and immoral Jacobin. His election in spite of his lack of piety reinforced the feeling of deep moral crisis. When in 1801 Jefferson offered Tom Paine passage on an American ship to come back from France, the opposition press had a field day. Jefferson received Paine at Washington, but there was no great public welcome for a hero of the Revolution, as there was to be in 1824–25 for the visit of Lafayette. Paine had returned to an America anxious about its future direction and increasingly turning to religious faith for personal meaning and social anchor. He died in 1809 in obscurity. Joel Barlow, who had published part 1 of *The Age of Reason*, advised against any biography on the grounds that Paine's writings "are not read at present." It was a measure of how quickly the dominant cultural tone of the nation had changed.[6]

The Second Great Awakening

Even while established churchmen were calling for a crusade against infidelity, a popular religious revival began that swept beyond their control and caused them almost as much anxiety as deism. The great wave of revivals known as the Second Great Awakening began with scattered and restrained outbreaks in New England and the South. In 1801 a great camp meeting at Cane Ridge, Kentucky, attended by over twenty thousand people, signaled a new form of religious expression. The sheer numbers in a sparsely populated country were part of its power over people's minds. The meeting lasted for several days; sinners were prayed over and exhorted by a dozen or so preachers, and hundreds converted in an emotional and physical release of hollering, singing, and falling in fits. For the next thirty years revivals broke out across America in one place after another; in some areas, like the notorious "burned-over" district of western New York, the revivalist fires swept through again and again. Sometimes revivalism meant essentially a deeper and more fervent piety among church members and particularly their children; sometimes, and especially in frontier areas, it meant the gathering into churches of the hitherto churchless and unorganized. Everywhere the revival emphasized emotion, a deeply felt commitment, and the religion of the heart, and it explicitly or implicitly jettisoned Calvinist belief in predestination in favor of a salvation open to all who would reach for it.

Above all, the revivals offered a more intense community life. At the heart of revival was the overwhelming individual experience of conversion. Yet evangelical Christianity was not the religion of the private person; professions were made publicly and the soul laid bare to the community, which provided stringent rules of conduct and the scrutiny to make sure they were followed. The new converts became members of a tightly knit group, joined by common experience, belief, and outlook on life, which would watch them and inquire into their welfare and activities. The evangelical churches not only took in but expelled as well, as members backslid into drink or immorality. The voluntary organization into churches of thousands of ordinary Americans was a spontaneous reaction against the growth of individualism and breakdown of traditional communities in the early republic.[7]

Revivals electrified cities as well as rural areas, cut across classes, captured black as well as white, and attracted all age groups, though some kinds of people were more susceptible than others. In urban areas in the North, for example, manufacturers and skilled artisans were more likely to be drawn into the evangelical domain than merchants or laborers. Above all revivals occurred among the young: the majority of converts were teenagers or in their early twenties. The drama of conversion was part of the resolution of the anxieties of growing up—a decision for a particular style of adult life. Women had been in the majority in American churches since the early eighteenth century, and the majority of converts continued to be female. Still, one effect of revivals, particularly those led by preachers who made a point of adopting a straight-talking masculine style, was to increase the intake of men, thus somewhat redressing, though not reversing, the male-female ratio in the churches.[8]

The evangelical message clearly answered a hunger for meaning in individual life and experience. Many of the Revolutionary generation who lived on into the nineteenth century, like Jefferson and John Adams, felt uncomfortable in the new emotional and evangelical world. They had lived the drama of the Revolution; their central role in it had given meaning to their own lives, and they continued to see in the creation of the republic, and in the progressive developments of the eighteenth century, a meaning to history. Yet for some of the Revolutionary generation, like Benjamin Rush, secular progress was neither sufficient nor, by the early 1800s, convincing. Many more of a younger generation—those who grew up during the 1760s and 1770s—were looking to religion, not politics, for personal and public direction. The lexicographer Noah Webster, for example, became a deist as a student. When he published a new edition of the *New England Primer* in the 1780s, he replaced the Puritan "A. In Adams Fall / We sinned all" by the more genial if less resonant, "A. Was an Apple-pie made by the cook." By the late 1790s his secularism was beginning to waver; the 1801 edition of the *Primer* restored Adam and sin. His wife and daughters were converted in 1808, and it was not long before Webster joined them. William Wirt followed a similar pattern of conversion from youthful deism to evangelical religion in the early 1800s, as did his fellow Virginian, the aristocratic Republican gadfly, John Randolph of Roanoke. In all three cases there had been prior conversion by women in the family, and all three felt disillusioned with the political and social state of the country. Religion offered a private world of solace and what Noah Webster came to call "our sheet anchor during our political storms."[9]

As the revivals spread, techniques were refined, adapted to new milieus, and routinized. At the same time, the process of Protestant fission accelerated as new sects, like the Republican Methodists, the Cumberland Presbyterians, and the German United Brethren, were spun off. The great gainers everywhere were the Methodist and Baptist churches with their more flexible organization, willingness to field ministers with minimal education, and openness to an emotional and popular style of preaching. The revivals transformed the ecclesiastical map of America. At the time of the Revolution, the largest denominations had been the Presbyterians, Congregationalists, and Anglicans; by 1855 the largest were the Methodists and Baptists, who comprised almost 70 percent of the members of American Protestant churches and were dominant in the South. The success of these hitherto "outsider" denominations emboldened them to attack the last remaining ties between church and state in America—the Congregational Standing Order of New England. After establishment was wiped out in Connecticut in 1818, New Hampshire and Massachusetts soon followed. The hegemony of Protestantism would be achieved in America without any formal ties with the state.[10]

The revivals were an integral part of the democratization of American culture in these years. In the heat of the revival experience, ordinary men and women were inspired to pray and exhort publicly. Revivalist attacks on coldness in the churches undermined the authority of the established clergy and gave expression to much smoldering popular resentment at the pretensions of elites. In the great expansion among the Methodists and Baptists, men without theological training, or much education at all, but with the power to preach, flocked into the ministry. The great Methodist itinerant Peter Cartwright recalled: "We could not, many of us, conjugate a verb or parse a sentence and murdered the king's English almost every lick. But there was a Divine unction attended the word preached." These men developed a colloquial, direct style, full of humor and anecdote, which spoke directly to a popular audience. Folk music makers adapted popular tunes of the day to their own religious verses and created a body of indigenous hymns and spiritual songs. Blacks, both slave and free, were attracted in unprecedented numbers to the gospel as preached by Methodists and Baptists, and the black preacher emerged as a major figure in black communities. By 1809 a defiantly radical new group had emerged, some 20,000 strong, calling themselves simply the Christians. Their leader, Elias Smith, began the first religious newspaper in the United States and used it to attack the genteel clergy as hirelings of the rich and to assert the right of the common people to read and judge the Bible for themselves without the intervention of educated ministers. In 1830 they merged with a similar group to become the Disciples of Christ, which by 1860 was the fifth largest denomination in America.[11]

The Christianizing of the republic proceeded on several levels: partly an attempt by traditional orthodox clergy to regain lost ground and cultural centrality, partly an upswelling of popular religious fervor, stimulated and led by new religious leaders from outsider denominations rebelling against the cultural dominance of the elite churches. All felt that they were engaged in the redemption of both individual souls and America. Whatever their initial distaste, most traditional church leaders succumbed to the new evangelical ethos. Eventually even educated ministers adapted the formal sermon to the new style. The fact that initial religious disorder seemed in the end to produce greater social order overcame many scruples. In Virginia the revivals were reported to have brought a strong diminution of "drinking, swearing, horse racing, fighting." Even "those who make no pretensions to religion" still appeared "under great restraint." Methodist circuit riders distributed plainly written religious books and pamphlets to poor and isolated families, bringing them within the print culture. In many sparsely populated areas of his state, reported the South Carolinian David Ramsay in 1808, Methodist and Baptist revivalists had provided religious instruction for the first time. Like missionaries to the "heathen" abroad, they had been engaged not only in "evangelizing" but in "civilizing . . . remote and destitute settlements." As Ramsay's remarks indicate, the Awakening not only transformed individual lives but acted as a socializing, or organizing, process. Even when enthusiasm eventually waned, new churches remained as permanent and stabilizing institutions. At its fringes the revival could produce the populist Christians and eventually the most radical social reformers, but as the center naturally cooled, its organizational and conservative elements tended to overwhelm its destabilizing potential.[12]

Liberal Christianity

As evangelical Protestantism became the dominant mode of American religion, it not only swept away deism but also restricted the influence of other forms of religious belief. While it fatally undercut the hold of Calvinism as a doctrine, it also halted the spread of what some had assumed would become the major religious form in America: liberal Christianity. Throughout the late eighteenth century there had been a strong drift toward liberal religion within the Calvinist churches of New England, and by the first decade of the century, Harvard University was firmly in the liberal camp. In reaction, some disgruntled orthodox ministers founded Andover Theological Seminary as a stronghold for orthodox Calvinist theology, but no definite schism developed until after 1815, partly because the liberals wished to modify the church from within. However, when the ultraorthodox Jedidiah Morse denounced the liberal group within the church as Unitarians and the next thing to outright infidels, the warfare was out in the open. This was more than just a storm in a Massachusetts teacup; when the leading Unitarian luminary, William Ellery Channing, published a formal exposition of the liberal position in 1819, it became one of the most widely distributed pamphlets in America, and it gave Channing a national reputation.[13]

The formal center of dispute between the two groups was the inability of the liberals to accept the doctrine of the Trinity and the divinity of Christ. The real heart of the dispute, however, was not the triune nature of God but His moral nature and, by extension, the moral nature of human beings. Liberal theology attracted those who could no longer stomach the stern Jehovah of orthodox Calvinism who allowed people to come into the world so utterly depraved by their very nature that they deserved the damnation that would befall all except the few predestined to be saved. Such a deity was not even a constitutional monarch, let alone a fit ruler for a republican people. "Should we not detest a human magistrate, who would be so unreasonable, vindictive and cruel?" asked the Unitarian Jared Sparks. "And how can we love that in God, which is so abhorrent to every principle of our nature in men?"[14]

Moreover, as liberals looked into their own hearts, they could not perceive there the depths of sin and depravity that orthodoxy seemed to require. Theologically cheerful, they lacked conviction of the omnipresence of evil. The essence of the schism between liberals and orthodox was seized by Leonard Woods of Andover when he concluded that the fundamental error of Unitarians was their blindness to *"the ruined state of man."* If they could only be "feelingly convinced" of this, then all other doctrinal difficulties would disappear. "The controversy," he added acutely, "appears, in this view, to be as much a matter of *feeling*, as of *reasoning*."[15]

By the late 1820s, recalled Harriet Beecher Stowe, "all the literary men of Massachusetts were Unitarians, all the trustees and professors of Harvard College were Unitarians. All the elite of wealth and fashion crowded Unitarian Churches." By that time there were Unitarian churches in New York, Baltimore, and several southern cities. Nevertheless, Unitarianism became just one of many American denominations rather than, as the liberals had once hoped, the basic mode of American Christianity. Moreover, it remained one of the minor denominations, its growth checked by militant orthodoxy and the sweep of revival. Outside Massachusetts, Unitarianism maintained a precarious foothold among small numbers of educated city folk, and even in New England it became almost entirely a religion of the well educated and the well off. Unitarians were to have a disproportionate influence on antebellum American culture, but it was through their central involvement in the creation of cultural institutions and attitudes rather than their impact on the religious ethos of the period.[16]

The liberals were temperamentally out of tune with the reviving religious spirit of their times. Both the terror of damnation and the promise of escaping it were central to the appeal of both orthodoxy and revivalism. "The words 'you are damned' and 'hell is your portion' thrilled through me like electricity," wrote one young woman of her experience at a revival meeting. Both of the denominations that effectively removed the threat of hell from their religious repertoire—Unitarianism and its more democratic and lower-class intellectual cousin, Universalism—remained minority churches, although the Universalist position, rejecting the idea of eternal punishment, would eventually be widely accepted. In the early nineteenth century, most Christians, it appeared, wished to believe that they could escape hell, but they also wished to believe in the certainty of deserved and definite punishment as well as rewards, in the next life if not always in this.[17]

"New School" Orthodoxy

Although the Unitarian threat turned out to be easily containable, this was not at all apparent in the second decade of the century. The orthodox clergy found themselves fighting on two fronts: against the liberals and also against the Methodists and Baptists who were fast making converts. The leaders in this battle were two of Timothy Dwight's students, Lyman Beecher, a famous preacher who organized a revival within the Congregationalist church, and Nathaniel W. Taylor, professor of didactic theology at Yale.[18]

Beecher was convinced that people were falling away from Calvinism because its doctrines had been clumsily explained. He even denied that Calvinists had ever taught that infants who died at birth might be damned. The question of infant damnation was becoming an important sticking point. The revulsion against it is probably not so much due to the influence of women in the churches or the growing sentimentality of religious culture as to the republicanization of theology in the nineteenth century—the insistence that Jehovah be held to the same standards of fairness as secular governments. The central problem of Calvinism had always been the difficulty of reconciling the absolute sovereignty of God with the free will (and thus justifiable culpability) of humanity. Beecher and Taylor realized they had to reassert orthodox doctrine in such a way as to absolve God from the charge of being an unjust tyrant. The corollary was that people could not then deny their obligation to obey divine law. To Beecher the most important thing was to hammer home the accountability of the individual to God.[19]

The most intellectually coherent exposition of what came to be called the "New School" came from Taylor, who summed up the essentials of his system in a famous sermon preached in 1828, "Concio ad Clerum." Taylor retained orthodox emphasis on human depravity but insisted that this was due to free human choice, not divine design, for only by depriving people of moral agency could God have created a world without sin. People had "freely and voluntarily set their hearts . . . on the world, rather than on God," and this was the "source of all their other sins." Taylor's final peroration revealed how completely his theology was involved in the evangelical world of repentance, conversion, and moral strenuousness. "Without derogating from the work of God's Spirit let us urge [man] to his duty—*to his duty—to his duty*, as a point-blank direction to business now on hand and now to be done."[20]

By the 1830s both Congregationalism and Presbyterianism were badly divided between the New School, which followed Taylor, and conservatives, who feared a downward slide into what they called Arminianism, "a tendency to cherish in the heart a feeling of independence and self-sufficiency." They were fighting a rearguard action, however, in a society in which fine points of doctrine and theology were becoming increasingly irrelevant as men and women turned to the religion of activism and the heart. As the orthodox churches slipped into minority, though still prestigious, status, Calvinism, quietly modified, adapted, and essentially denatured, ceased to be a dominant force in American religion.[21]

Reason, Religion, and the Bible

Although preachers increasingly emphasized feeling and aimed for the heart, they did not consider religion to be opposed to reason. For all its growing emotionalism, American Protestantism was thoroughly pervaded by a rather naive rationalism that assumed that religion rested on "truths," of which the intellect as well as the heart could be convinced. The great revivalist of the 1820s, Charles Finney, who started out as a lawyer, boasted that he addressed a revival meeting "as I would talk to a jury." Beecher liked to think that if only he could have got together with Lord Byron to argue with him man to man, he could have won him from infidelity to God through sheer force of logic. The colleges gave considerable attention in the undergraduate curriculum to Christian apologetics, the marshaling of empirical evidence for the existence of God, and the reliability of the Scriptures. William Paley's *View of the Evidences of Christianity* (1794) was one of the most widely used textbooks in America. Secure in their own considerable forensic powers, both Dwight and Taylor encouraged their students to debate religious questions and urged them to "think for themselves." "Follow the truth," Taylor told his classes, "if it carries you over Niagara." But of course he was confident that their explorations would eventually beach them snugly in the safe harbor of Taylorism.[22]

Even in frontier regions among the barely educated, there was a dogged insistence that points be proved. It was a great mistake, said one eastern orthodox minister, to think that half-educated ministers would do well enough to send to backwoods settlements in the South and the West. The people there might have very little book learning, but they were "accustomed to put everything they are required to believe to a severe test," and they were also accustomed "to hear in their courts, and on their hustings, addresses and arguments from the foremost men among them." For many ordinary people, disputation on politics and theology was the form that intellectual life took. Mormonism, for example, emerged out of a milieu in New York State buzzing with theological argument, and it combined, according to one critic, "every error and almost every truth discussed in New York for the last ten years." The young Joseph Smith left the Presbyterian church in 1820 at age fifteen because, after long pondering, he was convinced Presbyterianism was "not *true*," and in the *Book of Mormon* (1830) he produced documentary evidence for a new and quite complicated scheme of theology.[23]

The continuing psychological need for an objective basis for religion was evident in the increasing emphasis across the religious spectrum on the Bible and biblical studies. All the new religious seminaries made biblical study a large part of the curriculum, and laypeople as well as clerics undertook serious critical study of the Bible. Unitarians and religious liberals generally looked to the Scriptures as the repository of a core of essential, simple truths that provided the bedrock of faith. To get at these truths required the stripping away of what Andrews Norton, the Dexter Professor of Biblical Criticism at Harvard, called "the accumulated rubbish of technical theology" and the application of modern methods of philology, historical research, and literary criticism. It also meant judging the Bible in terms of modern standards of rationality and sensibility and discarding much, particularly of the Old Testament, as belonging to a more primitive and barbaric state of society.[24]

This was certainly the attitude of Thomas Jefferson, who while president began a serious study of the New Testament that he continued in his retirement, possibly in reaction to the political attacks on his lack of religion. Though staunchly anticlerical, Jefferson never doubted the existence of a benevolent God who had created the universe and wished His creatures to be good and happy. He was drawn to the Unitarian position, and although he rejected the divinity of Christ, he was attracted to Jesus as a moralist whose injunctions to universal philanthropy improved on the classical philosophers. Convinced that this "sublime" moral code had been almost buried by the additions and distortions of the compilers of the gospels and even more by the creeds and systems of power-hungry priesthoods, he compiled his own "testament" by extracting those verses describing the teachings and actions of Jesus that he felt to be genuine from "their style and spirit." To Jefferson, as to other liberals, the essence of religious truth was simplicity: getting at it entailed paring down and being prepared to throw out the accretions of history.[25]

Most Protestants, however, took the whole Bible as the inspired word of God, though there was a range of opinion as to how far verbal errors might have crept in in transcription or whether it had to be taken literally in matters of historical or scientific fact. Scholars could not long remain unaware of the disquieting new philological and historical criticism coming from Germany, but they resisted its implications. The foremost exponent of German methods of biblical criticism in America was Moses Stuart of Andover, who was convinced that he could use the German scholars for their "excellent matter . . . well arranged, and of real utility" without being in the least tempted by their conclusions that much of the Bible had to be read as myth. The crucial point was the acceptance (on, he was convinced, entirely rational grounds) of the book as authoritative; upon that acceptance it was the duty of the scholar to use the most rigorous means to get the meaning of what was written. This faith in the rationality of religion meant that within certain limits, piety was quite compatible with science and scholarship. Belief in the truth of Christianity as revealed in the Scriptures provided a fundamental paradigm within which all other knowledge was interpreted; since facts could never contradict the word of God rightly understood, people would never get into trouble as long as they stuck to empirical investigation. What was feared was not scholarship but "speculation," the mind unfettered by acceptance of fundamental "truths" and the minutiae of empirical research.[26]

Scottish Common Sense

The desire for a convincing philosophical underpinning for religion that would also be compatible with science accounts for much of the success of the Scottish school of Common Sense philosophy, which swept academic and intellectual circles in America in the late eighteenth and early nineteenth centuries. Even before the Revolution Americans had been well acquainted with some important Scottish thinkers, but it was in the 1790s that their books began to appear frequently in booksellers' lists and as college textbooks. As an explanation of human nature and the nature of the mind, Scots Common Sense was taught in orthodox Princeton and Unitarian Harvard; it appealed to all Protestant denominations and to those outside any, like Jefferson. When Americans began to write their own philosophy texts, they were firmly within the Scottish school.[27]

Scottish Common Sense was particularly appealing to educators because it underwrote both science and religion and was easy to teach. Moreover, it coped with the major problems that had emerged from eighteenth-century philosophy. John Locke and Sir Isaac Newton had been the two major pillars of the Enlightenment for Americans because they demonstrated the power of knowledge derived from direct empirical investigation of the world. David Hume, however, had called all in doubt by claiming that if, as Locke had maintained, all knowledge is acquired through the senses, we have, in fact, no way of being certain that our senses give us reliable information about the real world. Certainly they can give us no knowledge of causation; that is something we merely assume or imagine. Hume thus seemed to create an unbridgeable chasm between the human mind and the world outside it. Apart from anything else, this undermined the carefully worked out arguments for the existence of a God from the design of nature. Fortunately Hume's compatriots, the Scots professor Thomas Reid, and his more lucid disciple, Dugald Stewart, provided antidotes to Humean skepticism that were both intellectually respectable and adapted to minds averse to metaphysics.

Reid shared much of the instinctive impatience with useless speculation so common among nineteenth-century Americans. His answer to the problem of knowledge was a concept of the mind as not merely an empty receptor for sense impressions but as something already furnished with active, self-evident principles. These principles included the overwhelming belief in the existence of God, an orderly universe, and our own selves; in the reliability of perception; and in the reality of causation and other principles. As Levi Hedge of Harvard explained, such propositions as "I know that I exist," "Everything that happens has a cause," and "The events I remember really happened," are self-evident truths that we know by intuition; they are the foundation for all other knowledge, and one cannot go beneath them in an endless regression of doubt. Just as implicit belief in mathematical axioms is necessary if one is to do mathematics, implicit belief in these other intuitions of the mind is necessary if one is to get on with the business of living and producing useful knowledge. Reid and Stewart thus reaffirmed Locke's empiricism by refining and modifying his ideas, and they rescued the empirical method of science from the doubts Hume cast. "God himself," assured a commentator in the *North American Review,* had so ordered it "that there should be a perfect correspondence between our own minds and the onward progress of rolling events around us." "From this view of the subject," he pointed out, "not one dangerous or shocking consequence flows."[28]

Philosophy in early nineteenth-century America developed among those who were seeking not originality but a comprehensible system fitted to the education of young men for citizenship. The number of colleges expanded rapidly in the early nineteenth century, most of them under the control of orthodox ministers. At the same time, the colleges were plagued by student disorder, falling enrollments, and declining state appropriations. Determined to maintain both physical and intellectual discipline, the clerical college presidents encouraged piety and genteel revivalism on campus, cracked down on student rowdiness (Princeton expelled 125 students after riots in 1807 and Harvard 29), and geared education to the rational combat of dangerous ideas. The colleges and the academies became the key area where secular learning and the rationalism of the Enlightenment met the claims of Christianity.

The principal arenas for mediating the two were the various courses in philosophy that students were required to take, culminating in the senior year with a course in moral philosophy, almost always taught by the college president. This wide-ranging course covered the operations of the human mind and involved a discussion of all the moral duties of "man," defined implicitly as the male citizen, in both private and public life. Thus all students received a common framework to explain the natural and social world and their part in it in a coherent, scientific, and rational fashion without jeopardizing faith. As the writings of Scottish philosophers became dominant as textbooks, the text in turn came to dominate the course, so that the student did not so much study philosophy as study Reid or Stewart. As Professor Thomas Upham of Bowdoin College explained, if the student is presented with a mass of "conflicting statements, his mind becomes perplexed." It was safer to teach from one basic authoritative text, on which the professor might comment or make slight modifications but which he would not significantly undermine.[29]

Reid and his American followers used the term *Common Sense* for both those intuitions of the mind that everyone had in common and in the more everyday meaning of a sturdy defense of what ordinary people, unlike philosophers, had the good sense to take for granted. There was thus a built-in tendency in this philosophy toward a conflation of truth with what was generally accepted. As important as the idea of shared intuition of basic intellectual propositions was the Common Sense notion of a shared moral sense. To the Common Sense philosophers, the fact that all societies make moral distinctions, though the precise character of rules may differ, indicated that God had implanted in the human mind a conception of morality that allowed an immediate and simple realization of the path of duty. To Jefferson, a great admirer of Dugald Stewart, the moral sense was an absolute necessity for "an animal destined to live in society."[30]

A Christian Militia

The assumption of a "common sense" of humanity, which included a common conviction of morality, blended with democratic ideas to produce an increased awareness of the power of public opinion in America. Even before they lost the prop of establishment, men like Dwight and Beecher had realized that a well-organized Christian public opinion might to some extent replace the old deference and community controls that had restrained individual behavior in the past. No longer part of a Christian magistracy, the clergy could still guide the nation through influence and the organization of lay allies. The religion needed at the present time, declared the *Christian Spectator* in 1825, must be of "the diffusive, controlling, energetic kind."[31]

The vast effort to Christianize America entailed a great expansion in the number of the clergy and also in the means to train them. New colleges and seminaries were created, and by the 1820s New England colleges alone were graduating over three thousand men per decade, well over half of whom went into the ministry. The majority of these new recruits were young men from farm households, the first in their families to go to college, many supported by the contributions of the pious. "The prevalence of pious, intelligent, enterprising ministers through the nation," declared Beecher, drumming up financial support for ministerial education, "at the ratio of one of a thousand, would establish schools, and academies, and colleges, and habits, and institutions of homogeneous influence." The religious press also expanded prodigiously. The 10 religious journals in the United States in 1800 had grown to 850 by 1840. Some were devoted to professional clerical news or to missions; others, like the Unitarian *Christian Examiner* and its orthodox rival, the *Christian Spectator*, aimed at a wider educated audience. The Methodist *Christian Advocate* by 1828 had one of the largest circulation figures in the world. All helped to infuse the culture of the wide reading public with religion, a step toward the "more homogeneous character" Lyman Beecher felt necessary to the preservation of the republic, "a sameness of views, of feelings, and interests."[32]

Numerous voluntary societies devoted to various kinds of moral reform were an even more effective device for homogenizing and reforming values and behavior. Beginning with scattered examples in the 1790s in New England, by 1815 they were mushrooming all over the nation though concentrated in New England, New York, and Pennsylvania. Besides the many local moral societies devoted to the self-improvement of the members and pressure on local authorities to enforce blue laws, numerous associations sprang up after 1800 to distribute Bibles to the poor and organize Sunday schools for their children, to evangelize the heathen in the Mississippi valley and overseas, to rescue prostitutes, to advocate temperance, to combat dueling, and to distribute tracts. Although these societies were based on evangelical piety and enthusiasm, their aim was not directly conversion but the reformation of behavior through rousing the individual conscience and supplementing it with the pressure of organized public opinion. Associations, said Beecher, an energetic organizer, "teach the virtuous part of the community their strength, and accustom them to act, as well as to wish and to pray; they constitute a sort of disciplined moral militia." In the heady surge of nationalism and millennial optimism that followed the conclusion of the war with England in 1815, many of these associations were drawn together into national associations, headquartered in New York, Philadelphia, or Boston, with interlocking directorates. Dubbed the benevolent empire for their widespread influence, by 1830 organizations like the American Bible Society, the American Home Missionary Society, and the American Sunday School Union were dealing with an income of more than half a million dollars and were the most prolific publishers in the United States.[33]

The associations were interdenominational and basically lay societies in which the clergy shared leadership with prominent laymen of the commercial and professional classes. But the foot soldiers of the movement were drawn widely from the broad middle class and those who aspired to middle-class status. By the 1830s some 100,000 people, most of them young, had volunteered as Sunday school teachers. Women organized societies parallel to men's, and sometimes in advance of them, and threw themselves into the work of charity, fund raising, and tract distributing with a fervor that ministers could not but commend, though it made the more conservative a trifle uneasy. The world of benevolent and missionary associations offered women almost their only opportunity for a public role. Republicanism was a masculine affair, but the Christian call to benevolence in the world to some extent transcended the boundaries of sex.[34]

The direct impact on American behavior was probably greatest on those already within or on the edge of the respectable classes. The campaign against intemperance, for example, does seem to have made drunkenness less acceptable among the middle and upper classes, and after 1830 there was a decline in per capita consumption of alcohol from its all-time high of that year. The premarital pregnancy rate also seems to have begun to decline after 1820. Dueling as an upper-class practice died out in the northern states by 1830, although it lingered in the South until the Civil War. There clearly was a turn toward the behavior and attitudes that would later be summed up by the term *Victorianism:* a strict observance of the Sabbath, temperance (if not teetotalism), an emphasis on sexual morality, and a hypersensitivity to any suggestion of immorality in the arts and literature. In this sense the benevolent empire, even while it was devoted to the reformation of the republic, contributed to the privatization of the notion of virtue by associating it with moral behavior in the sphere of private life rather than in public affairs.[35]

Yet the distinction between private and public virtue was not one that nineteenth-century evangelicals would have made. In a society with few external restraints, in which the opportunities for individual self-aggrandizement at the expense of traditional mores and the welfare of others seemed to be opening up prodigiously, the ability of individuals to restrain their passions and desire for instant gratification seemed the only basis for a civilized and stable polity. Attacks on drunkenness, for example, ranged freely between denouncing drink as destroying families and portraying it as a fatal sap of public virtue. "I never see the drunken crowd on our public days celebrating their freedom," said the Reverend John Palfrey in 1827, "that I do not think they are then preparing themselves to part with it," and he reminded his audience that "the disorders of a depraved population almost demand a despotism." Even John Adams, who belonged to an earlier era and distrusted much of the evangelical crusade, was prepared to tell Benjamin Rush that the biblical "curses against fornication and adultery, and the prohibition of every wanton glance or libidinous ogle at a woman, I believe to be the only system that ever did or ever will preserve a republic in the world." Although much of the new moral tone of evangelical America easily degenerated into prudery, it reflected also a pre-Freudian sense of a basic opposition between civilization and the boundless drives of the human id.[36]

This recognition of the dangerous and demonic quality of human desire and capacity, which reason alone was too weak to govern, helps set off the evangelical world of the new century from the Enlightenment culture that it succeeded. It informed their more cautious and wary attitude toward the mind and those who lived by it. In particular, there was a keen sensitivity to any tinge of religious freethinking in those involved with the education of youth. Samuel Stanhope Smith, president of Princeton, outraged the trustees when he casually told a class that he could find no biblical reason for condemning polygamy. Jefferson found that he could not get the famous English chemist and freethinker Thomas Cooper appointed to the new University of Virginia because of religious opposition. The combative Cooper did manage to become president of South Carolina College and remained in office amid continual clerical sniping and two legislative investigations until 1834, when he finally had to go. In Kentucky, the Unitarian Horace Holley of Massachusetts had been appointed president of Transylvania University in 1818 by a liberal board of trustees. By 1827 he was forced out by a combination of orthodox objections to his religious liberalism and practice of giving Sunday evening parties with "instrumental music" and Democratic resentment at his Federalist politics, high salary, and "aristocratic" life-style.[37]

Many of the poorer and more isolated Methodist and Baptist churches, particularly in the West, were suspicious of the intellect and condemned music, dancing, and the arts. Condemnation of the theater was general among all evangelicals; among the better-educated congregations, fiction, poetry, music, and the plastic arts might receive a wary and conditional acceptance, and there was a strong commitment to education and science. But the life of the mind and imagination was held accountable at the bar of morality and tributory to faith and piety. The overwhelming deference paid in respectable circles to religion probably produced a good deal of instinctive self-censorship. Anyone who ventured deist opinion in polite society now, asserted Thomas Dew revealingly in 1833, would not be considered "a gentleman." "The imagination of the Americans," remarked Tocqueville commenting on the intellectual policing role of religion, "is circumspect and hesitant; it is embarrassed at the start and leaves its work unfinished."[38]

It is notable how much more optimistic clerical writers were by the 1830s than they had been at the beginning of the century about Christian prospects in America. They had not, of course, succeeded in making Christianity coextensive with the republic. The most commonly accepted estimate is that one of fifteen Americans belonged to a church in 1800 and one of eight in 1835. Actual membership does not include the much wider circle of people who regularly attended church, estimated at as high as 75 percent of the population by 1835. The clerical and evangelical campaigns had succeeded in bringing religious concerns and religious language to the forefront of public consciousness, and they had had considerable effect on behavior. The experience of revivals and participation in evangelical organization became part of the formation of a middle-class worldview. There was no national church in America and no national establishment, but the values and outlook of evangelical Protestantism came to permeate the culture and set its stamp on the new nation. A general assent to Christianity had become part of the axiomatic bundle of truths on which the nation rested—those assumptions that made everything possible and were not themselves disputable.[39]

Resistance to Evangelicalism

The triumphant march of evangelicalism did not go unchallenged, however; a number of "cultural worlds," even among the respectable, remained outside it. The Masonic lodges were among the most important. Many prominent figures in the Revolutionary generation had been Masons, and after the Revolution the order spread widely. Deistic in its religious orientation, Masonry was a relic of the Enlightenment, offering a relaxed, convivial world of masculine companionship; neither women nor teetotalism entered the lodges. It appealed especially to artisans, professionals, and businessmen, and its members tended to be affiliated with nonevangelical churches. Masons were also active in politics; a disproportionate number of officeholders and men in public life, including Andrew Jackson, belonged to the order. As a counterculture to the evangelical world of home and church, Masonry created a good deal of resentment among women, but on the whole it seems to have been a generally accepted and even respected part of American life until the 1826 disappearance and suspected murder of a renegade Mason in New York State. The ensuing scandal produced a full-scale religious and political movement against Masonry, and many lodges closed.[40]

The attempts of the evangelical crusade to change the behavior patterns of Americans also met with resistance. Missions and Sunday schools were greeted with hostility and suspicion in the poorer wards of northern cities and in many isolated areas of the South and West, where people resented their constant appeals for money and saw them as agents of alien, centralizing forces. One western Baptist denounced the mission societies as "verging close to an aristocracy, with an object to sap the foundation of Baptist republican government." Many Unitarians and other well-educated nonevangelicals shrank from the invasion of privacy, which they saw as characteristic of the whole evangelical movement. Submerged anticlericalism and fears of clerical despotism were triggered in the late 1820s when the Presbyterian Ezra Stiles Ely called for a Christian party in politics—a loose coalition of committed Christian voters pledged to support only avowed Trinitarian Christians for office and to prevent the election of deists or liberals. "We are a Christian nation," declared Ely, "we have a right to demand that all our rulers in their conduct shall conform to Christian morality." Although Ely protested that he was not calling for a union of church and state and that the civil rights of "Jews and Infidels" would not be compromised, the outcry his proposals provoked caused fellow orthodox clergy to disassociate themselves from his position. The fact that Ely's ideal Christian candidate was Andrew Jackson probably also gave them pause.[41]

A similar reaction met the great campaign launched in 1828 by Lyman Beecher and one of the major directors of the benevolent empire, Lewis Tappan, to get Congress to prohibit movement of the mail on Sundays. This was an important symbolic issue for the evangelicals. They had been lobbying for some time to get presidents and Congress to make an explicit acknowledgment of the dependence of the United States on God and a "distinct assumption for this nation of a Christian character." The Sabbatarians also urged Christians to withhold patronage from any businesses that operated on Sunday. The enormous opposition this campaign aroused took the evangelical forces by surprise. The South perceived it as another example of the Yankee propensity to manage everyone else's affairs. In the North, the urban working classes, shopkeepers, and tavern owners rallied in opposition, joined by upper-class people still attached to an older aristocratic life-style and by Universalists, Unitarians, and many Baptists, who saw this as an ominous portent of a new union of church and state. Ely's tactless term *Christian party* became for many irritated people a catchall phrase for the busy army of Sunday school teachers, moral reformers, temperance agitators, and tract distributors—all "the persons," as an Ohio anti-Sabbatarian rally complained, "who set themselves up to be better than their neighbors." In the face of the outcry and a report of the Senate's Postal Committee, which delivered a ringing affirmation of the necessary separation of church and state, the discomfited Sabbath Union disbanded in 1832.[42]

A Christian Nation

Yet most Americans would probably have agreed with Ely's assertion that "we are a Christian Nation." Certainly the assertion by Chief Justice James Kent of New York, in an 1811 blasphemy case, that Christianity was part of the common law of the state provoked no strong dissent. Kent denied that the expression of insulting opinions about Christ and his mother fell within the right of religious freedom: "To revile, with malicious and blasphemous contempt, the religion professed by almost the whole community, is an abuse of that right." It struck "at the root of moral obligation."[43]

Nowhere was the intertwining of religious faith and attachment to the political institutions of the republic clearer than in the millennial hopes that were such a striking feature of this period. In early nineteenth-century America expectations of the imminent millennium (calculated as anywhere between 1843 and the year 2000) were not a phenomenon of the lunatic fringe but were quite widespread among clergy and laypeople of the major denominations. The still-lingering Puritan idea of a special godly mission merged with the signs of religious revival to produce a heady belief that America must be the place where the millennium—a thousand years of peace and godliness preceding the Second Coming of Christ—would begin.[44]

The founding generation had seen the Revolution as a key event in the progress of the world toward knowledge, humanity, and political liberty; the millennial vision incorporated political and material progress into a divine scheme in which these secular goods were made an integral part of the triumph of Christianity. In the millennium, prophesied one popular account in 1818, "every cottage" would be "irradiated with science, as well as with religion." Moreover, Americans were convinced that there was a special affinity between republican institutions and godliness. Francis Wayland, the president of Brown University, addressing the Sunday School Union in 1830, claimed the dawn of the millennium for the United States, not only because America possessed the greatest number of "truly religious persons" but because it also enjoyed "perfect civil and religious freedom." Lyman Beecher was convinced that God had established the United States "on purpose to show the world by one great successful experiment of what man is capable."[45]

Such favor entailed a tremendous obligation to live up to divine expectations and to make sure that the world took proper note of the example it was being set. "I do believe that the option is put into our hands," urged Wayland. "It is for us . . . to say, whether the present religious movement shall be onward, until it terminate in the universal triumph of the Messiah." Such feelings of hope and obligation motivated the small group of young men at Andover Seminary who launched the first organized foreign missions in the late 1820s. The foreign mission field became one of the great enterprises of the nineteenth century as hundreds of young men and women dedicated their lives to bringing Christianity and modern civilization to the heathen in Hawaii or China or India. "I verily believe, the term of half a century would be sufficient to carry freedom and Christianity, in triumph, around the globe," proclaimed one churchman in 1829. The Americanization of the millennium gave the United States a special mission in the world—not to revolutionize it but to redeem it for the combined cause of Protestant Christianity and ordered liberty.[46]

three

The Problem of
Republican Culture

The cultivation of the liberal arts will not suffer men to relapse
into ferocity.

—*North American Review*, 1816, quoting an English review
quoting Ovid

The United States was still a provincial culture at the beginning of the
nineteenth century, dependent on British literature, science, tastes, and standards. "In relation to the British capital as the centre of English literature,
arts, and science," admitted the novelist and editor Charles Brockden Brown
in 1801, "the situation of *New and Old-York* may be regarded as the same."
The essence of any provincial society is that it looks outside itself for guid-
ance and for standards; it will necessarily be imitative though also prickly
about its tributary status. When the society is not only provincial but postcolonial as well, we may expect to see an acute self-consciousness among its
intellectual classes: on the one hand, still looking for acceptance and approbation from the old metropolis; on the other, concerned to demonstrate their
independence and their equality in the realm of culture as well as politics.
Facing the world as exemplars and defenders of the achievements of their
new country, they must also justify themselves to their countrymen as representatives of what may now seem alien activities and standards. In this
acutely anxiety-provoking situation, it is not surprising that culture is not
something that can be taken for granted but is endlessly discussed and ago-
nized over.[1]

The defining feature of early nineteenth-century intellectual life in the United States was not any particular set of intellectual achievements but a running discourse about culture carried on in periodicals, in commencement and Phi Beta Kappa addresses, and in the whole plethora of American orations. Until around 1815 the concern was not mainly that the new republic should have a particularly distinct American culture but that it should have culture at all. The small groups of people concerned about the intellectual and cultural life of the new nation were thinking in terms of American participation in the republic of letters, an international polity that obliterated the boundaries of space and time; they were looking for outstanding achievement which would gain international recognition. Nor were they differentiating among different kinds of intellectual endeavor. The terms *letters* and *literature* were comprehensive; in the early nineteenth century they encompassed not only imaginative literature but scholarship, philosophy, and often science too.

The educated classes of the American colonies had always been in touch with Western high culture. After the Revolution there was a general assumption that the new nation would begin to make a marked, even leading, contribution to it. These expectations were encouraged by the widespread notion that from ancient times, learning, art, and science had progressed geographically from East to West. "Westward the course of empire takes its way," predicted Bishop Berkeley's famous eighteenth-century poem and prophesied "another golden age" of the arts in the New World. Above all, Americans made an automatic connection between political freedom and intellectual creativity. Surely in a nation without the depressing effect of an authoritarian church or oppressive political establishment, learning, science, and art would flourish as never before. If they did not, the failure would cast a disconcerting shadow over liberty.[2]

The self-consciousness about their place in time was increased by awareness of the unique intellectual quality of the century just past. One of the more remarkable publications of these years was *A Brief Retrospect of the Eighteenth Century* (1804) by Samuel Miller, a young Presbyterian minister in New York City who later became a staunch pillar of orthodoxy. Subtitled "A Sketch of the Revolutions and Improvements in Science, Arts, and Literature during That Period," this was an early attempt at an intellectual history of the Western world in the eighteenth century and covered science and belles lettres, the arts, philosophy, linguistics, history, and medicine. Miller candidly admitted that he had not read all the works he discussed in the book—much of his information came from friends and correspondents—but its inclusiveness is an indication of his broad awareness of the wider intellectual world and his sense of the new republic as part of an international culture.[3]

When Miller turned his attention to the United States, he had to admit that the progress of American science and literature had been somewhat slow to date. Still, he was convinced that "the literary prospects of our country are brightening every day." Such confidence was harder to maintain, however, as the years passed and the glorious cultural achievements failed to materialize. Emerson later said of the Massachusetts of his boyhood that "from 1790 to 1820, there was not a book, a speech, a conversation, or a thought in the State." This was the hyperbole of a self-conscious rebel against the world of his fathers, and the implication of complete mental torpor was unfair, yet it was true, as educated Americans across the country were uneasily aware, that the new republic was not producing creative minds to stand beside the European greats. Even in an American context, there seemed a decline from the Revolutionary generation. No works of political theory emerged to rival the *Federalist Papers*; there were no scientists with the international standing of Benjamin Franklin or David Rittenhouse of the previous generation. A number of writers who had seemed harbingers of a new dawn of American literature in the heady days of the Revolution and just after petered out in the new century. Two of the major Hartford Wits, Timothy Dwight and John Trumbull, turned their talents to careers in the law and education. After an astonishing burst of creativity at the end of the century, Charles Brockden Brown gave up imaginative writing for more sober editorial and political work and died young in 1810. The truly talented Philip Freneau had already written his best poetry. When the young poet, William Cullen Bryant, summed up the state of American poetry in 1818, he referred to Freneau as "a writer in verse of inferiour note."[4]

The Conditions for Culture in the Young Republic

The first twenty years or so of the century were full of laments about the parlous state of actual cultural life in America. Yet the conditions for cultural achievement were by no means absent in the new republic. The population was still overwhelmingly rural certainly, and cultural life generally depends on cities, where universities, libraries, bookstores, theaters, clubs, and learned societies sustain intellectual interaction. The removal of the political capital from Philadelphia to Washington at the beginning of the century meant that the United States would never have a comprehensive capital city like London or Paris; when even state capitals were moved from major cities, a further division was made between political and cultural centers. Nevertheless, the new republic certainly had some cities with sufficient population density and wealth to support a lively cultural life.

In 1800 Philadelphia, with a population of 70,000, was not only the largest city in America; it was one of the largest cities in the English-speaking world and seemed set to become the major cultural center of the new republic. It possessed a rich and cultivated society and was the home of the oldest learned and scientific organization in the United States, the American Philosophical

Society, a remarkable museum and a notable medical school attached to the university. During its brief stint as the nation's capital, the city had attracted artists, and it was the mecca for French émigrés fleeing first the Revolution and then Napoleon, many of whom brought with them a taste for the arts. British and Irish radicals evading British prisons, like the publisher Mathew Carey, also gravitated to Philadelphia.

New York, with a population of 60,000 in 1800, was fast gaining on Philadelphia and would soon surpass it in wealth and population. By 1820 it contained over 100,000 people, and its first guidebook (1807) had already proclaimed it the "commercial metropolis of North America." It was becoming the hub from which foreign news radiated, and it sheltered a small, convivial world of literary clubs, theaters, bookstores, and taverns where young men with literary and artistic aspirations gathered. Boston was much smaller at the beginning of the century, with 25,000 people. The only other considerable cities, Charleston and Baltimore, were smaller yet, with populations of 18,000 and 13,000, respectively. Still, Edinburgh was not much larger than Philadelphia, and Weimar was about the same size as Hartford, Connecticut, and both were major centers of European culture. George Tucker of Virginia compared the United States with the other "English provinces," Scotland and Ireland, and wondered why they were both so much more culturally productive than his own country.[5]

By European standards, the United States was a highly literate society. It was often said to be a reading society too, although large numbers of literate people probably read only the Bible and religious tracts or the newspapers. By 1810 more than 22 million copies of 376 newspapers were in circulation annually, a larger circulation than anywhere else in the world. Recognizing the importance of the flow of information in a republic, the post office subsidized the distribution of newspapers through the mail, enabling people to obtain papers from major centers. Through the press, people in even remote areas could keep in touch with the wider world. A man in English Prairie, Illinois, for example, reported in 1817 that the Philadelphia daily papers arrived once a week, about a month late, and in them he could read extracts from English journals of the month before. Miller deplored the "profligate and scurrilous" character of most American newspapers, but he understood their potential role in developing popular intelligence. The newspapers often included pieces on the arts and sciences and extracts from books. Even the advertisements, with news of new books, inventions, and improvements, he pointed out were "well calculated to enlarge and enlighten the public mind."[6]

There was also a sharp increase in the publication and distribution of books at the turn of the century, although the book-reading public was much smaller than that for other kinds of printed matter. In New England, certainly the most "bookish" region, books spread as areas became integrated into a market economy. New Englanders were also disproportionately represented among producers of literature. In Virginia, on the other hand, over half of early-nineteenth-century estate inventories contained no books. The town-country distinction appears to be more important than wealth. With several spectacular exceptions, like Jefferson and John Randolph, even well-to-do planters did not participate much in the "book culture," whereas people with quite modest estates in the towns might possess fairly sizable libraries. In its general nonbookishness Virginia was more representative of the country as a whole than was New England.[7]

In newer western settlements, the book culture was even more thinly spread. "The people here," Timothy Flint noted reluctantly of Missouri, "are not yet a reading people." But settlers who had belonged to the reading classes in the East took some cherished books with them to their new homes and retained a hunger for them. It was such people who were behind legendary enterprises like the "coonskin library" founded by a small group of pioneer New England families in Ames, Ohio, who purchased books from Boston with their only currency: coonskins. These were pioneers who carried with them the old Puritan determination not to become "barbarians" in the wilderness.[8]

Publishing was very much a local enterprise, though Mathew Carey of Philadelphia was developing into a major national firm. In frontier areas cultural life began with the setting up of a printer's shop; quite small towns like Pittsburgh and Portland, Maine, became publishing centers for their region. Most of the books published, and read, were reprints of English books, for there was no international copyright and thus no royalties to be paid to an author overseas. Besides, the English authors had established reputations, and publishers knew they would sell. Native authors often had to bear the cost of publishing their works themselves or publish by subscription.

Books were not cheap, but the cost fell from the 1790s on through the spread of libraries. Besides college libraries there were the so-called social libraries, which were essentially owned by shareholders, and circulating libraries run as commercial enterprises. The social libraries, like the New York Society Library and the Boston Athenaeum, were elite institutions, with shares costing from twenty dollars (in New York) to a hundred dollars (in Boston). The circulating libraries, which could be joined for about six dollars a year or even pennies a day, offered mainly fiction and were an indication of the growth of a new kind of reading public.[9]

"This is a novel-reading age," proclaimed the *New York Magazine* in 1797. A growing taste for fiction began to create a popular market for books. Large numbers of novels were turned out, often to a formula, as the almost insatiable demand became apparent. Their popularity stimulated the proliferation of commercial lending libraries in practically every town. A large commercial library like that run by the French immigrant Hocquet Caritat in New York listed 1,500 fiction titles. By 1814 the postmaster general was complaining that the mails "were overcrowded with novels and the lighter kind of books for amusement."[10]

The majority of the novels Americans read were English imports, but about a hundred native works were produced between 1789 and 1820. In this period between the classic novels of Richardson and Fielding and before Scott, the most widely read novelistic genres were the Gothic terror romance and the "seduction" novel, in which the heroine negotiated the sexual hazards of young womanhood before the happy ending of a safe marriage or the tragic denouement of dishonor and death. The novel undoubtedly enlarged the reading public and drew in new readers, especially women, but at the turn of the century, it also aroused sharp censure from the clergy and most other educated men.

Many churchmen condemned the novel on the moral grounds that its emphasis on sexual passion made vice attractive. In addition, the prevailing Common Sense philosophy reinforced a distrust of the uncontrolled imagination. An inherently individualistic and private activity, novel reading created an intense imaginative identification with an alternative world more passionate and interesting than actual life, a world that might encourage moral judgments at odds with the conventions of society. This addictive private world was thought to be particularly dangerous to young women, and there was hardly an advice book or commencement address at a girls' school without a warning against novel reading. The extent to which novels became "real" to their readers is shown by the process through which people "identified" a particular grave in New York City with the fictional heroine of Susanna Rowson's best-selling *Charlotte Temple* (1791); it received many more visitors than the nearby graves of Alexander Hamilton or Robert Fulton.[11]

A new phenomenon was arising in the early years of the nineteenth century: a new intermediate cultural world between the high culture of the well educated and the mass of the barely literate who seldom read at all. Both the novel and the newspaper were adjuncts to the modern personality in that they enlarged the range of information and identification beyond the merely local and practical. Neither, in elite eyes, was entirely respectable; the newspapers were often scurrilous and full of party invective; the novels were sentimental, unrealistic, and faintly salacious. For men concerned with high culture, this growing number of people who were no longer part of the subliterate mass yet whose cultural tastes were escaping the direction of traditional leaders was deeply disturbing.

High Culture and the Professional Classes

High cultural life in the early republic was dominated by small groups of professional men: lawyers and doctors, some of the clergy, occasionally a journalist, a small number of college professors, with the addition of such merchants or landed gentry as had acquired a taste for literature and the arts, and a significant, but dwindling number of men in politics like De Witt Clinton and Robert Livingston of New York or John Quincy Adams of Massachusetts—and, of course, Thomas Jefferson. "In no other period in American history," according to the literary scholar William Charvat, was American culture "so completely and directly dominated by the professional classes; concomitantly, in no other period has the economically dominant class exhibited such an interest in the arts"—and one could add science and scholarship. This was the class that bought nonfiction books, and sometimes paintings, that sustained learned societies and periodicals, and that built up cultural institutions. They read the Latin classics and the Scottish philosophers, Locke and Adam Smith, Hume and Gibbon, Shakespeare and Milton, and, at the beginning of the century, they still read the French philosophers of the Enlightenment—Voltaire, Rousseau, and Montesquieu. Generally they took their cultural standards from England, and their knowledge of European intellectual developments was usually first filtered through English commentary. Their aesthetic tastes were primarily neoclassical; they admired correctness and clarity of style, polish, and balance. Addison, Steele, and Goldsmith were the models. Pope's *Essay on Man* went through 105 editions in the United States between 1790 and 1830, and the heroic couplet settled like a vice over American verse. But some were beginning to find eighteenth-century forms too artificial, and the early romantic poetry of William Cowper, James Thompson, Arthur Young, Thomas Campbell, and especially Robert Burns enjoyed considerable popularity.[12]

This professional gentry was also the culture-producing class. There were few professional writers as such at the beginning of the century and certainly no intelligentsia. There were professional painters, perhaps an index of the lower status of the plastic arts. But writing for the public was something that gentlemen did as part of their general leadership role in society. The scant scientific research was carried out mainly by medical men in time spared from their practice or by the small number of men employed in teaching scientific studies in the colleges. Lawyers, clergy, and politicians might do a little work in natural history, linguistics, or ethnology; they would certainly feel the need to keep abreast of major scientific or philosophical developments, for this was the tail end of a period when there was still a unified culture, and it was expected that the man of letters would have at least an overview of the entire universe of knowledge. Lawyers, followed by the clergy, dominated literature, turning out most of the essays, poetry, criticism, history, and biography of this period. A few, like Washington Irving and William Cullen Bryant, eventually left the practice of law for a professional literary life, but for most, writing was something they did, as they often said, in moments stolen or snatched from professional labors.[13]

Rather typical literary productions by this class were American versions of an already old-fashioned eighteenth-century genre—light satires on American society in the guise of letters written by a foreign traveler, such as *Letters of the British Spy* (1803) by William Wirt, *Inchiquin's Letters* (1810) by Charles Ingersoll, *Letters from Virginia* (1816) by George Tucker, and *The Letters of Shacoolen* (1802) written by the young Benjamin Silliman before he settled down to being a scientist. All published under pseudonyms to preserve gentlemanly anonymity, they mildly prodded the foibles of their compatriots. Didactic in an urbane way, they depended for effectiveness on a small, compact world of common values, where anyone of importance knew everyone else. The genre was parodied effectively by the young New Yorkers Washington Irving and James Kirke Paulding in their *Salmagundi* essays (1807).[14]

At the beginning of the century it was generally assumed that the great work of American literature would be an epic poem, the most prestigious and elevating literary form. To men reared on the classics, it seemed only fitting that the new nation should have an *Iliad* to celebrate its founding. A number of epics were dutifully turned out and almost immediately forgotten, but the most ambitious, and the most resounding failure, because the most was expected of it, was Joel Barlow's *Columbiad* (1807). Once a member of the Hartford Wits, Barlow had become a Jeffersonian Republican, and had spent the years between 1788 and 1804 in France. A friend of Jefferson and the scientific men connected with the American Philosophical Society, Barlow was a man of projects, interested in promoting internal improvements of every kind, from canals to a national university. He had even contemplated writing an epic on canals—"A Poem on the Application of Physical Science to Political Economy in Four Books"—but instead decided to rework an earlier poem of 1787, "The Vision of Columbus." The new version, *The Columbiad*, was in many ways another project for the improvement of his country. He wished, wrote Barlow, "to inculcate the love of rational liberty. . . . This is the moment in America to give such a direction to poetry, painting, and the other fine arts, that true and useful ideas of glory may be implanted in the minds of men here." Barlow disapproved of Homer for glorifying war; his own epic is built on the vision of future peaceful conquests of nature by science and technology, all flourishing under a free republican government. He used a number of new verbal coinages in the poem, one of which he adapted from the French, "to utilize"; his epic was an eighteenth-century vision of how the land might be utilized for the betterment of humanity.[15]

Barlow was wealthy, and he had the poem sumptuously produced, but neither the production nor the patriotism could secure its success. Its reception in America was respectful at best, derisive at worst. In Britain, the feared Francis Jeffrey in the *Edinburgh Review* denounced its style as "a curious intermixture . . . of extreme homeliness and flatness, with a sort of turbulent and bombastic elevation." "American republicans," he wrote, "bear no sort of resemblance to the Greeks of the days of Homer . . . but are very much such people, we suppose, as the modern traders of Manchester, Liverpool, or Glasgow. . . . They are just as likely to write epic poems, therefore, as the inhabitants of our trading towns at home."[16]

A much more successful "epic," artistically as well as commercially, was a spoof: *A History of New York, from the Beginning of the World to the End of the Dutch Dynasty by Diedrich Knickerbocker* (1809), by the twenty-six-year-old Washington Irving. Irving was the rather pampered youngest son of a well-to-do New York family who, while desultorily studying for the bar, hung out with a small group of literary and artistic young men and dabbled in writing. The *History* is a burlesque of pompous historical research and inflated political rhetoric. It included an extended satire on Thomas Jefferson, who appears as Governor William the Testy, the epitome of the impractical theorist in politics, whose regime was dominated by the "grand cabalistic word . . . economy." The book made Irving the talk of New York, and some old Dutch families never forgave him for ridiculing their ancestors. But it is Jeffersonian America that Irving was satirizing—and more sharply than he would ever do again.[17]

Probing the Question of Culture

As it became increasingly apparent that the expectations for a new cultural dawn in the United States were not being fulfilled, the old colonial fears of decline into barbarism crept back. Men of letters exhibited a growing malaise. Even if the republic survived, even if it prospered past all expectations, educated people worried that it would become not a new Athens or even a new Rome but a great barbarous empire, extended mindlessly across space, with here and there pockets of faint reflection from the corrupt but glorious culture of Europe. Americans had difficulty accepting the conclusion that political freedom might have no essential connection with scientific or artistic creativity and that the unfettered mind may not necessarily produce anything very interesting.

Part of the trouble was the discontent that came from being out of the mainstream. From Pittsburgh, Hugh Henry Brackenridge, only partly tongue-in-cheek, sighed for the "garrets of London," for he knew that they, not the frontier, were the proper habitat for genius. "Our elder brethren in Europe," wrote the botanist Benjamin Waterhouse in 1811, "know not the difficulties that the first settlers in science have to encounter." As his metaphor implied, these men were very much aware of themselves as a small band on the fringes of the international intellectual world of science, and they worried about being accorded recognition. The Philadelphia chemist Robert Hare in 1817 urged Benjamin Silliman of Yale University to send articles to

England for publication on the grounds that "it really seems bad policy to publish any thing in this country upon science especially in the first instance. It is rarely attended to in England and we are so low in capacity at home that few appreciate any thing which is done here unless it is sanctioned abroad."[18]

Perhaps even more important psychologically was the feeling of being no longer quite at home in the society at a time when alienation had not yet become a badge of honor for the intellectual. As society became more democratic, the authority of the man of letters fell away along with the authority of the patrician class to which he was allied. Brackenridge as a man of letters wanted to believe that there is "a natural alliance between liberty and letters" and that the people would willingly turn to the disinterested expertise of literary men. Yet allowing intellectuals to advise them was the leadership role that the people were least likely to grant. It was not "the want of learning that I consider as a defect," Brackenridge commented grimly of the society of western Pennsylvania, "but the *contempt of it.*"[19]

The educated classes felt themselves assailed on two fronts: by the philistinism of their compatroits and by sniping from the ex-mother country. Some British travel writers and literary critics were only too happy to portray the United States as a nation of uncivilized eye gougers, slave holders, and money grubbers. On the few occasions when the influential British reviews took notice of American works, they usually took the opportunity either to remark on the prevalence of barbarous Americanisms and the general inferiority of American culture or (even more galling) to bestow patronizing encouragement on these jejune efforts. "The style of Mr. Adams is in general very tolerable English," allowed the *Edinburgh Review* in 1809, reviewing John Quincy Adams's *Letters on Silesia*, adding, "which, for American composition, is no moderate praise." The *Quarterly Review* thought there was little hope for arts and literature in a society "characterized by mercenary speculation, and formed for individual aggrandizement." The most wounding of all was probably Sidney Smith's famous set of questions in the *Edinburgh Review* as late as 1820: "In the four quarters of the globe, who reads an American book? or goes to an American play? or looks at an American picture or statue? What does the world yet owe to American physicians or Surgeons? What new substances have their chemists discovered . . . ?"[20]

A number of American writers produced defensive replies to British attacks, but the most important response from the educated classes to these disappointments and humiliations was a promotional campaign for culture. "Who reads an American book?" was quoted over and over by culturally aware Americans as a mortifying reminder of their lack of standing in the republic of letters and as a goad to further effort. A Philadelphia medical and scientific journal printed, "What does the world yet owe to American physicians or Surgeons?" year after year on its title page as a spur to ambition. National pride could be a powerful weapon in stimulating intellectual effort and in tapping the increasing amount of money in the country for the support of arts and learning.[21]

In the face of a general indifference, if not hostility, it was necessary to formulate arguments to show why literature, arts, and the sciences were important. At the same time the culture promoters attempted to work out what had gone wrong. Why had high culture not flourished so far in America as expected? A number of arguments were offered, appearing again and again in different variations. American libraries were woefully inadequate for real scholarship. (A common example was that no library in the United States contained sufficient books to sustain an American Gibbon.) Scientific books, apparatus, and instruments were scarce. American colleges were inadequate, and the professors were expected to devote the bulk of their time to teaching, often at a quite elementary level, rather than to scholarship or research. The commercial spirit of the people diverted talented men into more immediately profitable paths, for where wealth is "the principal test of influence, the learned will experience but little reward either of honour or emolument." The thinly scattered population posed serious obstacles to the production and circulation of literature. The lack of "literary competition, rewards, and honours" meant that there was no incentive for real cultural effort, and, in any case, the American passion for politics made public office seem the only worthwhile avenue to fame. Early marriage or being expected to earn one's own living at too young an age deflected young men from the long and poorly paid apprenticeship needed for great intellectual achievements. The wide availability of English works crowded out and overshadowed American products. Finally there was "the entire absence of all government patronage, whether state or federal."[22]

One particularly disturbing point emerged from the soul searching: the development of high culture seemed to be retarded by some of the very elements integral to republicanism, such as the absence of a hereditary aristocracy. The Bostonian William Tudor pointed out that in great European families "a splended gallery of paintings, a magnificent library, descend to the inheritor, with the virtual obligation to cheer genius, to support science, to protect art." This kind of aristocracy was not compatible with American republicanism, and yet, "looking at the succession of ages, such establishments are the property of the publick, of which the apparent possessor, is only the hereditary keeper." It was disconcerting that in the unequal societies of Europe, certain kinds of "public things" were better taken care of than in a republic, where the tendency was always for wealth to circulate more widely among many private hands. The New England scholar Edward Everett, in a scathing attack on republican indifference and parsimony, pointed out that in Europe, major universities were supported by petty German principalities "whose whole revenues would not pay half the annual imposts of New York." They had been established by "dukes and princes, and electors and kings, by these natural enemies, as they have been called, of the people. It is these arbitrary lords and petty tyrants, who have done that for their states, which United America will not do for herself. . . . Who can see, without shame, that the federal government of America is the only government in the civilized world, that has never founded a literary institution of any description or sort?"[23]

To a considerable extent the question of culture came to center on the question of patronage: who or what agency would pay for cultural artifacts and support scholars, writers, scientists, and artists? High culture clearly could not be entirely self-sustaining in the popular marketplace, yet the resources for patronage in the United States seemed unpromising. There were only just beginning to be very rich men in America, and few had got into the habit of patronage as a necessary concomitant of status. Nor were American colleges wealthy enough to duplicate the fellowships available in Europe.

Literary men, however, tended to exaggerate, often in quite maudlin tones, the absence of support in their society. It was not entirely true that budding writers or artists had to struggle in a wholly cold and unsympathetic environment. There were considerable advantages to the fact that communities were still small. The educated men of any locality knew each other, and it was easy to spot the young man of talent who might be the up-and-coming American genius everyone was waiting for. The talented young were not lost in the mass or overwhelmed by competition. Modern students must envy young men like Edward Everett, Benjamin Silliman, and Henry Longfellow who, barely out of college, were first appointed as university professors and then packed off to Europe at college expense to prepare for the job.

Artists too received individual patronage. John Vanderlyn was first sent to study in Paris through the generosity of Aaron Burr; Boston merchants set up a trust fund for the artist Washington Allston; and in Philadelphia a group of young men who founded the Academy of Natural Sciences received generous financial support from the geologist-philanthropist William McClure. In a review of the poetry of Robert Treat Paine, after complaining that in America "the man of letters is almost an insulated being, with few to understand, less to value, and scarcely any to encourage his pursuits," Washington Irving had to admit that Paine had enjoyed considerable financial support from family and friends. His works had not only received constant flattering attention but had also made him a good deal of money. The collapse of his talent was due to his drunkenness rather than lack of appreciation.[24]

The culture promoters, however, wanted patronage on a larger scale and an official basis. Support from the national government would be the stamp of public endorsement to art and learning as valid American pursuits. Many voices called for federal aid to the arts and sciences. Some, like Charles

Willson Peale, the museum owner, and John Trumbull, the artist, petitioned unsuccessfully for aid to their own projects. President John Kirkland of Harvard wondered wistfully whether the federal government might be persuaded to subsidize a great library, "even at an expense equal to the cost of a single frigate." The national government did offer some slight support to science in sending exploring expeditions to the West and in 1816 authorizing a coastal survey, although Congress constantly harassed its director because he could not produce useful information quickly enough. Throughout the century diplomatic and consular posts often went to men of letters. State governments later supported science through the various state geological surveys in the 1830s and 1840s, and municipalities sometimes extended aid to learned societies by giving them rent-free space. But large-scale and systematic government aid was out of the question. The republican attachment to public economy translated, as the architect Latrobe pointed out, to "the dread of responsibility in the individual representatives of the people, converting all their notions of good government into the single anxiety to avoid expenditure."[25]

Republicanism and Culture

Apart from parsimony, there was a strong tendency in republican thought to equate the arts and learning with luxury, which implied decadence, effeminacy, and the end of virtue. John Adams's famous remark that he studied politics and war so that his sons might study mathematics and philosophy, geography, and natural history, so that their sons might study music and poetry, subtly denigrated the arts as fruits of the postheroic age. By the early nineteenth century this wary attitude had been reinforced by democratic suspicion of anything not obviously useful or immediately appealing to a wide popular audience, making it hard to justify spending public money on activities that the majority of people did not find particularly compelling.[26]

It might be thought that the intellectual interests and accomplishments of the president would have given some prestige to cultural activities. Jefferson was one of the most cultivated men of his generation; he remained president of the American Philosophical Society while serving as president of the United States. In fact, however, Jefferson's cultural and scientific involvements proved to be an Achilles heel, which his adversaries exploited. His skills in "impaling butterflies and insects" hardly fitted him as head of state, mocked one Federalist opponent. "He is a man of letters, and should be a retired one. His closet, and not the cabinet, is his place," declared another. John Quincy Adams mercilessly ridiculed Jefferson's interest in natural history and was justly punished some twenty years later by having his own considerable intellectual talents similarly mocked by his Jacksonian opponents. In both cases, the mockers were not necessarily anti-intellectual themselves, but they recognized that strong interest in learning or the arts was a political weakness that could be exploited.[27]

Jefferson himself was too thoroughly imbued with the self-denying quality of republicanism when it came to expenditure of public money to give impetus to public patronage of the arts or sciences, outside of the obvious need to put up public buildings. Perhaps he gauged accurately the temper of Congress and the limits of even his considerable abilities to manage it. Congress maintained an import tax on books for example, in spite of appeals from colleges and individuals, until 1816 when it exempted those destined for incorporated libraries and learned societies. But they refused to exempt the individual buyer, replying to a memorial from Jefferson that imported books were "extravagant expenditures" and "foreign luxuries," of benefit only to the "scholar of wealth and leisure."[28]

The equation of books with luxury, minority taste, and lack of general utility was clear in the debate over Jefferson's offer to sell Congress his own extensive library to replace the congressional library burned by the British in 1814. Men who still regarded Jefferson as the epitome of French immorality assumed that many of the books would be irreligious and improper. Moreover, the proposed sale could easily be construed as "corruption"—public money diverted into private hands. "The bill," declaimed the Federalist Cyrus King of Massachusetts, "would put $23,900 into Jefferson's pocket for about 6,000 books, good, bad, and indifferent, old, new, and worthless, in languages which many can not read, and most ought not." Although Congress eventually agreed to buy the collection, which became the nucleus of the Library of Congress, the rancor of the debate and the comparative smallness of the sum shocked the British diplomat Augustus Foster, who put it down as typical of republican stinginess.[29]

Even among those committed to promoting cultural life in America, many had internalized republican suspicion of esoteric interests. Republican focus on civic duty and commitment to the collectivity necessarily meant a distrust of purely private enjoyment or absorption in investigations whose benefit to the public good was not clear. Because men from the professional and upper classes still assumed that their major role was to lead society, there was considerable unease at the prospect of the man who might withdraw himself from community and public concerns, to become a literary "hermit," in "exclusive and solitary devotion to a single pursuit." This species of egotism was bad for the individual character and deprived the community of its due. While the republican gentleman was certainly expected to be a cultivated man, even a scholar or a man of letters, to be a "mere" (another favorite word) scholar or mere litterateur, even if one was prepared to bear the economic consequences, carried the implication of being something of a shirker. "To make literature one's main employment," in the early years of the century, recalled Richard Henry Dana, who did just that, "was held little better than being a drone."[30]

The career of the Reverend William Bentley of Salem, Massachusetts, is an instructive example of the ways in which internalization of the norms of civic involvement inhibited intellectual productivity. Bentley was a polymath who knew twenty languages, studied history, philology, the sciences, and the new biblical criticism, and corresponded with foreign scholars. His personal library of four thousand volumes was one of the largest private collections in the country. Yet Bentley left no monument to his learning; he wrote no books, and even his library, by his own wish, was divided up after his death. Bentley devoted his learning not to the creation of new knowledge but to the dissemination of information among as wide a public as possible. For nearly twenty-five years he devoted much of his leisure to turning out bi-weekly digests of the most impotent domestic and foreign news for local newspapers. These digests included notices of new books and important scientific discoveries and were designed to serve the public good by enlightening and elevating public opinion.[31]

While many professional men were also men of letters, they did not view such activities with ultimate seriousness and make literature their principal concern. Most were too involved with the public and social life of their communities and too concerned about the opinion of their own class. Professional men with a literary bent were torn between feeling that this elevated them above narrowness and suspecting that many of their colleagues would take them less rather than more seriously because of these abilities. John Quincy Adams, for example, contributed regularly to the Philadelphia literary magazine, the *Port Folio*, but requested that his poems remain anonymous since "no small number of very worthy citizens among us [are] irrevocably convinced that it is impossible at once to be a man of business and a man of rhyme." Weighty works of history were one thing; poetry had to be dealt with more carefully. It might well be regarded favorably, the Virginian St. George Tucker told William Wirt, as long as it was "given to the world in such a manner as to appear merely as a *jeu d'esprit*, the effusion of a leisure moment."[32]

Even those who were calling strenuously for a national literature made clear that literary activity should be consciously directed toward the public good. When Joseph Stevens Buckminster of Boston gave an extremely influential Phi Beta Kappa address in 1809, "Dangers and Duties of the Man of Letters," the "dangers" loomed rather larger than the duties. Buckminster urged his audience to contribute to a new "Augustan Age" in America, but his model of the man of letters was Cicero, whose learning and eloquence was dedicated to the service of the republic. The man who gave into the "luxurious leisure of study" and withdrew from active life was likely to find that "his learning becomes effeminate." He warned of the "solitary diseases of the imagination" and insisted that "in the eye of reason and of Christianity, simple unprofitableness is always a crime." As much as they valued learning and letters, early nineteenth century republicans were not ready to accept culture as an autonomous, self-evidently valid realm.[33]

The culture promoters still used the republican language of corruption and virtue as they tried to persuade the wealthy to contribute to the support of art and literature. Far from being a species of luxury, they argued, culture should be seen as an antidote to it. Literature and the arts might even redeem the nation from that gross materialism, that "physical, inelegant, immature, unsanctified, Carthaginian, perishable prosperity," that seemed to be becoming its most salient characteristic. The growing prudery and fear of sensuality of the early nineteenth century could also be enlisted in the cause of culture. As the republic became wealthier, spending money on the fine arts or the patronage of literature would prevent the purse from being poured out on sensual indulgence. Jefferson, accepting honorary membership in the Philadelphia Society of Artists, acknowledged grudgingly that patronage of the arts might "be able to give an innocent and pleasing direction to accumulations of wealth, which would otherwise be employed in the nourishment of coarse and vicious habits." The subscription memorial for the Boston Athenaeum spoke of the dangers of wealth and assured subscribers that membership would "check that dissipation which enervates and depraves." The liberal studies encouraged and made possible by the Athenaeum would "strengthen not debilitate, the mind . . . subdue, not inflame, the passions." Even the fine arts could be desensualized; the *Analectic Magazine* in 1815 maintained that the cultivation of artistic taste disentangled the mind from "appetite" and freed it from the "thralldom of sense" so that what "began in taste, may, as it is exalted and refined, conclude in virtue." Properly restrained, the arts could even become "the instruments of public morality." The proscenium arch of the Pavilion Theater in Cincinnati, built in 1822, summed up the argument in a prominently displayed motto: "The means, pleasure—the end, virtue."[34]

Creating a Cultural Infrastructure

It was within this context, in which national and civic pride and a wistful desire for a splendid cultural flowering blended with republican caution about its implications, that Americans began to create an institutional base for intellectual and artistic activity. Almost entirely without any governmental aid, professional and mercantile elites came together to found and support learned societies, art academies, and libraries and to establish magazines and journals, ensuring that at least some of the wealth and energy of the new republic would be channeled into the support of culture.

Philadelphia and Boston already had learned societies, peculiarly eighteenth-century institutions that emphasized the sciences and useful improvements, and brought together professional practitioners of science with the gentleman-amateur. New York lagged but acquired a Literary and Philosophical Society and a historical society by 1814. In New York and then Philadelphia, the two wealthiest cities, groups of gentry leaders created the American Academy of Fine Arts (1802) and the Pennsylvania Academy of the Fine Arts (1805), which both began by acquiring plaster casts of the most famous antique statues in the Louvre. To protect the more delicate sensibilities of American women, these were exhibited separately to ladies, and the male statues were provided with fig leaves. By 1816 even the cultural desert of Washington had the Columbian Institution, a learned society devoted to useful science, whose members included several congressmen.[35]

In the South, the absence of major cities retarded the development of the kind of cultural communities that formed in the North. Charleston, the most self-consciously sophisticated and culturally inclined of southern cities, founded the Literary and Philosophical Society in 1814, but such institutions proved hard to sustain in the context of southern life. A short-lived Fine Arts Academy got little support, as its founders complained, from "our wealthy and fashionable citizens." In the West, civic-minded mercantile and professional elites in the small but growing cities sought to translate eastern cultural institutions to the frontier. Lexington, Kentucky, had its Athenaeum, and in the 1820s professional men and literati met at the Kentucky Institute to read papers on subjects varying from theories of yellow fever to geology and Indian antiquities. In Cincinnati, the dynamic medical man Daniel Drake launched a campaign of institution building, founding a lyceum, a circulating library, a debating society, a medical college, a lunatic asylum, and an ambitious museum.[36]

The most successful city in creating long-lasting cultural institutions was Boston, where a fusion of professional and mercantile elites created a patrician class with an especially strong feeling of corporate responsibility for civic improvement. The architects they commissioned to build their new houses, Charles Bulfinch and Samuel McIntyre, created urban streetscapes of chaste elegance that expressed both status and a sense of urban form. Apart from considerable donations to Harvard College, the Boston elite also produced such lasting institutions as the Massachusetts Historical Society (1791); the American Antiquarian Society (1812), founded by Isaiah Thomas, a wealthy retired printer; and Massachusetts General Hospital (1811). Its most characteristic creation was the Boston Athenaeum, incorporated in 1807 and based on a similar institution in Liverpool, a provincial city whose wealth, like that of Boston, was based on commerce. A gentlemen's library and reading room, it was established "to contain the works of learning and science in all languages; particularly such rare and expensive publications as are not generally to be obtained in this country." By 1830 it was one of the largest libraries in America.[37]

Some of the most important cultural institutions established in these years were scientific journals and critical reviews. In New Haven in 1818, Benjamin Silliman of Yale University established the *American Journal of Science*, which became the foremost scientific journal in America and a major force in the development of science in the new republic. A number of critical literary magazines were established in the major cities, supported by small groups of congenial professional men who did most of the writing and editing. Launching a magazine was a risky venture, and many lasted no more than a couple of years. Critical standards were tentative, veering, as William Cullen Bryant complained, between extravagant praise of any product of an American pen and a reluctance to express enthusiasm about anything "till we see the seal of transatlantic approbation upon it." Nevertheless, the reviews provided American authors with a public reaction to their work and also served as a means of letting the educated public know what was going on in the world of culture and ideas. They created a community of readers.[38]

The most influential review of the early years of the century was Joseph Dennie's *Port Folio* in Philadelphia, founded in 1801 and lasting until 1827, the first American magazine to exist so long. It combined reviews with original essays, poetry, fiction, and politics. Dennie was an extreme Federalist with neoclassical tastes and standards; the journal held up the essays of the English eighteenth-century writers Addison and Goldsmith as models of elegant prose and as antidotes to the bombast and inflated rhetoric he deplored in America. His stated aim for the *Port Folio* remained to "revive classical discipline, create a passion for pure undefiled English, guide the taste and fortify the judgment of youth, multiply the editions of sterling authors, and absolutely eradicate every bad book in the country."[39]

The most successful attempt to mold cultural tastes was made in Boston. Out of considerable discussion about the problem of culture, came, first, the *Monthly Anthology*, which led directly to the founding of the Athenaeum, and then the long-lived *North American Review*, which lasted into the twentieth century. Founded by William Tudor, eldest son of a wealthy Massachusetts mercantile family, it soon became the most important intellectual magazine in the country. Specializing in the review essay, which took off from a review of several related works into a discussion of wider issues, it often excerpted large portions of books, especially those not widely available. Modeled on the English critical reviews, it ranged widely over natural history, the law, and economics, as well as history, philosophy, and belles lettres, and it often commented at length on important public addresses. Although its editorial board aimed to review every important American work, it also wanted to maintain the link between Americans and the wider international intellectual world, and it gave considerable space to discussing foreign literature. The journal was one of the earliest channels through which knowledge of intellectual developments in Germany came to America. By 1826 the *North American Review* had a circulation of three thousand, about the same as the circulation in America of the *Edinburgh Review* and the *Quarterly*. (The Methodist *Christian Advocate*, on the other hand, had a circulation of 25,000.)[40]

The men who edited the most important literary reviews were politically conservative, and their intellectual concerns blended with their political and social anxieties. The aim was to create and maintain a community of men of letters with a strong sense of moral responsibility to guide their culture in sane and wholesome paths. The reviews would be filters, admitting only those new ideas or literary modes from home or abroad that they judged to be worthwhile. "We are fully aware," wrote Tudor, "that the publick stands in need of literary guardians, and that it will not answer in any province of learning, to trust entirely to individual self government." The renewed religiosity of the early nineteenth century made a good deal of earlier literature seem rather coarse; from now on, works would be judged on criteria of "purity" and "refinement," as well as aesthetic form. Buckminster, a member of the *Anthology* group, likened the role of the critic in the republic of letters to that of the ancient Roman consuls, whose task was to ensure that the "commonwealth suffer no harm."[41]

The Problem of Language

The reviewers constituted themselves as guardians not only of the cause of American literature but also of the purity of the language. Rapid social change seemed to be producing marked changes in language. While a deliberate ideological attempt to coin a new American word, Samuel L. Mitchell's 1804 suggestion that the United States be renamed *Fredonia*, fell flat, ordinary Americans were zestfully producing an abundance of new words—adopting them from Dutch, German, and Spanish, combining English words in new ways or adapting them to new meanings, and developing new verbs like *to affiliate*, *to Americanize*, and *to boost*.[42]

Not only did these changes seem to augur linguistic anarchy, they impeded national unity. A wildly proliferating language, especially with regional differences, would add to the fragmentation of American life, whereas a uniform language would help to bind the union together. In 1821 a writer and language student, William S. Cardell, proposed an American academy of languages and belles lettres that would monitor changes in the language and form "as far as practicable, an English standard of writing and pronunciation, correct, fixed, and uniform, throughout our extensive territory." Linguistic change could not be stopped, but "some guiding influence may be exercised."

Cardell sought the support of leading politicians and men of letters, including Jefferson, who was quite relaxed about neologisms and not enthusiastic about any attempt to fix language officially. The academy seems to have consisted essentially of Cardell himself and disappeared after publishing three promotional circulars.[43]

The most famous proponent of linguistic uniformity was Noah Webster, another extraordinarily long-lived man whose active career spanned the Revolution through the age of Jackson. Webster's involvement with language was multifaceted. He wanted to reform English spelling drastically and wean Americans from slavish acceptance of British authority in linguistic and literary matters. In the 1780s he had looked forward to a time when American English would be as different from the parent tongue as Swedish and Dutch were from German. It was more important to him, however, that American speech be nationally uniform than nationally distinct. Although he was prepared to conceive of grammar as essentially descriptive rather than prescriptive, he still wanted national usage rather than local diversity and hoped that his spellers would bring this about.[44]

For many American men of letters, particularly those of Federalist politics, the purity of language had deeper implications than national unity. It was a question of unity with the past, of maintaining America's place as part of the civilization defined by the English language. As the *General Repository and Review* of Cambridge stated firmly in 1813, it opposed anything that might "tend to impair the character of our language, as the legitimate offspring of an English stock . . . and to prevent our being in a manner an acknowledged constituent part of this distinguished portion of the republic of letters." Keeping the language pure of neologisms was symbolic of maintaining civilized standards in the New World and holding the pass against the encroachments and debasements of democracy. Joseph Dennie, a great upholder of language standards, mounted a furious attack on new words like *lengthy*, which he denounced as a product of the "wigwam," by which he meant not that it was of Indian derivation but that it was a coinage of the sort of people who hung around Tammany Hall, the Republican party headquarters in New York. While the lower orders seemed to be taking over the politics of the republic, the educated classes could find a safe refuge in the transatlantic republic of letters—but only if they could convince British critics that the joint language was safe in their hands. Zealously the reviewers monitored American works for faulty grammar or "Americanisms," like *to advocate, to locate, to fix, progressive*—indications that civilization was declining in the New World and providing ammunition for America's critics. "We do not like to notice such faults in respectable writers," noted a *North American Reviewer* severely, after taking one to task for his word usage, "but we deem it to be our duty."[45]

The fear of being cut adrift from that "other republic" to which they wanted to belong was behind much of the opposition to Webster's great project of a new American dictionary. It was begun in 1800 and in the face of continual discouragement, even from Webster's friends, published in 1828, with a trial run of a small version in 1806. Webster was a staunch Federalist and increasingly conservative in his political and social views, but the mere fact that he wished to tinker with the language in various ways was enough to stir cultural anxieties. By the time the dictionary was published, however, the language front was calmer. Not only were new American words being used by respectable American authors, they were being picked up by the English too, and it was clear that the language was changing just as rapidly in England. Webster, moreover, had modified many of his own original views. Except for the minor changes (such as "or" rather than "our" in words like *color* and *labor*) he had given up on more radical spelling reform. More important, although he continued to defend the right to make new words (but included only about fifty American coinages in the *Dictionary*) and used American writers along with English as his authorities, he no longer looked forward to a fundamental divergence of the two branches of the language. In fact, by 1828 Webster had decided not only that British and American English were substantially the same but that this was desirable, though both parties should recognize that local circumstances would sometimes occasion new usages.[46]

By the 1820s, moreover, American writers were emerging who could not only do well with their works at home but were taken seriously in England too. After a hiatus of ten years in which he did some desultory editing and writing, Washington Irving departed for Europe, where he published *The Sketchbook* in 1819. This collection of essays and tales translated German legends to the Catskills so successfully that from then on those mountains became the abode of Rip Van Winkle and the Headless Horseman. The book was a tremendous success in both America and Britain. The feared Francis Jeffrey of the *Edinburgh Review* praised its "great purity and beauty of diction, on the model of the most elegant and polished of our native writers," remarkable in an author "entirely bred and trained" in America. Two years later *The Spy*, a historical novel of the Revolution by the New York country gentleman James Fenimore Cooper, was also a critical and financial success. By the time Cooper brought out his next novel, *The Pioneers*, in 1823, *The Spy* had gone through three editions, and *Niles Weekly Register* triumphantly flung back Sidney Smith's taunt: "Who reads an American book!"[47]

The success of these works at home and abroad encouraged others to test their talents in the literary marketplace and marked the emergence of a class of professional writers. Cooper was the first American professional author, one who earned his living by writing. He had a strong sense of himself as a republican gentleman, but for him writing was not the product of "idle moments" stolen from some more serious profession; it was his career. By the 1820s it was becoming possible for a man of quite traditional outlook like Cooper to regard fiction writing, if done by a man of "high character," as a way of exercising salutary influence in a republic.[48]

Although no outstanding researchers or theorists had emerged in the sciences by the same period, one historian of science concludes that there was a "flourishing scientific community," with the beginnings of "a well-developed institutional structure." The number of scientific periodicals had grown dramatically by 1825, providing opportunities for the publication and dissemination of American work, as well as access to the numerous British articles they reprinted. At the same time, colleges were beginning to increase their scientific offerings, and as the number of colleges expanded, so did the number of professional jobs for scientists.[49]

The leading historian of scientific societies in this period concluded that their record, though not brilliant, was "honorable": "Without them the scientific communities scattered over the face of the country would have languished for lack of communication among themselves and with each other." This judgment could be extended to the other forms of cultural institutions too. The organizational work of American elites indicated a serious concern for cultural and intellectual life, but original achievement and great minds did not automatically spring up in answer to this concern. As Gouverneur Morris quipped to a physician who had just come from founding the New York Philosophical Society: "But pray, Doctor, where are the philosophers?" Nevertheless, the network of institutions provided a foundation for discussion and community. They kept up morale and asserted to a skeptical world that the new republic was a civilized place, still part of the "republic of letters."[50]

Part Two

Man and Nature

four

The Science of Man

Know then thyself, presume not God to scan,
The proper study of mankind is man.
                                    —Alexander Pope, 1734

It is said to be the age of the first person singular.
                                    —Ralph Waldo Emerson, 1827

Alexander Pope's "Essay on Man" was probably the most widely read poem in turn-of-the-century America. It reflected the eighteenth-century belief that there was such a thing as "man"—that in all times and places, under all local variations, the fundamental attributes of the human personality and the workings of the human mind were essentially the same. This basic unity made it possible to discuss laws of the mind or the characteristics of "man." Of course, *man* comes in two sexes, as well as several different racial varieties, but the dominant tendency of eighteenth-century Enlightenment thought was to stress the ways in which a universal human nature was modified by environment and education. Thus many differences among races, and even some between the sexes, could be attributed to circumstances rather than to innate nature. After 1800, however, Enlightenment attitudes and categories gave way to greater preoccupation with human differences. For some, this meant a concern for individuality, for the uniqueness and distinctiveness of each personality, and for others, an interest in what distinguished definable groups of people. Approaches to understanding human nature and the human mind diverged, with some following the naturalistic methods of physical science and others taking the path of self-searching introspection as individuals became more engrossed with the workings of their own mind.[1]

71

The Materialist Approach to Human Nature

One quality that endeared Scottish Common Sense to clerical educators was its acceptance of a mind-body duality—a belief that mind was not material. This provided a comforting bulwark against the materialistic concept of humanity current in some English and especially French scientific circles. Materialism posited that the entire world, including human beings, consisted of various combinations of matter. Thus the human mind could be subjected to the same naturalistic methods of investigation as any other part of nature. While Common Sense accepted that information comes through the senses, materialists went further and assumed that thought itself was a function of matter and probably could be localized in various areas of the brain.

Benjamin Rush, the most influential medical man in early nineteenth-century America, accepted much of this outlook. Rush, a pioneer in the study of insanity and abnormal mental states, has been called the Father of American Psychiatry. In his "Lectures on the Mind," given at the University of Pennsylvania every year between 1791 and 1813, Rush insisted that every physician should have an acquaintance with psychology. Very much a man of the Enlightenment, he had all the eighteenth-century drive toward simplicity. "Truth is simple upon all subjects," he told his medical students, who must have been relieved to learn that "the essential principles of medicine are very few. They are moreover plain." This belief in a few basic principles led him to reduce all illness to one basic disorder, fever, for which the remedy was "heroic" bleeding and purging. Believing that mind and body constantly act and react with one another, he was one of the first Americans to think of madness as essentially a physical disease. When he published his *Observations upon the Diseases of the Mind* in 1812, he told John Adams that he had tried to bring mental disorders "down to the level of all the other diseases of the human body, and to show that the mind and body are moved by the same causes and subject to the same laws." To view human beings totally as natural organisms meant that every aspect, including the mind and the moral faculty, could be studied in terms of healthful or diseased functioning. Thus crime should be seen less as a sin than as the sign of sickness, a position that led Rush to oppose capital punishment.[2]

Rush was convinced that the health of both mind and body was dependent on the physical and social environment. In his practice with mentally ill patients at his asylum in Philadelphia, he prescribed carefully controlled diet and exercise, along with music and occupational therapy. The political environment of the wider society also had an effect on the physical and mental well-being of individuals. Freedom, Rush thought, was a factor that produced health. On the other hand, he believed that many aspects of American culture were particularly conducive to insanity, which he was convinced had increased since 1790. Intemperance was one such cultural factor, as was "an increase in avarice and ambition." In other words, the same unrestrained passions that undermined republican virtue also undermined physical and mental health.[3]

Rush combined a materialistic attitude toward mind and mental phenomena with a devout religious faith. He insisted that "there is no necessary connection between the immateriality and immortality of the mind," since God can confer immortality on matter just as well as on spirit. Materialist views, however, generally tended to be particularly attractive to men like Jefferson or his friend the chemist Thomas Cooper who were deists or free-thinkers of various kinds—people for whom the rooting of all thought in the physical sensations of the organism was allied with a faith in human capacity for ever-increasing knowledge. Joseph Buchanan of Kentucky was a materialist of this type. He is a fascinating example of both the brief flowering of intellectual life in the frontier state of Kentucky and the opportunities offered, as well as the problems posed, by the lack of specialization in a fluid and unformed state of society. Buchanan grew up in Tennessee with little formal education. A year at Transylvania University and a few months of medical study introduced him to the works of Erasmus Darwin, Locke, Hume, and David Hartley. In spite of this brief formal training, he was given a professorship at a proposed medical school attached to Transylvania, though the scheme collapsed before he could take up the appointment.[4]

In anticipation of his professorship, Buchanan wrote a series of lectures, which he published in 1812 as *The Philosophy of Human Nature*. In this book he maintained that mind is "an organic state of matter" and insisted that the investigation of human nature constituted "a science purely physical." To one alarmed reviewer, this position seemed likely "to exile everything like the idea of God and a future state." Only a thousand copies of *The Philosophy* were printed, however, and it was probably not widely read. John Adams, who did read it, found it valuable only as an example of "how vigorously Science and Literature [have] sprung up . . . in transalleganian Regions." Always plagued by lack of funds, in the remaining years of his life Buchanan became a politically active newspaper editor, started a short-lived school on the most advanced principles, studied and practiced law, invented an economical but somewhat impractical steam engine, wrote a book on the art of popularity, and brought up his son to be a precocious exemplar of his father's educational philosophies. He died in 1829 at the age of forty-four.[5]

By the 1820s European scientists were beginning to perform sophisticated physical experiments on the brain. Jefferson, who kept up with major scientific developments abroad until the end of his life, wrote excitedly to John Adams in 1825: "I have lately been reading the most extraordinary of all books," and he went on to describe the experiments of the Frenchman Pierre Flourens on the cerebellum and cerebrum of animals: "Flourens proves . . . that the cerebrum is the thinking organ." Adams was not impressed, but to

Jefferson Flourens's work seemed to disprove conclusively the religious insistence that mind and soul were nonmaterial entities. He associated a belief in a mind-matter duality with the metaphysical theorizing of the priesthood, which he thought had always tried to block the triumph of science. "On the basis of sensation, matter and motion," he assured Adams, "we may erect the fabric of all the certainties we can have or need."[6]

Considerable impetus to scientific study of the physiology of mind came from phrenology. Developed at the turn of the century by the German scientist Franz Joseph Gall, this quasi-science was widely discussed in the United States by the 1820s. It even had an American expositor, the physician Charles Caldwell, whose *Elements of Phrenology* appeared in 1824. Phrenologists held that the various "faculties" of the mind, such as judgment, memory, imagination, will, the capacity for religious belief, conscience, and emotionality, were located in different areas of the brain and revealed their various strengths and weaknesses in each individual in the physical configuration of the skull. As the art of reading cranial "bumps," phrenology became a tremendously popular fad in the 1830s and 1840s. Its growing popularity indicated the increasing interest in individual peculiarities and the differences among people as opposed to universal mental processes.[7]

Romantic Approaches to Human Nature

Emerson thought that in New England the year 1820 marked a new era. "The key to the period," he wrote, "appeared to be that the mind had become aware of itself. Men grew reflective and intellectual. There was a new consciousness." But the changes were recognized before 1820, and they were part of a basic shift in European and American culture: the transition from the Enlightenment to romanticism. Romantic styles of thinking emphasized individual subjectivity and an intuitive grasp of truth; they opened up new ways of looking at the world and perceiving the self. In art, romanticism preferred originality to "correctness"; in life, it valued will, passion, and the creative imagination over analytic reason. The idea of organic growth was central to the new attitudes; people increasingly perceived the world in dynamic rather than static terms. They demonstrated a strong interest in the exotic and the strange; in periods of the past that the Enlightenment had dismissed as regressive, like the Middle Ages; in natural scenery, which was wild and grand rather than beautiful and domesticated; and in extreme and even abnormal states of mind.[8]

In Europe the new attitudes were deeply involved with the break-up of the ancien regime and political rebellion but also with the reactionary defense of church and king—a facet of the movement not replicated in America, where the battle for national independence and political liberty had already been won under Enlightenment auspices. Nor was the flouting of conventional morality by many European romantics part of romanticism in American culture. Although Americans accepted romanticism as a movement in art and literature only cautiously, they were open to the more hopeful and optimistic changes in the zeitgeist.[9]

A growing cult of the individual self and its potential for growth was central to the new outlook. The intensity of child rearing in middle-class homes may partly explain this growing sense of self. As the number of children in a family began to decline, each child became more precious and more individual, and parents seem to have been paying much greater attention to their children. By the early nineteenth century men and women were becoming more introspective and more preoccupied with their own inner experience and developing personality. The nineteenth-century diary was more likely than its eighteenth-century counterpart to explore the distinctive feelings of the writer's inner self, a self deliciously unlike any other. "There is no reflection, which . . . draws with it such an association of delightful thoughts and anticipations, as that of our own individuality," wrote a contributor to the Boston *Monthly Anthology* in 1807. He went on to recommend a certain reserve in public, keeping much of one's thoughts private, a reserve "which belongs only to our own nature, and which constitutes the sovereignty of one's self." This was not self-sovereignty in the sense of self-mastery, an increasingly common usage, but in the sense of proud consciousness of one's uniqueness.[10]

The values assigned to expressions of personality began to shift. If in the Enlightenment the essential defining human quality was reason, to a later age it was the will, the quality of mastery of oneself and others. While reason could be seen as uniting human beings, the will, by its very nature, was individuating and distinctive. In Common Sense philosophy the will played an essentially executive rather than decisive role; it carried out the desires, but it was the task of reason to police these desires. However, by the early nineteenth century, a number of factors combined to give consciousness of the will a more important role. Theological disputes over human responsibility for sin helped to focus attention on freedom of the will. Nathaniel Taylor, noting that the soul could be torn by contesting principles of good and evil, singled out the will as the governor that allowed human beings to suppress their worst and emancipate their better nature.[11]

In 1829 the young president of the University of Vermont, James Marsh, dramatically demanded that the will must be conceived of as escaping the laws of cause and effect and as possessing an absolute freedom. Marsh was one of the first Americans to be influenced by the English romantic poet-philosopher Samuel Taylor Coleridge. In 1829 he published an extremely influential American edition of Coleridge's *Aids to Reflection*, with an introductory essay of his own. "Every man does, in fact," he wrote in that essay, "believe himself possessed of freedom in the higher sense of self-determination."[12]

Self-determination was distinguished from the independence of the eighteenth century by its dynamic quality; it implied not merely that the individual might maintain himself or herself against the encroachments of others but might burst out into a new mode of being. Self-determination had a hint of the limitless. In the United States as in Europe, the young were fascinated by Napoleon, the titanic, if demonic, figure who had imposed his will on much of the Continent. The glamor of his unconquerable will seemed to exempt him from the laws governing lesser people. In America the nearest approach to such a titan was Andrew Jackson, who from his victory at the battle of New Orleans in 1815 to his death was invariably described as a man of iron will. This will enabled him to triumph over bodily weakness, to stick to his purpose against all odds and opposition, to rise from obscurity and become a self-made man.[13]

"I was born an orphan, shelterless, penniless," wrote the young minister John Todd to his fiancée in 1823. "Obstacles were thrown in my way, everything opposed. I rose above all." He had gone to college unprepared, was ill much of the time, and had to work to pay his tuition, but "I pressed on, rose above all, and now stand where I can see my way clear." Self-made men were not a new phenomenon; Benjamin Franklin, after all, was the classic American example. But Franklin portrayed himself as triumphing through shrewdness and application in a world that was not described as particularly hostile. He had not depicted his ascent in quite the titanic terms that became commonplace in the nineteenth century.[14]

In popular usage, the term *will* was increasingly qualified by adjectives like *iron*, or coupled with phrases like "stern, unconquerable resolve." Such terminology implied a concept of the world as full of obstacles, which only the power of a "firm, decisive mind" could conquer. New opportunities were opening up for young people to choose lives different from those of their parents. More young men than ever were making their own way in a changed economy with little help from parents or patrons and finding new careers, often far from home. In these circumstances it was tempting to view the world as an obstacle race in which they were carried to success by their own determination. The prospect could be daunting, as well as exhilarating, and contributed to a high level of social anxiety. A popular gift for a young man was an 1805 essay by the English Baptist minister John Foster entitled "On Decision of Character." This essay, which went through nine American editions before 1830, singled out "a strenuous *will*" and "internal, invincible determination" as the essential qualities for the young man to cultivate in order to steer a successful course through the dangers of modern life. By the late 1820s a woman of the planter class, Ellen Coolidge of Virginia, believed that the best gift she could give her children was something her own late eighteenth-century upbringing had not provided her: "the habit of energy."[15]

The willful, restlessly striving individual seemed to many people in the early years of the century a menace to republican virtue. By the 1820s, however, this personality type was not only becoming acceptable but could be seen as contributing to the public good. "We are all striving in the career of life to acquire riches, or honor, or power, or some other object, whose possession is to realize the day dreams of our imaginations," wrote Lewis Cass, the military governor of Michigan in 1827. He added confidently: "And the aggregate of these efforts constitutes the advance of society."[16]

Differences of Sex

Cass and others who spoke confidently of the powers of the dynamic will were thinking in terms of the male character. The pattern held up to young women was quite different, yet it offered, though in a more restrictive realm, the promise of enhanced agency and self-reliance. In the first three decades of the century the position of women was not yet the controversial issue it was to become later. The experience of the Revolution had raised the consciousness of some women, yet there was little of the overt political action and demand for equal rights that had emerged in France. Mary Wollstonecraft's *Vindication of the Rights of Women* had been published and widely discussed in America in the 1790s, but by 1800 her views, taken as reflective of her "immoral" life, were generally denounced as part of the infidelity that had culminated in the French Revolution. When New Jersey in 1807 rectified the oversight that had allowed a few women property owners to vote, no one seems to have objected, not even the disfranchised women. Women were seen as dependents of the male citizen, quite outside the fraternal bonds of the republic. They were also associated with the fatal corrupting lures of luxury and self-indulgence. The most dire fate for the lapsed republican was to sink into "effeminacy."[17]

The other republic—the republic of letters—was far more hospitable to women. During this period the female literacy rate was fast catching up with that of males, at least in the Northeast. Samuel Miller thought that one of the most striking aspects of eighteenth-century civilization had been a new attitude toward female education and a corresponding development of women's minds, so that "a female of elevated understanding, and of respectable literary acquirements, is no longer a wonderful phenomenon." Not only were women a growing part of the reading public, they were also becoming authors. More than one-third of American fiction published before 1820 was written by women, and Charles Brockden Brown commented in 1805 that the great number of women who "pursue writing for a subsistence" was a "remarkable circumstance in the picture of our own times." Women writers were taken seriously by male critics. Madame de Staël was hailed as one of the great writers of her generation, and Andrews Norton thought Mrs. Felicia Hemans the greatest living English poet. When John Adams remarked testily of Mercy Warren's *History of the American Revolution* (1805) that "history is not the Province of the Ladies," it was more a reaction to her anti-Federalist politics than a considered position on women.[18]

The subordinate role of women was generally taken for granted but with less insistence than in the past upon their absolute natural inferiority. Evangelical clergy, seeing women as natural allies, began praising their instinctive piety and superior moral character. Enlightenment emphasis on the plasticity of human nature and the impact of environment led some people, by the late eighteenth century, to wonder whether the perceived mental inferiority of most women might be due simply to lack of education. Timothy Dwight, who had run an academy open to girls as well as boys in the 1780s, put as a debating topic to his Yale class in 1813: "Are the abilities of the sexes equal?" He himself believed they probably were, though a definite answer would have to wait until girls had educational opportunities as good as those of boys.

Rural and some town elementary schools had begun to admit girls, though they were usually taught separately from boys. And in both southern and northern states a number of female academies were opened, some with quite solid curricula. Emma Willard, asking for aid from the New York State legislature in 1819 for a female academy, stressed the negative effect of a frivolous education on female character and asserted women's rights as individuals to develop their minds. Women were not put in the world merely to please men, she insisted, "but reason and religion teach, that we too are primary existences." The arguments put forward for female education, however, generally evaded the egalitarian potential of Enlightenment environmentalism and instead stressed the functional necessity in a republic of making women more rational. Indeed, the education of women was viewed partly as a way of defusing their potential for erotic corruption. In the same appeal Willard warned that "republics have failed" through the influence of women given over to "luxuries and follies" from lack of a rational education.[19]

A new ideal of domesticity emerging by the late eighteenth century glorified the private world of the home as the place where true happiness was to be found, an ideal that elevated the position of woman as wife and, especially, mother. The growing literature on child rearing, which Americans first imported from England and then increasingly wrote themselves, emphasized the crucial role of the mother in fixing the moral character of the child and shaping the character of future republican citizens. This maternal role provided another, and more positive, reason that women should be given a more intellectual education than superficial accomplishments or purely domestic instruction. As presiding goddesses of the home, women could nurture virtuous habits in their sons, something that the public world of political life seemed increasingly unable to do. Virtuous homes run by virtuous women became part of the republican battery of props to the state.[20]

This new appreciation of female roles strengthened women's own self-respect by appearing to give them a vital role in the republic. "What an important sphere a woman fills!" exalted one young New England woman to her diary in 1815; "how thoroughly she ought to be qualified for it." Better education gave some middle-class women the self-confidence to take up extradomestic roles such as schoolteaching and the organization of various social welfare activities. At the same time this enhanced position was accompanied by a growing, and ever more elaborate, insistence that men and women were radically different in nature and therefore must move in quite separate spheres of activity. When Tocqueville visited the United States, he was particularly struck by this separation of powers between the two sexes. "In no country," he wrote, "has such constant care been taken as in America to trace two clearly distinct lines of action for the two sexes, and to make them keep pace one with the other, but in two pathways which are always different." The emphasis on sexual difference in some ways gave women more room for independent activity and a sense of a distinct identity; it also postponed tackling the question of equality.[21]

Differences of Race

On questions of race, however, emphasis on human differences had immediate repercussions for equality. For white Americans, who shared a continent with two other races, Indians and blacks, the question of how humanity came to diverge so much in appearance and possibly other characteristics had particular relevance. In the nineteenth century it became increasingly important to account for differences in human groups and to know what weight to give to these differences, especially as "scientific" evidence piled up on the question of racial distinctions.

Until about the 1840s most educated people accepted the biblical account of creation in which all people were descended from the original pair. Racial differences were explained in terms of the adaptability of human beings to differences of environment; for example, the skin of peoples who lived near to the equator became darker because of exposure to a harsh sun. But this view was being challenged by a new hypothesis that the different races were separate species, indeed separate creations. The widely influential Scottish polymath, Lord Kames, in *Sketches of the Natural History of Man* (1774), had maintained that the wide variety of human racial types could be explained only as separate creations by God after the Tower of Babel incident. The academic study of humanity in the early nineteenth century on both sides of the Atlantic was dominated by the quarrel between the monogenists, who clung to belief in unity of origin, and the polygenists, who asserted separate creations. The latter position always entailed a hierarchical ordering of these supposed separate species, with the white race at the top and the black at the bottom.[22]

How far were physical differences among races connected to differences in intelligence? How far were perceived cultural deficiencies the results of environment rather than rooted in nature? These questions were particularly important with reference to blacks. If black people were not even potentially equal to whites, were perhaps even a separate species, then slavery might be more morally acceptable. Certainly if they were free, their assimilation would be difficult, and perhaps impossible. The most important early American statement of racial inferiority was Jefferson's brief discussion of black capacities in his *Notes on Virginia* (1787), which remained influential into the nineteenth century. He wrote of the "real distinctions which nature has made" and refused to accept that the mental inferiority he ascribed to American blacks might be due to the condition of slavery. Jefferson did not commit himself on the question of whether blacks were a distinct human species from the beginning or had become so through the operation of time and circumstances, but he clearly felt that the distinctions that now existed were too great ever to be bridged. Jefferson did not doubt that slavery as an institution was immoral, yet he never overcame an instinctive aversion to blacks based on color. Moreover, his commitment to human equality rested on the assumption that this equality was founded in nature. If nature itself had made certain groups inferior, then they were presumably excluded from the complete range of rights properly belonging to those who were "born equal."[23]

The most influential statement of the environmental explanation of racial differences was a work by Samuel Stanhope Smith, president of Princeton, *Essay on the Causes of the Variety of Complexion and Figure in the Human Species*, which came out in the same year as Jefferson's *Notes*. Smith was primarily concerned with vindicating the biblical account of Creation against Kames and maintaining that unity of the human race on which he thought "the whole science of human nature" depended. All racial differences, he insisted, could be explained by the influence of natural causes. Climate and social factors, such as the degree of civilization, diet, clothing, and even different ideas of beauty, operated to modify aspects of the human appearance, and these modifications were then transmitted to future generations. Racial characteristics thus became fairly fixed, but it followed that what had been gradually produced by one environment could be gradually modified by another. In an enlarged 1810 edition, Smith took on Jefferson with considerable asperity. Jefferson's argument that the natural inferiority of blacks was proved by their lack of artistic or scientific achievement since being brought to America was exactly the same kind of argument European critics used to prove the "inferiority" of Americans. "Genius," he insisted, "requires freedom," reward, and competition in order to flourish.[24]

One trump card of empirical evidence for the notion that the human complexion changed in response to environment was the celebrated Maryland black, Henry Moss. A Revolutionary veteran whose skin was starting to turn white, Moss put himself on display in Philadelphia for a twenty-five-cent admission fee and caused a sensation. Here apparently was someone whose skin was responding to the temperate American climate by losing its protective black coloring. After examining Moss, Benjamin Rush came up with a rather different explanation for dark skin color, which still preserved the idea of the basic original unity of humanity. Blackness, he asserted, was the result of leprosy—congenital but no longer catching. A solution to the race problem waited upon finding a cure for leprosy, which would enable blacks to be returned to their "natural" color—white.[25]

By 1810, however, the growing science of comparative anatomy was dangerously undercutting a simple and sweeping environmentalism. In 1799 the English surgeon Charles White had dealt expressly with Smith's work in demonstrating that the numerous skeletal, cranial, and muscular divergences between blacks and Europeans could not possibly be the work of environment. White went further and insisted that the races were in fact separate species; moreover, in the ordered hierarchy of nature, whites were the superior race and blacks were lowest on the human scale. These views were expanded by John Augustine Smith, a Virginian who had studied medicine in London. As the subject of his 1809 inaugural lecture as professor of anatomy at the College of Physicians in New York, he chose the question of racial differences. Like White, he had measured and compared skulls, and he specifically, and condescendingly, attacked Stanhope Smith for his ignorance of anatomy.

The stumbling block for regarding the races as fundamentally and radically different was the biblical account of Creation. The problem of how environmental factors operated to produce so many distinctions in appearance was the weak link in the environmentalist position. In a devastating review of Stanhope Smith, Charles Caldwell, professor of natural history at the University of Pennsylvania, demonstrated that skin color could not be the product of climate and that no change in environment would ever change Africans into Europeans. Caldwell was a friend of Thomas Cooper and part of a group of medical and scientific men who resented clerical pretensions. He attacked Smith for his habit of branding people who disagreed with him as hostile to religion, an attitude that had "a direct and powerful tendency to check investigation and defeat argument." His irritation was indicative of the growing self-confidence of scientific men in repelling amateurs from matters they were coming to consider their own special province.

The first scientific treatise on comparative anatomy produced in America, John Warren's *Comparative View of the Sensorial and Nervous Systems in Men and Animals* (1820), supported Stanhope Smith's view of the basic equality of the races. Warren was professor of anatomy and surgery at Harvard, had studied in Paris, and was interested in phrenology. He had collected a large number of human and animal brains and found no correlation between the size or configuration of brain and intelligence. But Warren's work was overshadowed by that of the more famous Samuel G. Morton, who began to publish his investigations into the measurements of skulls in the early 1820s. Morton emphasized the differences in the crania of blacks and Caucasians, differences he insisted were just as clearly marked in three-thousand year-old skulls from recently excavated Egyptian tombs as at the present. Morton did not specifically argue for separate creations, but the massive amount of cranial data he accumulated would be used as strong evidence by the polygenists.[26]

The theory that blacks were a separate and unequal species did not necessarily imply a belief that slavery was the only condition for them. Jefferson acknowledged that ability was not a measure of rights. Conversely, belief in environmentalism tended to be inherently ethnocentric and imply that the white race was the norm, from which all other races had deviated and which they might once again approach under better conditions. The most extreme example of this is Rush's equation of blackness with disease. Still, an adherence to the essential unity of the human race, as all descended from the original pair, did tend to focus attention on the qualities people had in common rather than their differences. As evidence that Genesis was correct and that all humanity was descended from Adam and Eve, Archibald Alexander of Princeton pointed out that all people have "the same external senses, . . . the same natural passions and desires, . . . the power of reasoning, . . . the moral sense, . . . the faculty of taste," and "all men are capable of improvement." On the other hand, the scientific concentration on physical differences, which were increasingly correlated to implied differences in mind, and the accompanying drive to more minute and exact classification could make racial distinctions appear so fundamental that blacks could never be incorporated into the republic except within the total subordination of slavery.[27]

Emerging scientific ideas thus blended with and bolstered popular prejudice. Whatever the authority of the Bible, white inability to accept blacks as equals was pervasive. In schoolbooks, Africa was described as barbaric and blacks as "brutish" and inferior to whites. In the theater, black characters served as comic relief: a common way to satirize the vices of whites was to show black servants aping the vanity and foppery of their betters. A new artistic interest in verisimilitude and fascination with the peculiarities of different people led actors and writers to try to reproduce black English, along with other ethnic pronunciations of English, as accurately as possible. The effect was inevitably to associate the broken-English character with comedy. By the 1820s Negro songs—songs written in black dialect, often to Irish or English folk tunes, and performed by white actors in blackface—were popular features between the acts of a play or at the circus. In 1828 a white actor created the character—and song and dance—of Jim Crow, which he took on a triumphal tour of the United States and England. It was a forerunner of the fabulously popular black-face minstrel shows of the next decade.[28]

The willingness to see blacks as an inferior and separate species dulled white conscience about slavery. It was not, in fact, difficult to reconcile slavery with republicanism. The republican freedom of Greece and Rome had been the freedom of citizens supported by a slave labor force. In its more modern incarnation, republicanism was the freedom of a people from oppression. Since they could not conceive of blacks as part of "the people," spokesmen of southern states like John Taylor were not embarrassed to talk in terms of resistance to enslavement by an overbearing national government. Although the existence of slavery still troubled many consciences, major political leaders never defined it as an urgent national problem. In spite of his hatred of slavery, Jefferson never made any public effort as president to encourage Americans to think seriously about how emancipation might be accomplished, nor would he lend his prestige, even after his retirement, to antislavery efforts. By general agreement slavery was excluded from national politics after the Revolution.[29]

No attempt had been made to prevent settlers taking slaves into the new lands of the Louisiana Purchase. Since the rate of slave reproduction was about the same as that of the white population, with every decade the number of slaves grew larger, and slavery became more geographically widespread and more economically important. As early as 1806 a southern congressman was candid enough to admit, "I will tell the truth. A large majority of the people in the Southern States do not consider slavery as even an evil." Few leaders of the slave-holding states were yet willing to go so far. However, much of the antislavery sentiment aroused by the Revolution faded away in post-Revolutionary America.[30]

Since northern states had emancipated their slaves after the Revolution (though in the case of New York so gradually that some blacks still remained in bondage as late as 1827), slavery was increasingly a sectional matter. Still, for northerners a mixture of growing racism and growing patriotism combined to mute antislavery feelings. When three northern writers, Timothy Dwight, James Kirke Paulding, and Robert Walsh, wrote replies to some particularly stinging British attacks on American civilization in 1816, for example, they felt obliged to offer defenses of slavery as it operated in the American South. In an argument that later became standard among southern defenders of slavery, they insisted that the American slave was generally well treated and in any case considerably better off than the operatives in English factory towns.[31]

Free blacks found themselves in an increasingly precarious position as the social and intellectual climate became more hostile, especially after 1815. In the South manumission was made more difficult, and many southern and western states prohibited the entry of free blacks. Southern states feared the unsettling example of free blacks on their slaves, especially after the slave revolts in the French sugar islands and revolts in Virginia in 1800 and Louisiana in 1811. In the free states, blacks were prey to periodic attacks of white violence and chronic discrimination in employment. As a symbol of their pariah status in the republic, it became customary to exclude blacks from Fourth of July celebrations. Nor did the churches resist the growing racism. Even among the Methodists, who had been the denomination most open to black participation, blacks increasingly met discrimination in seating and exclusion from positions of power in the church. In 1816 a number of black Methodists responded by seceding and creating an entirely new denomination: the African Methodist Episcopal Church, the first independent black church in America.[32]

One aspect of democratization was that the political rights of blacks were undermined at the same time, and as part of the same process, as the voting rights of white men were extended. By the Civil War, only the five New England states and New York allowed blacks to vote. The objections to black voters reveal the assumption that blacks were ineradicably a separate people and could never be assimilated as Americans. "When the distinctions that now prevail shall be done away," said a delegate to the New York Constitutional Convention of 1821, "when the colors shall intermarry—when negroes shall be invited to your tables," only then might it be possible to allow blacks to vote. A republic had to be a society of equals, founded on some kind of fraternal bond, and entrenched white feeling was such that blacks could never be accepted as equals at this deeper and more fundamental level. There was a widespread assumption that civil and political equality for blacks would mean intermarriage, a possibility that produced almost universal revulsion. "We will not, must not, expose ourselves to lose our identity as it were," wrote the Philadelphia editor and critic Robert Walsh in a defense of the color line against British criticism; "to be stained in our blood, and disparaged in our relation of being towards the stock of our forefathers in Europe." American identity rested not only on distinctive republican institutions; as the restriction of naturalization to free white aliens in the first naturalization law of 1790 had already made clear, Americans conceived of their nation in terms of European "racial" identity.[33]

The assumption that blacks were unassimilable was the primary motive behind the 1817 founding of the American Colonization Society, in many ways a typical member of the benevolent empire of reform associations, with the same leadership of Protestant clergy and conservative gentry. It was supported by a number of people prominent in public life, including John Marshall, Henry Clay, James Madison (its third president), and James Monroe. The society proposed to solve the race problem by colonizing free blacks in Africa. Even those unwilling to accept that blacks were by nature inferior still could not imagine their acceptance into American society because of the depth of white prejudice. Strong feelings about race seemed to be among those in-built principles of the mind that existed prior to any actual experience and were not amenable to reason. The historian Jared Sparks in endorsing the program of colonization spoke of "the customs of society whose power no arm of flesh can counteract." He acknowledged the unreasonableness of race prejudice but accepted it as a fundamental aspect of human nature, which was impossible to eradicate. "Let the fact be as melancholy as it will, it is nevertheless a fact, and one with which we must be contented."[34]

In 1822 the society shipped out its first load of blacks, but any large-scale effort would require massive federal funds and initiative, and in an era of increasing sectional tension and suspicion of central governmental power, that was not forthcoming. After 1819 Congress never again voted any money for colonization. Some free blacks, especially from the middle class of skilled craftsmen, despaired of equality in America and were willing to emigrate, but the majority were not. The practical, not to mention the moral, problems of resettlement were so enormous that the whole scheme was always a fantasy. This fantasy appealed so deeply to white Americans' mixed feelings of guilt and aversion toward blacks, however, that colonization gained much support in both the slave-holding and the free states.[35]

The growing belief in the fundamental importance of racial categories and the fixity of racial hierarchies, the low level of antislavery activity, and the growth of the colonization movement sent an unmistakable message of exclusion to the free black community. Black leaders responded with various self-help and benevolent associations, and they vigorously protested discriminatory legislation, like the 1813 attempt in Pennsylvania to require the registration of every black inhabitant of the state. Black protests invoked the services of blacks in the Revolution and insisted that the "principles, which have been the boast of this republic," applied to them too.[36]

In 1829 a young Boston black, David Walker, wrote *An Appeal to the Colored Citizens of the World*, denouncing the damage that learned speculation about black inferiority inflicted on the prospects and the self-respect of blacks. Written in a heat of fury and humiliation, this passionate polemic excoriated the cruelties of slavery, lashed out at the white race as vicious and imperialistic throughout history, and deplored the ignorance and servility Walker found among his own people. His special target was Thomas Jefferson's remarks on black inferiority in *Notes on Virginia*. "I hope you will try to find

out the meaning of this . . . its widest sense and all its bearings," he urged
his fellow blacks. "Whether you do or not, remember the whites do." Those
speculations on black inferiority, "having emanated from Mr. Jefferson, a
much greater philosopher the world never afforded, has in truth injured us
more, and has been as great a barrier to our emancipation as any thing that
has ever been advanced against us." He closed the pamphlet by printing the
preamble to the Declaration of Independence. "See your Declaration Americans!!! Do you understand your own language?"[37]

The Vanishing Indian

"Next to the case of the black race within our bosom," wrote Madison in
1826, "that of the red on our borders is the problem most baffling to the
policy of our country." In frontier areas Indians were still a physical threat
to white settlers, and Indian tribes still retained vast land holdings in the
South and Southwest. The elections of 1824 and 1828 revealed the strength
of anti-Indian popular sentiment among whites exposed to Indian warfare or
with a direct interest in taking over Indian land. Only in eastern areas, where
Indian tribes were no longer a physical threat, were whites free to contemplate the Native American in the mode that had become fashionable in Europe in the eighteenth century—as the noble savage.[38]

There was considerable intellectual interest in the Indian as a natural phenomenon of the New World. Stanhope Smith in 1784 had suggested that
scientific societies send investigators to live among the Indians "on a familiar
footing; dress and live as they do; and to observe them when they should be
under no bias or constraint." This plea for a participant-observer anthropol-
ogy was premature, but the various state historical societies founded from
the 1790s onward undertook the collecting of information on the Indian.
De Witt Clinton of New York urged that as much as possible of the Indian
languages and culture should be recorded before it was too late. Indian agents
too were instructed to collect systematic information, and when Jefferson
dispatched Lewis and Clark on their exploring expedition to the Pacific in
1803, he gave them detailed instructions on observing and systematically
describing the Indian tribes they would meet. These explorers, who inter-
viewed, collected artifacts and vocabularies, and made drawings, were pioneer ethnographers.[39]

The question of Indian historical origins intrigued many people. It was
generally assumed that they had made their way from Asia via a land bridge
that no longer existed, though some surmised that they might even be descended from the lost tribes of Israel. There were puzzling relics of earlier
civilizations in the ancient mounds, large, rectangular earthworks scattered
throughout New York State and the Mississippi valley, which on investiga-

tion proved to be great communal graves. These were genuine American antiquities, and some people thought they indicated a much higher level of civilization among the Indians in the past. Others assumed that they must have been built by a lost race. The mounds presented evidence that the continent had once supported a population much larger than the first settlers found and offered the tantalizing prospect of an exotic past before recorded history. They fascinated the popular as well as the scholarly mind and were incorporated, along with the Indian, into the *Book of Mormon*.[40]

Indian languages were also a topic of interest. Late eighteenth-century European philosophers had raised interesting questions in comparative philology. Did the structure of language reveal basic properties of mind? What would language reveal about the origin of races? Was there even perhaps an ur-language, a universal grammar from which all particular languages had developed, thus proving the unity of humanity? Studying Indian languages provided a way for Americans to participate in an international scientific endeavor. On these questions they were uniquely placed to provide crucial information, and the collecting of data could be accomplished by intelligent amateurs. Jefferson, who was fascinated by language, compiled over many years a list of Indian words from some fifty different tribes, unfortunately largely destroyed when his baggage was stolen in 1809. Albert Gallatin and the prominent lawyer Peter du Ponceau devoted much of their leisure to important studies of Indian languages.[41]

Few of the people interested in philology worked with Indians in the field. They got their information from travellers, traders, and Indian agents, but lack of a standard orthography for Indian languages made studying them scientifically difficult. Indian languages were complex, and few whites mastered them; most missionaries never became fluent in the language of the tribe they were assigned to, and many never tried. The Cherokee leader Sequoyah realized the advantages of literacy, but he wanted his people to be literate in their own tongue and developed an alphabet for Cherokee. It was enthusiastically adopted by the Cherokee, who rather quickly became a literate people, but it met with far less welcome among whites. After all, if Indians were to become assimilated into the republic, they would have to abandon their languages in favor of English.[42]

Intellectually and aesthetically, Americans responded quite differently to blacks and Indians. Whites perceived Indians as physically more like themselves than blacks were and often commented on the handsomeness of native Americans. "My God, how like a Mohawk warrior!" exclaimed the painter Benjamin West on being shown an ancient Greek statue of Apollo in Rome. It is clear that educated American opinion was far less hesitant to accord the Indian an essential natural equality with whites, even if Indians were now culturally inferior. This was partly, no doubt, because Indians were seen as part of the American habitat; to denigrate them was somehow to depreciate the continent. Jefferson, who was so dubious about the natural abilities of blacks, was far more sanguine about the Indians. He never changed the opinion expressed in his *Notes on Virginia* that "we shall probably find that [the Indians] are formed in mind as well as in body, on the same module with the 'Homo sapiens Europaeus.'"[43]

The idea of intermarriage between whites and Native Americans was much more acceptable than between whites and blacks. Jefferson (for whom black-white "mixture" was horrifying) saw marriage between Indians and whites on the frontier as a useful method of assimilation. Secretary of War William Crawford told Congress in 1816 that government policy was to "let intermarriages between [Indians] and whites be encouraged" as part of the policy of acculturation. Lydia Maria Child's novel of the colonial period, *Hobomok* (1824), featured a marriage between an Indian man and a white woman, and in the same year the true account of an American woman who, captured as a girl, had lived a happily married life among the Seneca was a runaway best-seller. It is true, however, that when two Christianized and educated Indian men in Connecticut married white women in 1825, there was such a furor that the Indian school where the young men had studied had to be closed. Nonetheless, Indian-white marriage could be discussed and even advocated by respectable people, whereas a black-white union was totally unacceptable.[44]

While blacks were increasingly understood by physiological models of anatomical difference, Indians were subsumed under a historical model of cultural development. Here again Scottish philosophers provided a framework within which to interpret American experience. According to the widely read Adam Ferguson, humanity naturally progressed through set stages of development. In the beginning, all peoples were "savages": hunters, without private property, with few arts and minimal government. The natural progression was then upward to agriculture, accompanied by private property and monogamy, the essential basis on which all further development of the arts and sciences would rest. Each stage of development, including the savage, had its particular virtues, which the more civilized might genuinely admire. This was a framework that preserved human unity and made progress toward increasingly refined civilization natural to all human beings. Ferguson and his American followers saw in the Indians perfect examples of the earlier savage but heroic stage of human development, somehow frozen in time. There was a certain allure to the savage life, felt by many whites who came in contact with it, particularly the freedom from the relentless need to work imposed by civilization. But a modern, civilized America could not coexist with this living reminder of an earlier, perhaps freer state. To white policy makers, either Indians must be hurried into the agricultural stage or, in the inexorable logic of history, they must disappear.[45]

From George Washington to John Quincy Adams, the eastern elite who dominated American political life hoped that white expansion could take place without the wholesale destruction of the Indian. They never doubted that the earth belongs by right to those who will till it and make it fruitful, but they hoped that Indians could be assimilated into the republic by giving up their hunting economy and tribal organization and becoming farmers, learning English, and adopting white norms of marriage, family descent, individual property, and the work ethic. If the Indians persisted in hanging on to their own way of life, however, they would have to be removed from contact with whites; there was no room in Jeffersonian America for cultural pluralism. The safety and the rising glory of the republic depended on the vision of a continent, as John Quincy Adams said in 1811, "destined by Divine Providence to be peopled by one *nation*, speaking one language, professing one general system of religious and political principles, and accustomed to one general tenor of social usages and customs."[46]

A writer in the *North American Review* caught the dilemma in the assimilationist position in a discussion of a report by Jedidiah Morse to the secretary of war. Morse was a defender of the Indians and regretted the poverty and distress into which the remnants of eastern tribes had fallen. In order to preserve them, he recommended that these remnants be gathered into "education families" as wards of the federal government and be taught the skills of modern American life. They were to become Christians, farmers, and owners of private property and to forget their native languages. "Is there anything left then," asked the reviewer, "that we wish in fact to preserve?" Since Morse also advocated intermarriage, the assumption was that in time even their color would disappear.[47]

The assimilationist position was becoming less tenable. After 1815 there was intense pressure on Indian lands from southern states, which openly advocated removal, not assimilation. At the same time, by the 1820s the Enlightenment faith in the almost infinite educability of people was declining even among educated easterners, and there was a growing doubt that the policy of assimilation would work. Too many Indians exhibited a stubborn preference for the ways of their ancestors; too many whites were determined not to give Indians the room and the time that assimilation would need. Ordinary whites in contact with Indians were less ready than elites to accept them as potential equals. The most that "public opinion would concede to the Indians," according to Georgia Governor George Troup, would be to "fix them in the middle station between the negro and white man." As John C. Calhoun candidly pointed out to a cabinet meeting, the problem in Georgia and Tennessee was not the totally unassimilated Indian but those like the Cherokee who had adopted many of the white man's ways. In response to southern pressure, President Monroe began to explore the question of removing the eastern tribes. The election of Andrew Jackson in 1828 meant that removal became official government policy.[48]

The debate over removal was accompanied by the growing acceptance of the idea that the Indian must naturally disappear, or "extinguish" as Jefferson put it, in a curious intransitive use of the verb that conveniently obscured the agency. By the 1820s the idea of the Indian as a race destined to disappear before the expansion of the stronger and more advanced Europeans allowed many whites to assume the fate of the tribes of Massachusetts and New York who had become extinct as a fait accompli for all the race. As Enlightenment categories of thought faded, Indians were not demoted from the ranks of humanity, but they were increasingly interpreted in relation to the natural habitat of North America and their fate associated with the virgin forests. As the forests fell before the farmer's axe, so must their inhabitants give way before the advance of civilization. The impoverished and drunken Indian, the pathetic remnant of once-proud tribes who lurked around the fringes of white settlement, was a sign that civilization could degrade as well as destroy. Indian nobility, it appeared, could not withstand contact with whites; it could be preserved only in death. Thus, in quite a different sense from the vulgar frontier usage, the dead Indian was the good Indian.[49]

This expectation of their general doom allowed whites far removed from contact to contemplate the Indian's fate with a mixture of melancholy, complacency, and guilt. It was not just a question of outright brutality on the part of whites; the mere contact between whites and Indians seemed to spread a blight over native societies. In the midst of a centennial paean to the founders of Salem, Massachusetts, Justice Joseph Story paused to remember the original inhabitants whose subsequent extinction was disturbing and somehow unaccountable: "By a law of their nature, they seem destined to a slow but sure extinction. Everywhere, at the approach of the white man they fade away."[50]

This oration was much excerpted in the following decades in school readers, which usually contained at least one essay or poem with titles such as "Melancholy Decay of the Indians" or "Melancholy Fate of the Indian." Whereas in the captivity narratives of the seventeenth and eighteenth centuries, the Indian appeared as a live, satanic threat, the vanishing Indian now took center stage in the American imagination. The realization that Americans were building a civilization not on virgin land but on the ruins of another people recurs in numerous poetic images of the Indian burial ground, turned up by the white man's plough:

> A noble race! but they are gone,
> With their old forests wide and deep,
> And we have built our homes upon
> Fields where their generations sleep.[51]

As Americans tried to fashion a distinctive culture, particularly after 1815 when the Western world was swept by the vogue of Walter Scott's historical tales, it seemed that the American Indian might furnish a unique resource for romance. "From its offering so many advantages to the writer of imagination," declared one reviewer in 1820, "the history of the Indian will, hereafter, undoubtedly form the classic lore of American literature." In the theater, "Indian" dramas began to associate the native American with the high theme of the destiny of America. Several popular plays dealt with the Pocahontas story; others, like George Washington Custis's *The Indian Prophecy* (1828) or *Metamora* (1829), featured a noble Indian chief who expired eloquently in the final act, symbolically bequeathing the continent to whites.[52]

The writer who did most to fix the Indians in the world's imagination was James Fenimore Cooper. Cooper was the son of a prominent Federalist judge who had made a fortune speculating in frontier lands. Born in 1789, James grew up in the New York frontier village founded by his father. The changes he witnessed gave him a vivid sense of the development of the country and also an experience of the precariousness of wealth and position in the new nation. His father eventually lost much of the family fortune, and Cooper, the only surviving son, began to write to pay off the family debts. But his novels were also an expression of civic purpose: to reflect back to his country some sense of its history and meaning.[53]

In Cooper's epic series of novels, the Leatherstocking saga, the clash between white and red was central to the development of the American nation. The theme of the novels is the struggle for possession of a continent and their setting, the frontier, in the particularly American meaning of that word as the always-shifting ground where civilization and the wilderness meet. Cooper's sense of historical process was not of evolution but of violent struggle and displacement. His Indians are doomed figures; the "last of the Mohicans" can stand emblematically for the whole race. Cooper did not doubt that civilization is preferable to savagery or that the elimination of the Indian was inevitable, but he saw the struggle as between two modes of life, each with its own integrity. A European critic, George Sand, caught the implication of Cooper's work better than his contemporary compatriots. Cooper laments, she wrote, "a noble people exterminated; a serene natural world laid waste. . . . The American let loose from his breast this conscience-stricken cry: 'In order to be what we are, we had to kill a great people and devastate a mighty land.'"[54]

This may not have been Cooper's conscious intent. Outside the novels—for example in his commentary on contemporary American life, *Notions of the Americans* (1828)—Cooper wrote quite conventionally and complacently about the decline of the Indian and the advantages of removal. In *Mohicans* he had Leatherstocking say to his Indian companion Chingachgook: "But everything depends on what scale you look at things. Now, on the small scale, the 'arth is level; but on the large scale it is round." The larger perspective of history allowed most Americans to place the fate of the Indian within the necessities of the historical process. But the artist worked with a different moral geometry, and from the perspective of the woods, the clash of white and red lost the cloak of progress and took on the shape of tragedy.[55]

The literature on Indian themes often served to veil actualities, since it tended to treat the "vanishing" Indian as already vanished. Cooper's novels take place in the previous century, and Cooper was at pains to remind his readers that they were reading about the past. Some 125,000 Indians were still living east of the Mississippi in 1820. The first three books of the Leatherstocking series were published in 1823 (*The Pioneers*), 1826 (*The Last of the Mohicans*), and 1827 (*The Prairie*), in the midst of the debates over removal. The message of these novels, however, was that the drama was already over. Similarly, the artist George Catlin, about to embark on his career as painter of the Indians, wrote that for many years, he had contemplated the "noble races of redmen . . . melting away at the approach of civilization . . . and I have flown to their rescue—not of their lives or of their race (for they are '*doomed*' and must perish), but to the rescue of their looks and their modes." Although an "acquisitive world" might "crush them to death," they would rise and "live again upon canvass."[56]

The realization that the arrival of Europeans in the New World was a disaster for other races spread a chill over notions of progress and belief in American mission. As De Witt Clinton said grimly to the New-York Historical Society in 1811: "When we consider, that the discovery and settlement of America, have exterminated millions of the red men, and entailed upon the sable inhabitants of Africa, endless and destructive wars, captivity, slavery and death," there was reason to fear the "retributive justice" of God. Andrew Jackson, however, offered a different kind of reflection, probably more representative of white attitudes, in his 1830 annual message to Congress: "To follow to the tomb the last of his race and to tread on the graves of extinct nations excite melancholy reflections. But true philanthropy reconciles the mind to these vicissitudes." Could anyone genuinely regret the march of progress? "What good man would prefer a country covered with forests and ranged by a few thousand savages to our extensive Republic, studded with cities, towns and prosperous farms, embellished with all the improvements which art can devise or industry execute, occupied by more than 12,000,000 happy people, and filled with all the blessings of liberty, civilization, and religion?"[57]

While Americans responded intellectually to Indians and blacks in different ways, in practical terms the program for both turned out to be virtually the same: slavery or removal for blacks, extinction or removal for Indians.

By the 1830s the lines between the sexes and the races were more clearly drawn. The unity of humanity was less clear; the differences seemed more obvious and more important. Americans were thinking less about "man" and more about men and women, whites and other "lower" races; less about how differences could be reduced and more about how the republic could be preserved as an arena for the expansion and self-development of whites.

Thomas Jefferson. Illustration by Cornelius Tiebout, 1801. *From the collections of the Library of Congress.*

Andrew Jackson. Engraving by James Barton Longacre, after Thomas Sully, 1820. *From the Print Collection, Miriam and Ira D. Wallach Division of Art, Prints and Photographs, New York Public Library, Astor, Lenox and Tilden Foundations.*

Bald Eagle. Illustration by Alexander Wilson, from *American Ornithology*, vol. 4 (Philadelphia: Bradford and Inskeep, 1811). *From the Bancroft Library, University of California, Berkeley.*

Robert Fulton's *Paragon*. Drawing by Pavel Svinin. *From the Metropolitan Museum of Art, Rogers Fund, 1942 (42.95.7).*

Boston Townhouses, designed by Charles Bullfinch. *From the Boston Athenaeum.*

Eastern State Penitentiary, Philadelphia, designed by John Haviland, 1829. Illustration by Charles Burton. *Courtesy of the New-York Historical Society, New York City.*

The Second Bank of the United States in Philadelphia, designed by William Strickland. Photograph by Cervin Robinson. *From the Historic American Buildings Survey Collection, Library of Congress.*

The University of Virginia, designed by Thomas Jefferson. Lithograph by C. Bohn, 1856.
From the Prints Collection, Special Collections Department, University Archives, University of Virginia Library.

Marius Amidst the Ruins of Carthage, by John Vanderlyn, 1807. *From the Fine Arts Museums of San Francisco, Gift of M. H. de Young.*

Landscape Scene from "The Last of the Mohicans," by Thomas Cole, 1827. *From the New York State Historical Association, Cooperstown.*

The leopard with the harmless kid laid down,
And not one savage beast was seen to frown.

The wolf did with the lambkin dwell in peace,
His grim carnivrous nature there did cease;

The lion with the fatling on did move,
A little child was leading them in love.

When the great PENN his famous treaty made,
With indian chiefs beneath the elm-trees shade.

Peacable Kingdom, by Edward Hicks, ca. 1835. *From the New York State Historical Association, Cooperstown.*

five

The Possession of Nature

It is this idea of destruction, this conception of near and inevitable change which gives in our opinion so original a character and so touching a beauty to the solitudes of America. One sees them with melancholy pleasure. . . . The idea of this natural and wild grandeur which is to end mingles with the superb images to which the march of civilization gives rise. One feels proud to be a man, and at the same time one experiences I know not what bitter regret at the power God has given us over nature.

—Alexis de Tocqueville, *A Fortnight in the Wilds*, 1831

Americans in the early republic faced the task of taking mental as well as physical possession of the expanding natural world of which they were now freehold owners. In 1800 there was still no accurate geography of North America, and the Louisiana Purchase of 1803 added a huge unmapped terrain to the national territory. The few late eighteenth-century works in natural history had barely begun to catalog the array of American fauna and flora. Nature had to be both domesticated to human purposes and possessed by the national imagination before the new nation could sit easily on the continent. It was time to take, as Edward Everett put it, "an inventory of the glorious inheritance we are called to possess."[1]

The American Habitat

Jefferson, a great collector of Americana, was eager to grasp the opportunities for new knowledge of the natural world offered by the West. Like many others, he was fascinated by the prospect of a water passage across the continent, opening China and the East to American trade via the Pacific. All of these prospects lay behind Jefferson's commissioning of the Lewis and Clark expedition in 1803 to explore the upper Missouri, cross over the mountains to the Columbia River, and proceed down to the Pacific. The president provided detailed instructions: besides discovering a passage to India and making contact with the Indians, the explorers were to note the topography, the quality of the soil, and the weather; make maps; note new species of flora and fauna; and make a thorough description of the territory that would be of use to science, traders, and future settlers. The aim was to extend "the boundaries of science" for citizens of the new republic and "to present to their knowledge that vast and fertile country which their sons are destined to fill with arts, with science, with freedom and happiness."[2]

No one in the expedition had any scientific training, but Meriwether Lewis, Jefferson's secretary, had an amateur's interest in natural history, and Jefferson sent him to Philadelphia for a crash course by leading members of the American Philosophical Society in map making and longitudinal measurement. The president impressed upon him the importance of keeping regular and detailed journals of observations, with second copies for backup in case of accident. From the beginning it was assumed that the results of the expedition would be published. This was a mission to make known to the American people and to the rest of the world what lay hidden in the interior of the continent. There is always an element of the predatory in exploration, an element expressed in the poem by Joel Barlow to hail the return of Lewis and Clark. The Nile and the Niger might still conserve their secrets from Western eyes, but

> Columbus, not so shall thy boundless domain
> Defraud thy brave sons of their right;
> Streams, midlands, and shorelands elude us in vain,
> We shall drag their dark regions to light.[3]

Yet Meriwether Lewis found that the expedition could not be merely a project of utilitarian discovery. He seems often to have been overwhelmed by the grandeur of the terrain and the problem of conveying some of its emotional impact. He tried to conceptualize the stunning jagged country of the Missouri Breaks in terms of architectural ruins. However, by the time the expedition reached the Great Falls of the Missouri, Lewis had given up the attempt at adequate description, wishing that he were either a great artist or a great poet, "that I might be enabled to give to the enlightened world some just idea of this truly magnificent and sublimely grand object, which has from the commencement of time been concealed from the view of civilized man."[4]

Although the Lewis and Clark expedition returned in September 1806, it took another eight years for an official account of their epic journey to be published. Because the federal government had no facilities for storing or analyzing the specimens of animals, birds, Indian artifacts, plants, and samples of soil and minerals the explorers had sent back, they were scattered to various locales. It is an example of the paradoxical nature of Jefferson as a cultural leader that he would take pains to give the expedition scientifically useful instructions but then fail to ensure a thorough follow-up. The plants were sent to the famous naturalist Benjamin S. Barton in Philadelphia to be described and classified, and the animals and birds were deposited in Charles Willson Peale's museum, where a number of naturalists made good use of them. But Barton neglected his part of the project, and the plants were eventually described by Frederick Pursh, a German botanist who published his *Flora Americae Septentrionalis* (1814) in London. Lewis, who was made governor of Louisiana Territory on his return, seems to have made no effort to prepare his journals for publication, and when he died in 1809, probably by suicide, the project was turned over to the Philadelphia banker and editor Nicholas Biddle. Biddle eventually brought out a tidied and smoothed-out version of the journals, with a disappointingly slight scientific appendix, in 1814.[5]

The *Journals* did not sell well. An apocryphal account, partly cobbled together from other travelers' tales, had already creamed off much of the popular interest. The expedition had also exploded some cherished fantasies, particularly the dream of a water passage across the continent. Nor, as a gleeful John Quincy Adams pointed out in an anonymous poem, had they found any of the other exotic legends about the West, like Welsh-descended Indians, a salt mountain, or a living mammoth. Nevertheless, particularly through the magnificent map Clark drew that accompanied the Biddle edition and incorporated information from the later Zebulon Pike expedition of 1805–7, Americans now had a much more accurate picture of the basic geography of the continent. The Rocky Mountains were not, as had been thought formerly, a single, long, narrow range running parallel to the Pacific but massive multiple ranges, a far more formidable barrier. The 1820 expedition of Major Stephen Long provided more, though rather depressing, information about the regions west of the Mississippi valley. The area should be designated the "Great American Desert," wrote Long, for it was unfit for any but a nomadic population. Providence, it appeared, had thoughtfully placed this arid area as a perpetual barrier "to keep the American people from ruinous diffusion" and as a convenient dumping ground for Indians removed from the East. The new information was only slowly assimilated. As late as 1819 the most widely used American geography, Jedidiah Morse's *American Universal Geography,* had still not incorporated the data from Clark's map. By 1823, however, the botanist Jacob Bigelow could confidently assert: "Any one who surveys the map of North America at the present day, and compares its features with those which it wore scarcely more than twenty years ago, cannot fail to be struck with the great changes it has undergone."[6]

At the beginning of the century the long-standing debate among European scientists over the quality of the American continent as a habitat was still unresolved. Did this environment, as the notable French scientist the comte de Buffon had charged in the mid-eighteenth century, produce degeneracy in animals and people? The American climate was unhealthy and too extreme for civilization. In his *Notes on the State of Virginia,* Jefferson had argued that the American climate was in fact becoming more moderate, probably due to forest clearance. This view was echoed by the French writer François de Volney in *A View of the Soil and Climate of the United States,* published in a translation by Charles Brockden Brown in 1804. Volney predicted that the continent would become even more temperate as civilization progressed. But Americans were becoming less sure. In the notes to his translation, Brown vigorously denied any change in the climate at all; Noah Webster in 1806 asserted that the clearing of forests had not so much moderated the climate as made it more "inconstant." Was this fluctuating climate, together with the "miasmas" from swamps no longer absorbed by forests, connected to the endemic fevers of America, particularly the great yellow fever epidemics in Philadelphia and New York in 1793 and 1795? Or were these diseases due rather to Americans' generally unhealthy and immoderate style of living and their lack of self-discipline in keeping cities clean, as Benjamin Rush and the physician-historian of South Carolina, David Ramsay, suggested? In what has been described as "the first long-term scientific research carried out in America," the surgeon-general of the army required all army doctors to begin recording the weather at their posts. The aim was to try and uncover connections among climate, terrain, land cultivation, and disease.[7]

Recording and Investigating Nature

Sensitivity about the quality of nature in America stimulated Americans' interest in natural history. National self-respect required that "their" natural world had to be at least as beneficent as the Old World's. In addition, the continent was teeming with life, much of it different from European species, which still awaited naming, description, and classification. European naturalists were already usurping this role and naming and describing American flora and fauna; urgent calls began for Americans to take up the task.

In this period natural science was concerned largely with the collection, description, and classification of specimens, usually according to the Linnaean system of easily observable surface characteristics. Amateurs as well as professional scientists could make useful contributions through careful observation. Josiah Meigs, commissioner of the General Land Office, in 1817 requested his agents to keep records of temperature, wind, and weather thrice daily and to note flowering times of plants, bird migrations, hibernation of animals, droughts, and "memorable facts relative to the topography of the country." Starting in 1825 the State University of New York required its faculty to keep records of weather, times of flowering, harvesting, first frosts, and so on. Networks were set up to exchange information and specimens. The *Portico* of Baltimore urged gentlemen traveling across the country to pay systematic attention to its geology, "whose investigation, while it will open new sources of entertainment to themselves, may add considerably to the general stock of useful science."[8]

Botany was the most popular branch of natural history because of the ease with which it could be undertaken by the interested amateur. American botany labored under both advantages and disadvantages in the early nineteenth century. On the one hand, it was a vast field still open for new research, and there was an established network of contacts with English and European naturalists. On the other hand, almost all American botanists were either practicing medical men, like Benjamin Barton of Philadelphia, or clergymen, like Manasseh Cutler of Massachusetts, whose botanizing had to be part time and their fieldwork close to home. There were only a few botanical gardens in which they could study, notably William Bartram's in Philadelphia, the Elgin Botanic garden in New York, and others in Charleston and at Harvard University, and getting funds to support even these over the long haul was a constant problem. The South Carolina naturalist Stephen Elliott deplored "the want of books, the want of opportunities for examining living collections or good herbaria, the want of coadjutors." "No one in Europe," he complained, "can appreciate correctly the difficulty of the task in which I have engaged."

Outside major centers like Philadelphia, European reference books were hard to find. Publishers were unwilling to publish the fruits of native research because illustrations would be difficult and expensive to produce and the likely audience would be small. Most important scientific studies of botany in America were by Europeans, who had been able to range widely over the continent and then return to Europe to work up their collections and to publish. The first work on American oak trees (1801) and the first general account of North American botany (1803) were produced by the Frenchman

André Michaux; both were published in Paris, with illustrations by Redouté. As late as 1826 John James Audubon went to England to publish his *Birds of America.*[9]

But the study of natural history in America was becoming better organized. Major Long's expedition, unlike that of Lewis and Clark, included trained naturalists and artists to record and collect specimens. In Philadelphia, the Academy of Natural Sciences, founded in 1812 with the proud aim of rendering "ourselves as independent as possible of other countries and governments," began to build sizable collections. By the 1820s, the young botanist John Torrey; the entomologist Thomas Say; zoologists George Ord, Richard Harlan, and John Goodman; and others were ready to make recording and classifying American nature an American business.[10]

An important figure in this enterprise was Charles Willson Peale. Peale had been a highly successful portrait painter before the Revolution, but his interests turned increasingly toward natural history and invention. Throughout his long life (he did not die until 1827 at the age of eighty-five) he was a classic tinkerer who developed a paleograph and porcelain false teeth, besides arranging illuminated displays for public celebrations. A member of the American Philosophical Society, Peale was also an entrepreneur of science. In 1790 he opened his museum, which he ran with the help of various of his eleven children, all named after famous painters or famous scientists. The exhibits were mainly natural history specimens, arranged carefully according to the Linnaean system of classification, together with portraits of American Revolutionary heroes and displays of Indian costumes and artifacts. For twenty-five cents admission, patrons could also examine insects through a microscope, listen to organ music, have their likeness taken in profile by a special machine, and sometimes hear lectures on natural history by Peale or others.

Peale believed that nature existed not only for use but for moral education. The museum was to be a "world in miniature," designed to make nature an "open-book," accessible to all, "more powerful to humanize the mind, promote harmony, and aid virtue, than any other School yet imagined." The lectures on natural history and the dramatic display of stuffed animals against painted scenic backdrops attracted a good deal of popular interest, and the collections themselves were an invaluable resource for scientists. As a commercial enterprise the museum was fairly successful, but Peale's dream of securing federal patronage and making it a national institution in Washington was never fulfilled. His son Rubens took over the business in 1809 and found that, in order to break even, he had to put increasing emphasis on various kinds of "wonders" and shows to attract the public.[11]

Peale's collections were particularly useful to the first great American ornithologist, Alexander Wilson. Wilson, a weaver and a poet who had arrived penniless from Scotland in Philadelphia in 1794, had no training in science, but he was astonished by the birds of his new country and determined to become their recorder. Peale's museum provided numerous specimens from which he could work, including, after 1806, the birds brought back by Lewis and Clark. But Wilson was a field naturalist, making up for whatever he lacked in scientific preparation with the accuracy and acuteness of his observation, and he rambled extensively to observe birds in their natural habitat. In the days before photography, the naturalist had to murder to depict, and Wilson was no exception; he drew from birds he or others had shot and mounted. In 1808 the first volume of his projected multivolume *American Ornithology* appeared, a high-quality production with splendid drawings. When Wilson died in 1813, eight volumes had been completed; the final volume of the series was produced by his friend, the wealthy Philadelphia businessman-scientist, George Ord.[12]

Wilson's achievement inspired later naturalists like Audubon, Thomas Nuttall, and Charles Bonaparte. Like William Bartram, whose *Travels* (1791) had influenced Samuel Coleridge and the English lake poets, Wilson was lyrical in describing the landscape and the birds he studied. Sometimes his feelings burst out of prose, and a number of poems are scattered through the *Ornithology*. He shared with his contemporaries an approach to nature that was both scientific and rhapsodic, describing natural history as an activity that was both "rational" and "sublime."[13]

Nature and Nature's God

However far they departed from the religious orthodoxy of an earlier era, American naturalists still worked firmly within a tradition that regarded the study of nature as a means to "look up through Nature to Nature's God." Painstaking observation and attention to nature were acts of natural piety. "To whatever portion of the vast chain of created beings we direct our research," declared Wilson in the prospectus for his *Ornithology*, "the wisdom, power, and benificence of the Deity, in its formation, in the harmony of its parts, and in the provident care exercised for its preservation, fill us with wonder, delight and awful veneration." To scientists entrenched within a theistic worldview, every evidence of adaptation in nature was an indication of design—yet another sign of the benevolence of the Creator in precisely fitting His creatures to their world. No close observer, declared Samuel Willard in the *North American Review*, can fail to be struck with the "wonderful manifestations of infinite goodness" by which the bodily powers of animals are adapted to their manner of life, so that those "destined to obtain their food by violence," for example, "are furnished with weapons of attack and defence."[14]

Occasionally a few men allowed themselves to wonder about the utility of some elements of the Creator's design. "What end could creative wisdom propose," mused Timothy Dwight contemplating the Green Mountains, "in forming such masses of solid rock . . . unfit for habitation and apparently useless to man? . . . Why, the mind instinctively asks, were these huge piles of ruin thus heaped together?" Channing also was troubled by the inexplicable wastefulness of nature. "The light and heat of the sun on the ocean may seem unprofitable," he acknowledged to his diary on a sea voyage, but hastily added, "Not so." Since the heat was absorbed and eventually condensed into rain, "good done by raining, at sea, as well as on land."[15]

Potentially troubling questions arose from the discovery of remains of unknown animals. Farmers had been digging up huge bones for some time. The scientific and popular sensation of 1801 was Peale's reconstruction of a "mammoth," which he had dredged up from a farmer's marl pit in New York. Peale's monster, eleven feet high and over seventeen long from head to tail, was exhibited to great crowds at fifty cents admission. Peale sent casts of the bones to the celebrated French scientist Georges Cuvier, who proclaimed it a member of a new genus and named it the mastodon. Jefferson, who had earlier presented a memoir on similar remains dug up in Virginia to the American Philosophical Society, encouraged the continued collecting of bones. Many of these were deposited with the American Philosophical Society, where Caspar Wistar began to classify and describe them, beginning what was to become a distinguished school of paleontology in Philadelphia.[16]

The question aroused by these skeletal remains was whether these animals were still somewhere in existence or whether they had become extinct. Jefferson refused to admit the possibility of extinction and insisted that living examples of the mammoth must still exist somewhere, possibly in the remote interior of the continent. What seemed to be at stake was the idea of the design of nature, perfect from the beginning. Why would God have created a species only to eliminate it later? Could nature make a mistake? "If one link in nature's chain might be lost," Jefferson insisted to the American Philosophical Society, "another and another might be lost, till this whole system of things should evanish by piecemeal." Scientific men of his generation like Benjamin Rush repudiated the notion hazarded by Erasmus Darwin that advanced animals might in fact have evolved from other lower animals. But clinging to the fixity of the natural design was becoming old fashioned. The botanist Benjamin Smith Barton was quite prepared to accept, as he told the Philadelphia Linnaean society in 1807, that North America had once been inhabited by several species of animals that "there is reason to believe, now no longer exist." Most scientific men were becoming willing to accept the fact of extinction as part of the process of nature—a position that perhaps made it easier to accept the idea of the extinction of a race, as in the case of the American Indians.[17]

The increasingly important science of geology raised touchier questions. After much speculation on the formation of the earth, geologists by the early nineteenth century were divided into two camps: the neptunists, followers of the German Abraham Werner, who held that the strata of the earth were precipitates of a vast primeval ocean, and the vulcanists, followers of the Scot James Hutton, who held that the structure of the world was the result of the constant process of erosion together with volcanic upthrusting from below. Both theories required long periods of time, far longer than the six thousand years hitherto generally accepted as the age of the earth. The distinct fossil contents of earth strata implied not just the extinction of some species but catastrophic natural events in which they had been destroyed. In some ways this view of nature disturbed deists like Jefferson and the Scottish immigrant geologist James McClure more than orthodox Christians, whose theology provided more room for the unexpected. Both Jefferson and McClure in fact preferred to avoid speculation about the origins of the earth altogether and restrict geology to purely empirical investigation, concerned with turning up useful knowledge for the miner and engineer.[18]

In the early nineteenth century all educated men paid intellectual allegiance to Francis Bacon. To Jefferson, Bacon was one of the three greatest men who ever lived (the other two were Isaac Newton and John Locke), and Joel Barlow hailed Bacon in the *Columbiad* as the genius who taught men to give up "their unproved systems" and informed them "what to learn and how to know." Bacon was credited with having swept away the cobwebs of scholasticism, encouraging men to look at the facts and from them induce the laws of nature. This inductive method was assumed to be *the* scientific method and, indeed, the key to all real knowledge. Nature was open to human investigation but only through careful and humble observation. The true disciple of Bacon would eschew "speculation" and "wild" hypotheses— indeed hypotheses at all. It was more scientifically useful, maintained one geologist, to avoid theorizing that always tended to both begin and end in "doubt and painful uncertainty" and concentrate on "matters of fact, where we are less in danger of being misled by imagination." American scientists were characterized by what one historian has called "naive rationalistic empiricism."[19]

The reluctance of American scientists to speculate, coupled with the fact that the most influential figures in American geology, with the exception of McClure, were devout Christians, meant that churchmen in the early nineteenth century were generally able to take scientific work in paleontology and geology in stride. When Samuel Miller wrote his *Brief Retrospect*, he could assert that once scientists gave up vague speculating and buckled down to empirical investigation, the facts of geology would be found to support the

Mosaic account of creation. It soon became clear that the account would have to be interpreted with a certain license, but Miller was right in sensing no immediate threat from geology.

A leading figure in interpreting geological discoveries within the paradigm of divine creation was Benjamin Silliman. Having persuaded the Connecticut legislature to set up a new professorship of chemistry and natural history at Yale University, in 1798 President Dwight picked the twenty-two-year-old Silliman, a recent Yale graduate with no particular scientific training, as its first incumbent. Silliman had been converted in a recent revival and had the advantage from Dwight's point of view of being "born and raised among us and possessed of our habits and sympathies." Orthodoxy was the important quality. An intelligent and diligent young man could pick up the science, and Silliman was dispatched to Philadelphia and then Edinburgh to learn his craft. Silliman did not become a front-rank researcher, but he was an excellent teacher who connected science with admiration for the sublimity of nature's design and humility toward its creator, and he passed on this attitude to his many students. He introduced geology into his science courses at Yale, published geological research in his *American Journal of Science*, and trained most of the prominent American geologists before the Civil War. Silliman was convinced that geology did not contradict the Bible. He pointed out in 1829 that the great length of time geology revealed as necessary to the creation of the present earth could be resolved by interpreting the six "days" of creation as referring to "periods of time" rather than twenty-four hours, a resolution of the problem that became widely acceptable.[20]

Like most other American geologists, Silliman was inclined to the neptunian position, which could more easily be reconciled with Genesis. To the eye of faith, however, vulcanist theories could also be made compatible with religion. Silliman's student Edward Hitchcock, a devout Congregationalist who became professor of chemistry and natural history at Amherst College, was prepared to accept that the earth might be three hundred thousand years old. Hitchcock maintained, however, that geology in fact bolstered Christian revelation. In place of the Enlightenment's Creator who set in motion a self-sustaining world, the newer geology indicated an interventionist God who shaped a world through volcanic action and catastrophic floods and created new species as earlier ones were extinguished. Once the increased age of the earth was reconciled with the Creation story, this prospect of almost infinite time could be assimilated as giving added depth and grandeur to the world. When he reissued *The Prairie* in 1832, Cooper added a new introduction describing the origin and date of the "Great American Prairies" as "one of nature's most majestic mysteries."[21]

So solidly entrenched was the biblical paradigm that there was little danger as yet that God would be dethroned or that humanity would be left alone in the world. The universe still bespoke purpose, even if that purpose was now more mysterious and veiled. Few doubted that the universe was friendly and that nature was made for human beings to use and exploit, to understand and contemplate, and to receive intimations of divinity and immortality. "The material organs of sense, especially the eye," as Channing remarked, "wake up infinite thoughts in the mind. . . . The universe in which we live, was plainly meant by God to stir [us]."[22]

Nature and the Sublime

As Americans sought a way of apprehending imaginatively the expanding natural world, they turned instinctively to the concept of the sublime. Popularized by Edmund Burke in the eighteenth century, it connoted the feeling of religious awe inspired by the sight of grand and wild scenery, of jagged mountains or raging torrents. More than merely an aesthetic term, the sublime encapsulated the aesthetic, the moral, and the religious and was as likely to be used by the scientist as by the poet or the artist. It was a category that unified different realms of experience and brought science, art, and literature together in a new appreciation of the works of nature. As Americans set to understanding and assimilating their environment through both science and art, the idea of the sublime provided a major mode of shaping intellectual and emotional response.[23]

It certainly provided a way for artists to cope with the problem of rendering the essence of the American landscape. In terms of contemporary aesthetic theory, the American landscape lacked the essential quality to produce great art: poetic associations of romantic legends, or great deeds from a glorious misty past. It was not a written landscape; there was no bridge of human communication between it and the observer. The concept of the sublime allowed the artist to bypass these deficiencies and invoke the vast and limitless qualities of American nature as cultural assets of the new nation to set against the European superiority in history and literary associations. "If we then are destitute of the antiquity of human institutions," Walter Channing pointed out, "we should never forget that we possess the antiquity of nature." An orator told the American Academy of Fine Arts in 1825 that in America "nature needs no fictitious charms" and "the eye requires no borrowed assistance from the memory." He insisted that it was now time, however, to make the land present to the American imagination through art and "adorn our houses with American prospects and American skies."[24]

As American painters began to tackle the landscape, the major problem was finding a technique to convey an impression of the vast and the wild. John Vanderlyn took on Niagara Falls in 1802, adopting a panoramic technique that emphasized horizontals and thus the breadth of the falls, forcing viewers to sweep their eyes from one side of the picture to the other to take it all in. Alexander Wilson, in an engraving to accompany a long narrative poem, drew only part of the falls, but from underneath, thus emphasizing the overwhelming height and the impact of the descending water.[25]

The first important artist in America to make the wildness of untouched American nature his central theme was Thomas Cole. Cole arrived in the United States from England in 1818 at the age of seventeen, with no artistic training; he began his career as a member of that numerous tribe of portrait artists who tramped from town to town painting likenesses of local worthies. But he had fallen in love with American nature and soon devoted himself to learning how to paint it. Three landscapes he painted from a trip up the Hudson in 1822 were bought immediately, and when they were exhibited at the New York Academy, they took the art world by storm.

Cole's landscapes display full blown the idea of nature as sublime: wildness, infinity, the centrality of towering mountains, dangerously plunging clefts, extreme contrast between darkness and light, and the human figure reduced to insectlike size, overshadowed by the dominating forms of the natural world. Like the naturalist Wilson, Cole was a prodigious walker who tramped for miles over wild terrain, drinking in the scenery with romantic enthusiasm and making sketches. These sketches were later combined in the studio, after a deliberate lapse of time, into landscapes designed to capture the "truth" of nature rather than a literal representation of an exact spot. Cole's patron, the Baltimore merchant Robert Gilmore, complained of his lack of strict fidelity to actual landscapes, but Cole wanted to elevate painting above a mere "dead imitation of things" and make it, like poetry, an exercise of intellect and imagination, able to "enforce a truth." In his landscapes, nature became metaphor, a "visual correlative" for the "drama of the soul." This approach eventually took him beyond the painting of American scenery into grandiose allegorical works, but his earlier works founded a tradition of American landscape painting.[26]

Approached in terms of the sublime, nature began to serve an essentially conservative function. In the Enlightenment, the concept of nature had operated radically, furnishing a ground of authority to free people from outworn forms and customs. American writers and painters now turned to nature to evoke reverence for something outside imperious human will. The message of nature, if indistinct, nevertheless suggested, in the words of the poet William Cullen Bryant, "the idea of unity and immensity, and abstracting the mind from the associations of human agency, carried it up to the idea of a mightier power, and to the great mystery of the origin of things."[27]

Bryant's poetry exemplified the fusion of religion and nature. Bryant grew up in the foothills of the Berkshires, the son of a doctor who was an enthusiastic naturalist and taught his son to observe and admire nature. Influenced by William Wordsworth's *Lyrical Ballads*, which he read at sixteen, Bryant believed that the poet must draw correspondences "between the things of the moral and of the natural world." His first important poem, "Thanatopsis," gave him an enduring reputation on its publication in 1817. As he moved from a vague deism to Unitarianism, his poetry became more specifically religious. In "To a Waterfowl" (1818), the poet trusts that the bird's flight will be guided by "Him," who also "Will lead my steps aright," and in "A Forest Hymn" (1825), the woods are a temple, and God is not merely the creator of the natural world but palpably present in it: "But Thou are here— Thou fill'st / The solitude . . . the barky trunks, the ground, / The fresh moist ground, are all instinct with Thee." The natural world is a school in which errant humanity may be chastened: "And to the beautiful order of Thy works / Learn to conform the order of our lives."[28]

Nature and the Individual

Nature could also have more anarchic implications however. The popular cult of Daniel Boone demonstrated the lure of an individual relationship to nature unmediated by society. The first settler into Kentucky in the 1770s, Boone quickly became a myth in his own lifetime. He had been celebrated in John Filson's early history of Kentucky as the harbinger of civilization, a theme developed in Daniel Bryan's epic poem on Boone, "The Mountain Muse" (1813). In this work, already old fashioned in its diction and increasingly in its sentiment, Boone was chosen by the "Spirit of Enterprize" to bring Civilization, "Social Love," and "Refinement" to the wilderness. Meanwhile, popular mythmaking was transforming Boone into the rootless loner, the man who could not abide seeing the smoke from another cabin and so had constantly to move on.[29]

Cooper based Leatherstocking on Boone. A hunter and trapper who ventures alone into the wilderness far in advance of settlement, Leatherstocking is a trailblazer for civilization yet himself estranged from it. He seemed to embody a vision not of ordered liberty in community but of an absolute freedom, available only to the male and to be found only apart from society and ties to women and children. Cooper was careful to insist that his hero does not become an outlaw, because he is still voluntarily bound by the law of a benevolent nature. He had an instinctive piety toward the God he found in the woods, and his morality was in many ways superior to that of people in the "clearings." The novels seemed to indicate that a white man could have the freedom of an Indian without becoming a savage; the popularity of Leatherstocking, in Europe as well as America, testified to the chord he struck in modern urban minds.[30]

The imaginative appeal of an individual specially linked to nature could be seen in the popular cult of Andrew Jackson. His miraculous victory at New Orleans in 1815 demonstrated that elite, trained British troops could be soundly drubbed by a bunch of wild, untrained Kentucky riflemen. Frontiersmen did not need military training because they had learned in the school of nature to be dead shots. In the presidential races of 1824 and 1828, publicists found ready to hand both popular prejudices and metaphors from nature that allowed them to play off Jackson, one of "Nature's great men," against the effete and overcivilized John Quincy Adams. "He grew up in the wilds of the West," wrote one, "but he was the noblest tree in the forest." His untutored "natural" genius enabled him to grasp the right course intuitively and take decisive action, while lesser men were bound by society's petty rules and legalities. In the cult surrounding Jackson, nature did not so much invoke awe as provide an arena for the unrestrained exercise of human will.[31]

The Transformation of Nature

The works of Bryant, Cooper, and Cole appeared when popular interest in natural scenery and exposure to famous natural wonders was growing rapidly. There was a great vogue for travel literature in this period. The reading public enjoyed the feeling that they knew what places they had never seen looked like. "It would be difficult at this time," wrote a weary reviewer in 1827, "to write a new thing on either the Hudson river, the Niagara Falls, or even the Grand Canal. Indeed, through the medium of books of travels, tours, sketches, diaries, and the like, almost every nook and corner of the United States, within the reach of stage-coaches, steamboats, or even pedestrian enterprise, has become familiar to every reader." By the 1820s improvements in transportation were expanding the possibility of travel for pleasure. A steady stream of tourists ascended the Catskills and the White Mountains, where there were now shelters to receive them. On top of Mount Washington climbers found a thoughtfully provided sheet of lead and an iron pencil with which they could write their names. The opening of the Erie Canal in 1825 made Niagara Falls accessible to the pleasure traveler, and thousands arrived to gaze upon this prime example of the American sublime. Nature was soon improved by showmanship. In 1827 thousands came to Niagara not to gaze in awe at the work of the Almighty but to watch a leaky old schooner loaded with circus animals be set adrift over the falls; even more turned up two years later to watch Sam Patch jump over them.[32]

Although people of sensibility knew that untouched nature was sublime, for the majority terms like *wilderness* and *forests* still almost automatically conjured up accompanying adjectives such as *desolate, barren, monotonous,* and *gloomy* and stimulated the immediate desire to subdue them, populate them, and cover them with corn fields, villages, and towns. Recording his reactions to the White Mountains of New Hampshire, Timothy Dwight observed, "In so vast an expansion the eye perceives a prevalence of forest which it regrets, and instinctively demands a wider extent of smiling scenes and a more general establishment of the cheerful haunts of man."[33]

Dwight's aesthetic taste in this case was probably like that of most ordinary people. It is notable that in the flourishing world of "primitive" art, there were few scenes of wild, untouched nature. Thousands of amateurs painted in America. They painted portraits and sometimes scenes from books. As engravings and commercial prints became more widely available, the amateur painter often used such pictures as models. Landscapes were a popular subject, but the scene was usually of a farm or village rather than wilderness. The most famous of these primitive painters is the Quaker Edward Hicks, whose successive obsessive renderings of the verse from Isaiah about the lion lying down with the lamb have become one of the most famous of American images. He painted his first *Peaceable Kingdom* in 1820 after seeing the collection of stuffed animals in Peale's museum. He drew his moral, however, straight from the biblical text rather than directly from the book of nature.[34]

Most Americans probably regarded nature less as a source of spiritual uplift than as raw material for transformation. Works like Timothy Flint's immensely popular *Condensed Geography and History of the Western States* (1828) were concerned with nature, particularly in frontier regions, essentially in terms of economic possibility. Flint, a New England clergyman who had spent twelve years living and traveling in the Mississippi valley, felt his imagination chiefly stirred by the "unparalleled advancement in population and improvement" he had witnessed in that time, "that transformation, as if of magic, which has converted the wilderness to fields and orchards."[35]

That transformation, however, often involved violence. In his 1819 bestselling *Sketchbook*, Washington Irving had praised the way in which the English landscape had been shaped over centuries by a "delicate tact," a cooperation between people and nature. Such affectionate patience with nature did not come easily to most Americans. The willingness to disregard features of the landscape in order to facilitate acquiring and recording land is clear in the imposition of the grid pattern of surveying on western lands. The grid shaped new city development too. When New York City in 1807 decided to plan for the future development of Manhattan, it imposed a rectangular grid over the island that completely ignored topography. Made up of uniform lots designed to facilitate private housing, the plan also omitted any provision for ornamental public spaces, offering instead an impersonal and egalitarian framework for individual initiative to provide the content. A symbol of the triumph of the rational mind over the irregularities of nature, by 1820 this grid concept, with all its inconveniences, had become an integral part of the national inheritance.[36]

By the opening of the nineteenth century, the wasteful habits of American farmers and their stubborn resistance to good advice were the despair of others devoted to useful improvements. The availability of land led to extensive rather than intensive farming, to "an overweening desire of possessing *many acres*, rather than *well managed farms*." The common method of clearing land "by the destructive and truly inconsiderate and savage practice of burning," wrote the agricultural reformer John Lorain, destroyed in a day or two the natural "animal and vegetable matter" that had accumulated over a long period. A little observation would teach that "nature did not cut, rend, or mangle either the tops or the roots of the plants, and by this means debilitate, and procrastinate the growth of them." The slash-and-burn method produced a few bumper crops and then sterility, but the abundance of land allowed wasteful farmers merely to move on. John Taylor of Caroline, who devoted much of his life to turning his own Virginia plantation into a showplace of scientific agriculture, blamed the desire for quick profits. The problem appeared to be that most farmers and planters lacked the kind of "piety" that would lead them to learn from nature and cooperate with it, sacrificing quick returns for long-term benefit.[37]

The American farmer was the man with an ax, his sweep across the country symbolized by the rotting stumps of the trees he cut down. The tree stump was a feature of the American environment noticed and deplored by every traveler. Yet as Timothy Flint acknowledged in 1826, "To the eye of a Kentuckian the huge stumps that remain after cultivation has commenced, are pleasant circumstances," clear evidence that the wilderness was being brought under human control. Flint had to confess that personally he preferred the prairies, "where there are no dead trees, nor stumps, but a clear stage, 'tabula rasa,' and the first aspect of cultivation is as smooth, . . . as it will be after the lapse of a century."[38]

Wildlife also fell victim to what sometimes seemed a compulsion to destroy. Alexander Wilson resorted to verses to impress farmers with the idea that certain birds kept down insects and should not be shot on sight: "Some small return, some little right resign, / And spare his life whose services are thine." Cooper was a strong critic of American destructiveness; one of the most powerful scenes in *The Pioneers* depicted the mass shooting of flocks of pigeons with rifles, arrows and even a miniature cannon, until the ground was covered with dead and wounded birds. Leatherstocking hunted only for food and denounced the men of the clearings, the "Yankee choppers" as he called them, for their "wasty ways," their extravagant destruction of nature, "without remorse and without shame."[39]

One of the most popular songs of the 1820s was George P. Morris's "Woodman, Spare that Tree / Touch not a single bough; / In youth it sheltered me, / And I'll protect it now." The appeal of this tearjerker indicated some faint recognition that economic development endangered the irreplaceable. In the song one man could rescue one special tree, but even among the thoughtful who tried to teach Americans to be less ferociously wasteful toward nature, there was a fatalistic recognition that much of what was distinctive about the New World land must, like the Indian, disappear before the onslaught of an otherwise admirable civilization.[40]

"A century hence," mused the wandering naturalist John Audubon in 1826, the rivers, swamps, even the mountains of America, "will not be here as I see them, Nature will have been robbed of many brilliant charms, the rivers will be tormented and turned astray from their primitive courses, the hills will be levelled with the swamps, and perhaps the swamps will have become a mount surmounted by a fortess of a thousand guns." His language suggested not only the inevitability of the process but the violence with which it was accomplished. A long way from the raw edge of new settlement, a few people like Taylor or Cooper realized that the power people had used against nature could ultimately turn against them. In "An Indian at the Burial-Place of His Fathers," Bryant has his despairing Indian warn the white man about his destruction of the land:

> The springs are silent in the sun;
> The rivers, by the blackened shore,
> With lessening current run;
> The realm our tribes are crushed to get
> May be a barren desert yet.[41]

As Americans leanred more about nature, their image of it changed. No longer what Philip Freneau called a "vast machine" "constant, still the same," nature was now coming to seem older, more complex, prodigal and capricious, always in the process of *becoming* rather than fixed and regular. Its grandeur and remoteness inspired awe and humility. Yet as some were coming to realize, even nature was vulnerable to the relentless march of humanity, and for the thoughtful observer its sublimity was tinged with pathos.[42]

Part Three

Democracy

six

The Influence of
America on the Mind

> Though there is scarce such a thing as a capital picture in this
> whole country, I have seen more beautiful, graceful, and con-
> venient ploughs in positive use here, than are probably to be
> found in the whole of Europe united. In this single fact may be
> traced the history of the character of the people, and the germ
> of their future greatness.
>
> —James Fenimore Cooper, *Notions of the Americans*, 1828

Returning from Germany in 1819, Edward Everett was amazed "at the astonishing development of intellectual energy in this country." The heightened vitality came both from the confidence generated by the War of 1812
and by the injection of new ideas from abroad. The end of the Napoleonic
wars in 1815 meant that Americans could travel freely in Europe. As transatlantic travel became easier and quicker, more and more made the
pilgrimage.[1]

Americans and Europe

American attitudes to the Old World were complex. For most Americans
Europe meant the heritage of the past. American painters, for example, generally responded more readily to the antique or to the Old Masters than to
contemporary European artists. Writers approached Europe as the history
from which the New World had broken free but which still exercised an

inescapable fascination. Washington Irving, who left America for a long stay in Europe in 1815, sought "romance" in the Old World as an escape from the stark actualities of the New. "I longed," he wrote in *The Sketchbook* (1819), "to loiter about the ruined castle—to meditate on the falling tower—to escape in short, from the commonplace realities of the present, and lose myself among the shadowy grandeurs of the past." To some travelers, however, those who went to look at Manchester and other industrial cities or who studied in German universities, Europe meant a modernity of considerable power but morally disturbing implications.[2]

Always the impact of Europe was to make travelers more aware of being Americans. They were appalled by the inequality and poverty there compared to the United States. At the same time they were usually unprepared for the sensuous appeal of European life. The painter Washington Allston was overwhelmed by the "gorgeous concert of colors" in Titian and Veronese; the Protestant Cooper felt himself yielding to the art and music of Catholic churches; the Quaker educator John Griscom, in the public gardens of Paris, was startled by the seminude statues, which in the United States would be "only placed behind screens in exhibition rooms." When Thomas Cole returned to England for further study in 1829, Bryant was sufficiently nervous to write a farewell sonnet urging him to preserve in his heart "a living image of our own bright land," and, though surrounded by the seductions of Europe, to "keep that earlier, wilder image bright."[3]

His wariness was not ill founded, for several of the talented painters who had been studying in Europe before the war and returned after 1815 found the adjustment to American conditions hard. Their calling did not enjoy the same esteem as in Europe, and it was almost impossible to make a living except by portrait painting. The latter paid fairly well: "everybody is anxious to see his own phiz on canvas," said the irreverent *Salmagundi* in 1807. It was a mark of a growing sense of self, as well as growing disposable income, that quite ordinary people aspired to have their portraits painted. Men like Gilbert Stuart and Thomas Sully made highly successful careers in America out of portraits. But to equally talented younger painters, like Samuel F. B. Morse, son of the formidable pillar of Massachusetts orthodoxy Jedidiah, the South Carolina aristocrat Washington Allston, or John Vanderlyn, the portrait smacked too much of colonial days when the artist was basically an artisan, traveling from town to town and executing portraits or shop signs on demand. In Europe these men had developed a much more exalted sense both of themselves as artists and of the function of art.[4]

Neoclassic in their taste and followers of the laws of painting laid down by Sir Joshua Reynolds, they believed that the highest type of painting was the great historical picture (a term loose enough to include biblical and religious subjects). Large in size, painted nobly in what was called the grand manner, and concerned with some great significant human action, the history painting was intended not so much to please as to elevate and inspire. It was the furthest remove from the artisan-portrait since it was "intellectual," not a mere copy of nature, and required thought and education.[5]

While in Europe, Vanderlyn, Morse, and Allston did good work in the grand manner. Vanderlyn's classical *Marius amidst the Ruins of Carthage* won him a gold medal from Napoleon. Back in America, however, his career was frustrating, and his later work did not fulfill the earlier promise. On his return, Morse became increasingly disgusted with the American art scene and eventually abandoned art for invention. (That is why he is mainly known to history as the inventor of the telegraph.) Washington Allston presented a particularly sad case. His thirteen-foot-tall *Dead Man Restored to Life by Touching the Bones of Elija* won him election to the Royal Academy and was bought by the Pennsylvania Academy of the Fine Arts for $3,500. Allston was widely expected to be the genius of his generation, but he sunk into decline once he returned home in 1818. He brought back with him the half-finished canvas of another huge picture, *Belshazzar's Feast*, which was to be his masterwork. Instead it became an albatross—long awaited but never finished. Though he continued to paint, he never fulfilled the expectations people had had of him.[6]

The rather disappointing careers of these genuinely talented men once they returned to America seem at least partly a result of their commitment to the grand manner and the historical painting. History painting was in fact as suitable an aesthetic for a republican nation as neoclassical architecture. But because it was a public art, it needed display in public space and, thus, government patronage, which most of the time was not forthcoming. The only way a painter could make money from a noncommissioned large history painting was to send it out as a touring exhibit. Sometimes this paid off, and sometimes it did not. The commitment of these artists to this kind of didactic painting was an assertion of the dignity of art and their own and their country's participation in the great Western tradition, but it blinded them to other possibilities. They were never much attracted to American landscape or to genre paintings of everyday American life. They had returned from their European sojourn with a theoretically appropriate but in practice dysfunctional aesthetic.[7]

Other men who went to Europe to study successfully resisted absorbing attitudes that might have alienated them from American society. A good example is the young New Englanders who went to do advanced work at the University of Göttingen after 1815. Germany was to be the great fount of new ideas. Although few Americans as yet knew much about Germany or read the language, scholars were becoming aware that German universities were on the cutting edge of European scholarship, particularly in the study of the classical languages from a historical perspective. When Harvard picked the young minister Edward Everett for a new professorship of Greek,

Göttingen, rather than Oxford, Cambridge, or Edinburgh, was the obvious place to send him for advanced training. Everett went in 1815 along with George Ticknor, scion of a wealthy Boston family; Joseph Cogswell followed a year later, and the future historian George Bancroft went out in 1818.

Göttingen was something of a shock. From their experience at Harvard, the young Americans had no idea what modern advanced scholarship entailed. "What a mortifying distance there is," Ticknor wrote home, "between a European and an American scholar. We do not yet know what a Greek scholar is; we do not even know the process by which a man is to be made one." The cultural distance was most evident in the library at Göttingen. In Germany the university "consists in the library," he wrote to the steward of Harvard, whereas Americans erected buildings and founded new professorships and colleges, "but we buy no books."[8]

The freedom of discussion and publication was also startling. Ticknor reported to Jefferson that every day, books appeared that elsewhere in Europe would be suppressed by the state "and in America would be put in to the great *catalogus expurgatorius* of public opinion." Bancroft, who expected to become a minister, was appalled by the flippancy with which religious matters were discussed, by the general use of profanity, and by the slovenliness of the German students. The narrowness of the new model scholars was also deeply disturbing. Coming from a New England where it was assumed that a scholar was also a gentleman, a Christian, and a citizen, committed to a responsible role as leader and guide of the community, Bancroft found the new breed of specialist, whose standing in the roped-off world of scholarship depended solely on his expertise, hard to accept. "He who can instruct me best in Greek metres," he complained in a letter home, "is a man, who has not found time from his studies to ask if there be a God, or a world in which we are to act. He, who can teach me to understand Horace, does not know that there are such things as morality and good manners." One result of apparently unlimited freedom of investigation, he noted in his journal, was rapid obsolescence of research. There were no unassailable authorities held up as models "offering the highest sublimity," and the earliest investigators were forgotten. Worst of all, scholars "neither guide public opinion nor form it. . . . The learned write for the learned."[9]

While the Americans admired the prodigious achievements of the new scholarship, they did not find the German scholar an attractive model. When they returned home, only Ticknor remained in university teaching for any length of time. Both he and Bancroft became distinguished men of letters—Bancroft as a historian of America, Ticknor as a commentator on Spanish literature—but neither adopted the new rigorous methods of German scholarship. Ticknor and Bancroft wrote for the wide cultivated public, not for other specialists.

Despite the American students' discovery of the importance of a large research library, little of the German university pattern made its way through
them into American higher education. The career of Edward Everett shows
how easily the German experience was sloughed off in America. Back at
Harvard, Everett taught a lecture course on the history of Greek literature
(Emerson, a senior at the time, said that the undergraduates found a "new
dawn" opening to them, though this seems to have been a minority opinion).
Everett also published a couple of articles and translated a German Greek
grammar. By 1824, however, he was restless and tried, unsuccessfully, to get
a diplomatic appointment in Greece. In the same year an emotional Phi Beta
Kappa address on national literature brought him such public acclaim that
he was nominated to Congress and elected by a landslide. Giving up his
professorship, Everett went on to a successful career as governor of Massachusetts, president of Harvard, secretary of state from 1852–53, and one of
the foremost orators of the day. He maintained his interest in literature, but
far from becoming an American example of the new type of German research
scholar, he adhered instead to the old pattern of the man of letters in public
life.[10]

The Problem of Higher Education

While a few people were arguing that at least some American colleges should
become universities devoted to advanced scholarship and research on the
German pattern, many more were demanding that the colleges should become more popular institutions, teaching agriculture and business and thus
offering a truly useful education to everyone, not just a classical education
appropriate only to future lawyers or ministers. A few colleges instituted
nondegree courses allowing students to avoid Latin and Greek and concentrate on modern languages or the sciences. At Harvard, Ticknor attempted
to introduce reforms designed to raise the standard of instruction but found
that President Kirkland and other faculty dragged their feet. Teaching was
still based on the recitation method and tied to the text, which meant that
much of it was essentially drill. The most vital intellectual activity probably
went on outside the formal curriculum in voluntary student literary societies,
which maintained their own libraries and sometimes published magazines,
and whose members read modern literature and history, wrote, and debated.

There was a fairly widespread feeling among people in higher education
that reform of some kind was necessary. The number of colleges had grown
dramatically: there were twenty-six in 1800; by 1828 there were fifty, most
of them under denominational influence. Most, however, were underen-
dowed and undersupported, with small student bodies and small overworked

and underpaid faculties. Although there were more institutions, the proportion of the American population attending college was in fact declining. In 1830 no graduating class was as large as a hundred. An increasing number of people considered a college education irrelevant to the opportunities of American life. In addition, state legislatures were questioning the worth of what went on in colleges and cutting back on funding.

In 1828 the faculty of Yale, in response to legislative hints at drastic reform, issued a report on the functions of higher education, which, reprinted in Silliman's *American Journal of Science*, was widely discussed and extremely influential in guiding the development of American college education until after the Civil War. It defended the basic structure of the existing system, with its lack of specialization, its classical core curriculum, and its reliance on the single basic text in each course so as not to let the students loose in the library where their minds might be confused by divergent views. The report reaffirmed the commitment to the paternal college ideal in which the moral and social education of the young was even more important than their intellectual improvement. The American college was to be neither a professional school nor an institution dedicated to research and the development of new knowledge. Rather, it was to offer a liberal education at a fairly basic level, providing the future leaders of the nation with a common culture.[11]

Romanticism and Cultural Nationalism

Although the example of the German university was rejected, German literature and German romantic critical ideas had considerable influence. The first widely read introduction to German ideas in America was Madame de Staël's *Influence of Literature on Society*, published in translation in Boston in 1813. This brought to America an aspect of romanticism that seemed to speak directly to its postcolonial situation: the emphasis on national identity. Madame de Staël spoke of literature as reflecting the unique national spirit of a people. Breaking away from the universalism of the Enlightenment, romantics like de Staël began to interpret literature as an expression of national experience and personality. There was a spirit of the people, just as there was a spirit of the age, and the great writer was a vehicle for both. One reaction to these ideas in America was an increased interest in foreign but non-British literature. There was a spate of articles on the literature and culture of Germany, France, southern Europe, and even India and the East. Most of all, there was an increased self-consciousness about the extent to which American literature could be said to represent the national character.[12]

Numerous calls went out from orators and periodicals, gathering strength in the 1820s, for a national literature. These calls went beyond insisting that Americans should take their due place in the universal republic of letters; the

United States needed a literature that was distinctly and recognizably American. The *North American Review* was particularly active in encouraging writers to take up specifically American themes. The romantic linking of literature and national spirit endowed the man of letters with a sacred task: not merely to vindicate his country in the eyes of the world but in a sense to create it. Until it was reflected back in works of imagination, the nation could hardly be said to have a character or a consciousness.[13]

A practical example of how nationality could find life in literature came from the enormously popular historical novels of Sir Walter Scott. The hero of *Waverly*, as the *American Monthly Magazine* pointed out in 1817, was not the conventional young man who gives the book its title "but Scotland." The immense market for Scott's works stimulated American publishers to new entrepreneurial heights. In Philadelphia, Mathew Carey was able to rush a new Scott novel from the ship to typesetters working around the clock and have it in the bookstores within forty-eight hours. It is surprising how quickly the English best-sellers got to western towns. Scott's *Rob Roy*, brought out in Edinburgh in early 1818, was in Lexington, Kentucky, by the end of March of the same year. American writers complained bitterly that the flood of British reprints blasted their own prospects and retarded the production of indigenous works, and one Boston publisher estimated in 1820 that three-quarters of the books read in America were by English authors. In fact, literature feeds on literature. Scott created a public that would storm the bookstores or ride many miles to get his latest work. He enlarged the reading public and stimulated native writers to undertake new forms and subject matter.[14]

According to Cooper, Scott raised the novel "to the dignity of the epic." He certainly made it morally and intellectually respectable and thus a suitable form in which to deal with American themes. One problem, however, was the widespread assumption that the highest imaginative literature depended on a subject matter more elemental and mysterious than modern life in a republic could afford. Could a "new" country like the United States, wearing "a spick-and-span new aspect, . . . in the broad garish sunshine of everyday life," furnish sufficiently exciting and interesting material for the poet, the dramatist, or the novelist?[15]

The answer came in 1821 with the instant success of Cooper's *The Spy*, set during the Revolution. The *North American Review*, in the first review it had ever given to an American novel, trumpeted the viability of American material for works of fiction. Scores of American historical novels followed. Meanwhile, Catharine Sedgwick was exploring the extent to which a contemporary novel of manners could be constructed out of American materials in *A New England Tale* (1822) and *Redwood* (1825), and in Virginia the lawyer George Tucker produced the first fictional depiction of plantation life, *The Valley of Shenandoah*.[16]

In spite of the success of novels on American themes, disillusion began to set in rather quickly, even among critics who had called most loudly for the use of American materials. Some found that the Indian rapidly wore thin as a fictional subject; others suggested that "the rise of republican liberty is too much the creation of common sense to be very applicable to the purposes of fiction." When Cooper left the United States in 1826 for an extended stay in Europe, he indicated that the vein that he had mined so successfully was played out. The surface of American life was too uniform and prosaic, he felt, too "bald" to spark the imagination, too likely "to repress passion." "I have never seen a nation so much alike in my life, as the people of the United States," he wrote in 1828, "and what is more, they are not only like each other, but they are remarkably like that which common sense tells them they ought to resemble."[17]

"There are no annals for the historian," Cooper lamented; "no follies . . . for the satirist; no manners for the dramatist." The thinness of the American scene as material for poetry, novels, or romance was the subject of ritualized complaints for the rest of the century. The most familiar is Henry James's famous formulation: "No sovereign, no court, . . . no palaces, no castles . . . no cathedrals, nor abbeys, . . . no Oxford, nor Eton, . . . no Epsom nor Ascot!" Sometimes these complaints were really criticisms of European conventions, with the implication that plain, commonsense American materials were just as good, if not better, for real art. Sometimes they turned the tables with a ringing defense of the supposed deficiencies of American life. "Here are . . . no old castles . . . whose melancholy history informs the curious traveller that their foundation was bedded in tyranny," declared one patriot staunchly. "America has none of these costly ornaments . . . of oppression. I thank God she has not."[18]

The question of what constituted Americanism in a work of literature continued to be vexing. Did it mean writing exclusively about American society and American places? Did it require the assertion of the right political principles? the infusion of some spirit of nationality? the repudiation of foreign models and influences? Something more seemed to be needed than merely substituting the bobolink for the nightingale, but by 1830 it was still not at all clear what.

The Romantic Sensibility

Some aspects of romantic sensibility and aesthetics were assimilated cautiously, but by 1820 there had been a definite shift away from the canons of neoclassical taste among both writers and the reading public. Americans were not yet interested in Keats or Shelley, and Wordsworth was not widely accepted until the late 1820s, but the rage for Scott signaled an end to the reign of the heroic couplet as the mode for American poetry and a demotion of Pope as the preferred pattern for poets.

Thousands of young people learned Scott's long poems, "The Lady of the Lake" and "Marmion," by heart. The poetry of Lord Byron was even more captivating, for it was backed up by the notorious immorality of his life. Byron made the poet's own persona and sensibility the subject of poetry and released in his readers a voluptuous surrender to their own subjectivity. Readers as various as John Randolph of Virginia and James Marsh of Vermont found their own feelings validated in his. The young Marsh, while still a divinity student, was disturbed by his own passionate response to Byron. The deeply religious young man could not approve Byron's morals, yet "he seems to me," he acknowledged, "to *live* more than other men." Reading Byron, he confessed, "gives me new vigor and I seem in reality to live a being more intense." Byron's example stimulated a number of respectable, though now largely forgotten, imitators, and practically every village, according to the publisher Samuel Goodrich, suddenly sprouted its moody and romantically misanthropic Byronic youth, who might also write some poetry.[19]

Cautiously American critics modified their literary standards and moved away from slavish neoclassicism. Edward Tyrrell Channing, the younger brother of William Ellery, pleaded in the *North American Review* in 1816 against the timid crampedness produced by always feeling bound to classical and Augustan models of correct taste. He fused this stylistic rebellion with cultural nationalism: every nation "must be the former and finisher of its own genius." In 1819 Channing became the second Boylston Professor of Rhetoric at Harvard, where he taught many future New England writers, including Emerson and Thoreau.[20]

The language of the eighteenth century began to appear labored and unnatural, its stately periods a prison preventing the expression of feeling and spontaneity. Bryant denounced the pernicious effect of the English Augustans on men like Barlow, Dwight, and Trumbull, providing models of "balanced and wearisome regularity" and an "artificial elevation of style." John Neal, an extraordinarily prolific essayist, poet, and novelist, proclaimed in the late 1820s: "I hope to God . . . I never shall write what is now worshipped under the name of *classical* English." American authors needed to capture the language of people as they "*do* talk, in our language, every day, in the street."[21]

Richard Henry Dana, Sr., gave up a law career to become a full-time man of letters. In a brief period as assistant editor of the *North American Review* in 1818–19 he championed the poetry of Wordsworth, whom he proclaimed as the most important poet of the age, and passionately asserted the romantic doctrine of the creative imagination, rather than analytical reasoning or laborious fact gathering, as the way to the highest truth. Backing away from the severely judgmental role of the neoclassical critic, he insisted that the critic must be sympathetic to an artist's intentions and be open to new ideas and new forms: "Original minds will be peculiar and individual; and it is not for us to haggle at every thing new." What he valued in poetry was passion and intensity of feeling, which could no longer be contained by frozen forms. Nor could the subjective truths of the poet's imagination be made plain to all and sundry: "it is but a small class of society that can see or feel them." It should not be surprising "if the larger portion give the name of mysticism to what they were not born to understand."[22]

The eighteenth century had distinguished between the educated classes and the vulgar, but within the ranks of the educated, it had assumed a literature equally accessible to all, with the onus on the writer to be intelligible. To the romantic sensibility, however, profundity and obscurity were bound together, and only certain choice spirits would be able to penetrate to the deeper truths. In 1826 William Ellery Channing published in the new *Christian Examiner* a long essay on Milton that attracted considerable notice in the United States and was published to critical acclaim in London. Two particular marks of the new romantic sensibility stood out in this essay. One was the perception of modern life as "dreary" and modern civilization as "tame and uninteresting"; thus, one of the major functions of great art was "to meet the "thirst . . . for . . . something . . . more powerful, lofty, and thrilling, than ordinary and real life affords." The other was the scornful abandonment of clarity. In defense of Milton's prose style, he maintained that "to be universally intelligible is not the highest merit. A great mind cannot, without injurious constraint, shrink itself to the grasp of common passive readers." What the great mind required was the "gifted reader."[23]

Despite the attractions of the individualism and personal expansivism of romanticism, most Americans continued to resist its anarchic and solipsistic tendencies. Critics condemned writers who did not consider "the common susceptibilities" of the majority of readers, writers who, as the *North American Review* noted severely in 1823, stood "apart from and above the world" and wrote the "poetry of soliloquy." Dana's attacks on classical standards and his tendency to mysticism were too much for the group who ran the *North American Review*, and he was edged out. Even Dana could never yield entirely to the imagination without misgivings. In some short stories in the early 1820s, he explored the darker workings of the unconscious mind but drew back from the more radical implications of subjectivism. Converted during a revival of 1826, he found in Christianity an assurance of universal truths and meaning existing independently of the human mind and anchoring the artist to the community and to the world.[24]

Americans were not prepared to divorce art from morality. There were no advocates in America, wrote George Bancroft in 1827, for the theory that holds beauty as "something independent of moral effect." He submitted his translations from Johann Wolfgang von Goethe to two clergymen before attempting to publish them; even so, the poems were rejected. Bancroft himself condemned Goethe not only for the "immorality" of some of his work but for his refusal to take the progressive side in the great political struggles of his time. Friedrich Schiller's popular play *The Robbers* was roundly denounced for making a criminal the hero and showing in one character "the most contradictory moral qualities as existing together." Milton was a hero to Channing not only because he was a transcendent talent but because he had devoted that talent to the service of God and liberty. Lecturing to the New York Athenaeum in 1826, Bryant insisted that poetry has an important bearing on the "virtue and welfare of society. . . . It cherishes patriotism, the incitement to vigorous toils endured for the welfare of communities."[25]

New Views of Culture

American men of letters were often doubtful about democracy and critical of the materialism of their country, but they were not disaffected from the fundamental institutions of America or from its promise. By the mid-1820s, a new readiness to embrace the turbulent world of American democracy appeared among younger men of letters. When Irving revised his early *Salmagundi* essays for a new edition in 1824, he cut out much of his bitter satire against Jefferson and considerably toned down his criticisms of "mobocracy." As they absorbed German ideas about culture as an expression of national spirit, men of letters began to reevaluate the criteria by which a civilization should be judged.[26]

Perhaps critics had been looking in the wrong place for the flowering of American culture. If the essence of the United States was its free political life, then perhaps one should look for its most authentic cultural expression not in books but in the fundamental political currency of the spoken word. The best literary work in America, wrote J. G. Palfrey in the *North American Review* in 1820, was to be found not in belles lettres but in "the speeches of our barristers and statesmen, the lectures of our academical men, and the sermons of our divines." He made this remark in a review of Joseph Buckminster's sermons, which had been published six years earlier. Palfrey reviewed them now precisely because he wanted them to be considered a species of literature. Similar judgments were made frequently by Americans returning from England with the impression that English parliamentary and forensic eloquence was far inferior to the American.[27]

American culture gave extraordinary emphasis to public speech. Rhetoric was important in the college curriculum because it was assumed that professional gentlemen would find it necessary to speak in public. John Quincy Adams, Harvard's first Boylston Professor of Rhetoric, told his students to mold themselves on the orators of ancient Greece and Rome, for in republics "eloquence was POWER." Both Congress and the courts provided opportunities for long, eloquent harangues, as did the frequent elections. And the sermon, of course, was central to Protestant religion. In addition, Americans created numerous communal occasions on which the oration or discourse was the centerpiece: the Fourth of July and other commemorative days, commencement exercises in colleges and academies, meetings of literary and scientific associations and Phi Beta Kappa chapters. A good speech at one of these occasions could launch a young man on a public career. "There are few men of consequence among us," said John Adams in 1816, "who did not commence their career by an oration on the fifth of March" (the official commemoration day of the Boston massacre). The history of the American Revolution, he suggested, could be written as commentaries upon its great speeches.[28]

While much public speaking was aimed at persuading people, more often it involved preaching to the converted. The crowd at a Fourth of July rally did not need to be persuaded that the Revolution had been a glorious event; the commencement audience was already convinced that learning must be encouraged in the republic. Orations on these occasions were essentially rituals of community in which the content of the message was less important than its presentation by the spoken word in a face-to-face context, generating an emotional bond between speaker and audience. Everett thought such occasions essential to counteract the isolating tendency of print, which enabled individuals to develop their thoughts independent of "the action and reaction of society."[29]

Nevertheless, America was becoming a print society, and most major orations were quickly published as pamphlets. Newspapers often printed complete speeches, and periodicals reviewed important ones at length, thus considerably expanding the audience. As a mode into which many talented Americans poured, or compressed, their thoughts, the oration had certain disadvantages. It was comparatively short and it was exhortatory rather than analytic. Not everyone was congratulatory about so much widespread "eloquence." There were complaints that a declamatory style spilled over into everything, so that all American speech and writing was infected with the virus of inflated rhetoric. America, Irving had grumbled in *Salmagundi*, was not so much a republic as a "logocracy."[30]

A broadening of the definition of culture was evident too in a greater appreciation among men of letters of the widespread material evidence of popular intelligence. "A prevalent error," insisted a writer in the New York *Atlantic Magazine*, "is that which estimates the intelligence of a people, by their published literature alone—which considers no information valuable which is not written, no truth available which is not printed, no learning applicable which is not presented in all the tangible and intelligible attributes of a book. It is time to understand better the true claims of a nation to the respect and admiration of mankind."[31]

The best example of this new tack was a celebrated 1823 address before the American Philosophical Society by Charles Ingersoll, "The Influence of America on the Mind." Ingersoll boldly asserted that the essence of the American achievement was to be found at the base of the cultural pyramid. In the United States the mass of the people were better educated than Europeans, and Americans could boast that "every husbandman understands the philosophy of politics better than many princes in Europe." In addition, the four thousand patents for useful inventions issued over the last thirty years demonstrated the inventive creativity of the people: "If a ship, a plough and a house be taken as symbols of the primary social arts of navigation, agriculture and habitation, we need not fear comparisons with other people in any one of them. . . . The houses, ships, carriages, tools, utensils, manufactures, implements of husbandry, conveniences, comforts, the whole circle of social refinement, are always equal, mostly superior here to those of the most improved nations." The United States had been as busy building internal improvements like roads and canals as any European country: "Five thousand post offices distribute intelligence throughout the United States with amazing celerity and precision over eighty thousand miles of post roads. . . . There are twelve thousand miles of turnpike roads. . . . The New York canal and the Philadelphia water-works are not surpassed, if equalled, by any similar improvements in Europe within the period of their construction." This was not just a celebration of material progress. All these things were offsprings of the fertility and exuberance of what Ingersoll called the "American mind."[32]

The Technological Sublime

It was a mind that expressed itself most characteristically in the conquest of matter for utility and power. There was a striking tendency for cultural commentators after 1815 to discuss fine arts, literature, and mechanical invention in the same breath as products of the same creative impulse. Addressing the New York Academy of Fine Arts in 1816, De Witt Clinton made only a few remarks on art and devoted the bulk of his speech to the invention of the steamboat. Americans, declared Jacob Bigelow in 1816, are entitled "to the character of a nation of inventors." Bigelow, a physician and botanist, was appointed in 1816 to a newly endowed Harvard chair for the application of the sciences to the useful arts. In 1829 his Harvard lectures were printed with a newly minted word in the title: "Elements of *Technology*." They were virtually hymns to technological progress. The time was approaching,

Bigelow was convinced, when this kind of knowledge would be "essentially requisite to a good education."[33]

Eli Whitney's cotton gin and the water-powered machinery in the Lowell mills were already profoundly transforming American life. The iron plough developed between 1800 and 1820, with its cheap, interchangeable blades, modernized the age-old symbol of agriculture. But the most spectacular form of technological progress was steam. One great American invention was the steamboat, developed by Robert Fulton under the patronage of Chancellor Livingston of New York. The first successful run was in 1807, and in 1811 (the same year as a spectacular comet and an earthquake in New Madrid) the first steamboat went down the Mississippi. The boats soon became a familiar sight on western waterways. As they became increasingly elaborate and ornate, the sight of the floating palace steaming down the Mississippi through untouched nature became emblematic of the close conjunction of civilization and wilderness in America. The foundation stone of the first American railroad, the Baltimore and Ohio, was laid on 4 July 1828 by the ninety-one-year-old Charles Carroll, the only surviving signer of the Declaration of Independence. That signing, he declared, was the proudest act of his life, but a close runner-up was "the laying of the first stone of the work which is to perpetuate the union of the American States."[34]

In the early nineteenth century machinery came to seem particularly expressive of American values. It was both useful and democratic, offering to all the possibility of saving labor and creating comfort hitherto available only to the few. Nineteenth-century Americans very quickly associated machinery with the sublime and learned to give it the same kind of emotional response as Niagara Falls. After visiting the cotton factories of Manchester, John Griscom exclaimed, "Can it be possible that any man can contemplate such a train of machinery . . . and regard all this as the offspring of thought and reflection, and yet remain a materialist!"[35]

Thoughts of the sublime were immediately roused by a major project of this period, the Erie Canal, begun in 1817 and completed in 1825 under the auspices of Governor De Witt Clinton. This canal, thirteen times longer than any previously attempted, connected New York City with the Great Lakes and the Ohio valley. It was recognized not just as enhancing trade but as vindicating republican institutions by demonstrating what republican minds were capable of. "All hail! to a project so vast and sublime!" exulted a song written for the splendid opening ceremonies by the popular poet Samuel Woodworth. It was not just the new economic opportunities that made the moment sweet; rather "'Tis, that Genius has triump'd—and Science prevail'd. . . . It is, that the vassals of Europe may see / The progress of mind, in a land that is free."[36]

Embracing their country in all its democratic turbulence and material

abundance, Ingersoll and other educated Americans like him did not abandon their hopes for a high culture in traditional European terms, but they
became considerably more relaxed about the time frame in which this could
be expected to take place. They argued more frequently than before that the
United States was a young country whose infancy had been spent in subduing the wilderness. As it matured, it would inevitably acquire new cultural
trappings. It was really no reproach if art, literature, and science were still a
little thin; the mere passage of time would remedy the defect. "That those
arts, which suppose wealth and leisure and a crowded population, are not
yet so flourishing amongst us as they will be in the course of a century or
two," declared the South Carolinian Hugh Legaré confidently in 1823, "is so
much a matter of course, that instead of exciting wonder and disgust, one is
only surprised how it should even have attracted notice."[37]

In 1824 Everett delivered a fervently nationalistic Phi Beta Kappa address,
"The Peculiar Motives to Intellectual Exertion in America." Like Ingersoll
he was abundantly optimistic. He was determined to concentrate on those
conditions of American life favorable to the life of the mind. He transmuted
those aspects of the American scene that many commentators had seen as
militating against high culture—westward expansion, material prosperity,
political excitement—into sources of national greatness that the "American
scholar" should celebrate: "Instead of being shut up, as it were, in the prison
of a stationary, or a slowly progressive community, the emulation of our
countrymen is drawn out and tempted on by an horizon constantly receding
before them." Everett was still trying to assert leadership for men of letters
in the republic—no longer, however, as upholders of "civilized standards"
but rather as the nation's inspired spokesmen, articulating for it its own
thoughts: "The character, energy, and resources of the country are reflected
and imaged forth in the conceptions of its great minds. They are the organs
of the time; they speak not their own language, they scarce think their own
thoughts; but under an impulse like the prophetic enthusiasm of old they
must feel and utter the sentiments which society inspires. They do not create, they obey the Spirit of the Age."[38]

The End of a Common Culture

In claiming this role for "great minds," Everett assumed that there was a
common mind that scholar and artist could interpret and elevate. But in fact
American culture, like all other modern cultures, showed signs of fragmentation. Fissures were developing between experts and amateurs, between the
proponents of the new and difficult and the generality of the cultured classes,
and commercial popular culture was going its own exuberant way, unintim-

idated by elites. This separating process was especially clear in the development of the physical sciences, which were becoming increasingly opaque to the lay public.

American science was increasingly separating itself from learning in general. The sheer accumulation of new data, the problems of generalization raised by that accumulation, and the proliferation of technical terminology made it difficult for cultivated amateurs to keep abreast of developments. As early as 1806, Jefferson complained of chemistry that "the common herd of philosophers seem to write only for one another." Thirteen years later a Boston physician, John Ware, deplored the fact that chemistry had become "so unsettled and obscure." Antoine Lavoisier's system of classification had been "simple and beautiful", but it broke down under the pressure of new discoveries, with the result that chemistry became more complicated and far "less captivating to the general scholar." "A tolerable knowledge of chemistry cannot now," he wrote in a review of a new text by the professor of chemistry at Harvard, "be obtained by attending a few lectures, performing a few experiments, and studying some short and familiar exposition of its principles." Ware recognized, however, that it was necessary to have specialists, as in Europe, if the United States was ever to contribute its "full share to the science of the world."[39]

Although botany remained open to amateurs, progress in natural history inevitably meant greater technicality. All the new plants, insects, and animals that were being discovered entailed a huge expansion of names, and amateurs seemed to be squeezed out by this development. "The general reader," as one complained, could no longer be "as well versed in these matters as those who claim exclusive right to a technical acquaintance with the subject." By the late 1820s professionals too were worried about the unceasing proliferation of new names and new species. Some were realizing the problems of the Linnaean system of classification and moving toward the "natural" system of Antoine Laurent de Jussieu, which had already been widely adopted in Europe. This system, based on structural relationships rather than easily observable characteristics, was much more difficult for amateurs to grasp. Similarly, in mineralogy, classification by surface characteristics was being replaced by a system requiring chemical analysis. Jefferson had thought that classificatory systems should be based on "such exterior and visible characters as every traveller is competent to observe, to ascertain and to relate." Instead, science was becoming esoteric and professionalized.[40]

The community of practitioners and interested laypeople who joined learned societies was still important, but strains were beginning to show. Practitioners found it increasingly irritating to have to make themselves understood to people outside the guild of specialists. In 1819 the chemist Robert Hare wrote to Benjamin Silliman about a scientific paper he had given: "I was told in New York that many said they could not understand my memoir, who considered their standing such as to feel as if this were an imputation against me rather than themselves." To have made his work intelligible to the nonspecialists would have made it too "commonplace for adepts." "We cannot," he concluded, "write anything for the scientific few which will be agreeable to the ignorant many." As scientific practitioners became more separated from other learned men, they became more nervous about pretenders. The controversial naturalist Constantine Rafinesque was ostracized by leaders of the profession and was unable to publish in the *American Journal of Science* after 1819, less because of his radical views about evolution than for his propensity to discover too many "new" species, which the more cautious thought brought American science into disrepute.[41]

In an unsuccessful attempt to bridge the gap between specialist and layman—and also between classes—the Franklin Institute was founded in 1824. The goal was to give mechanics a theoretical understanding of their craft through a program of lectures on chemistry and natural philosophy. The program failed because workingmen had too little scientific knowledge on which to build. The Institute flourished only after it was taken over in 1829 by Alexander Dallas Bache, who steered it toward original research geared to industry.[42]

Impatience with amateurs led to the founding of specialized scientific societies like the Lyceum of Natural History, founded in New York in 1817. With the exception of Samuel L. Mitchill, the charter members were young, many of them recent graduates of Columbia University or the College of Physicians and Surgeons. The rules of the society required that each member give a formal scientific paper within twelve months of his election. Serious laymen were not excluded, but their role was distinctly secondary. In 1817 the organization voted against making De Witt Clinton a member in spite of his substantial scientific interests. Young members did not take him seriously as a scientist, and they were not sufficiently awed by his status as civic leader to accord him a place in a professional society. By the 1820s the lyceum had begun to dominate the scientific life of the city, and in recognition of the new separation of disciplines, the Historical society, which had originally combined natural and civil history, turned over its cabinet of specimens. In Philadelphia, the process of specialization led to the founding of the Academy of Natural Sciences in 1812. By the mid-1820s rifts in this society were apparent. Some members conceived of natural history as primarily a matter of systematic naming and classification, and others were more interested in a popular descriptive approach to animal habits designed to render the study of natural history "pleasing and intelligible."[43]

A similar set of tensions disturbed the arts. The art academies founded in New York and Philadelphia were intended less to train artists than to educate the taste of patrician laypersons and cultivate an interest in art in the community. The New York academy in particular spent more of its money on buying "old masters," some of them of dubious authenticity, than on patronizing living American artists. In addition, artists complained that the gentlemen shareholders in the academy tended to treat them as inferiors. In reaction, Samuel B. Morse and others in 1826 formed the National Academy of Design, which was to be both an art school and a gallery where artists could exhibit their work. "The encouragement of national genius is more directly promoted by giving *practice* to our own artists," said Morse pointedly, "than by any efforts to place before them the best *models*." Most important, this association was to be controlled by practicing artists. "Every profession in a society," said Morse, "knows what measures are necessary for its own improvement." A letter of support in the *New York Evening Post* pointed out that "courts of justice are not placed under the control of physicians; medical degrees are not conferred by lawyers. . . . Why, then, should the concerns of the Artists be thought in better hands than in their own."[44]

Popular Culture

As the world of professional practitioners separated from the general world of elite culture, the world of popular culture also went off in its own direction. In cities and towns a lively commercial culture, driven by mass tastes for excitement and novelty, had little respect for elite tastes or leadership and remained stubbornly resistant to the direction of the "wise and good." Sensational magazines and papers offered tales of the bizarre; cheap pamphlets detailing gory crimes were a popular subliterary genre. By 1831 a temperance magazine was complaining that crime stories "now form the 'Domestic News' of every journal. Once it was not so." Heroes of popular culture arose who were the direct opposite of the character ideals preached by churchmen, educators, and other promoters of "virtue." A new genre of frontier humor was emerging by the 1820s, featuring characters like Mike Fink, the legendary keel-boatman, who lied, cheated, stole, and destroyed his way through fantastic and violent adventures. Masters of the tall tale, these frontier characters spun the language into ever wider spirals of exaggeration. "I'm a regular tornado, tough as hickory and long-winded as a nor'wester," "half a horse and half an alligator."[45]

Veering between violence and sentimentality, popular culture also harbored a strong streak of parody, a delight in pricking the pretensions of elites and deflating the genteel. Sam Patch the "jumper" began his career as a popular hero by an impromptu leap into New Jersey's Passaic Falls in order to upstage the pompous opening ceremonies of a new pleasure ground for the refined and respectable. In similar mockery of their betters, a poor district of Philadelphia in 1825 elected as colonel of their militia regiment a deformed ostler, John Pluck, to lead his contingent in a militia day parade. The escapade deflated the pageantry of parade, drill, dinners, and high-flown oratory, taken so seriously by the city's upper-class militia regiments. When two New York newspapers brought Pluck to New York and took him on a grand tour, he became, briefly, a popular culture hero.[46]

Most of the time popular culture could exist alongside the respectable culture of the genteel without causing too much alarm. In the world of the theater, however, the power of popular tastes to shape and dominate was obvious. In many ways the theater still mirrored the old-fashioned social order: the fashionable were in the boxes, the middling sort in the pit, and the lower orders in the gallery. Yet all participated in the same amusement, with tolerance of the raucous behavior of the gallery and the area traditionally set aside for prostitutes. It was, however, this socially as well as sexually promiscuous quality that now led many people to shun the theater. Most churches denounced it as a sink of iniquity, and when the Richmond, Virginia, theater burned in 1812, killing seventy-three people, the tragedy was a ready-made subject for a sermon. Still, in that same year a minister complained that more and more people had come to consider the theater a "lawful amusement for Christians." Between 1820 and 1830 four new theaters were built in New York and two in Philadelphia, all major cities had their own theatrical companies, and both American and English companies regularly went on tour.[47]

Theater was the most democratic of all art forms. Unlike literature, where a press run could to some extent be varied according to the probable size of the readership, the economics of theater determined that halls had to be filled for a manager or company to stay in business. Thus theater managers were extremely sensitive to popular tastes and unwilling to take too many risks. The preferences of the majority of the theater-going public determined what would be shown. The popularity of Shakespeare has been taken as evidence that culture had not yet divided into highbrow and lowbrow, but the plays were usually cut heavily to make room for a short farce at the beginning or end or comic turns between the acts. The greatest box-office draw was the melodrama, a democratic form featuring ordinary people, whose plots revolved around various villainous attempts on the virtue of the heroine. At the happy ending she was rescued by the hero, who carried her off to a life of blissful domesticity; thus in melodrama, virtue was equated with virginity and marriage. Even more than sentimental plots, audiences craved variety and spectacle. Managers competed to put on the most impressive scenery and the most elaborate special effects, such as a fully rigged warship filling the whole back of the stage or "Grand eruption of Mt. Vesuvius. Terrific Explosion!!"[48]

Literary men bitterly criticized the debasing effect that the commercial power of popular taste had on drama. Despair at democratic taste bedeviled the theatrical career of the multitalented William Dunlap. Another entrepreneur of culture like Charles Willson Peale, Dunlap, besides his work in the theater, was also a professional painter and a historian whose *History of the American Theatre* (1832) and *History of the Arts of Design* (1834) remain valuable. In 1796 he became manager and part owner of the American Company of New York. Full of idealism about the latent cultural interests of a democratic audience waiting to be awakened, he was soon stuck with commercial realities. Since the new Park Theater with seating capacity of 2,000 had to be at least half-filled to break even, Dunlap found that he had to compromise artistically to keep going financially. He hired juggling and acrobatic acts, including the Antipodean Whirligig, a man who could dance on his head, with firecrackers attached to his heels, to perform during the intervals of plays. He staged a number of patriotic dramas, complete with battles and splendid tableaus, and then discovered the great money-maker, the German dramatist Kotzebue, the pioneer of the melodrama, and translated and produced a number of his plays. Beset by squabbles among rival actors, Dunlap could not stave off financial disaster for long. In 1805 he went bankrupt and turned back to portrait painting and writing for a living.

Reflecting on his experience in 1834, Dunlap complained of many problems that have remained central to the theater ever since. He deplored the star system and the construction of theaters that were too large, which meant that the uppermost problem was that of filling them. Managers said, "'We must please the public.' But their public becomes that public which is filled with glitter, parade, false sentiment, and all that lulls conscience or excites to evil." The New York writer and critic James Kirke Paulding, in an analysis of the state of American drama, concurred. Theater managers pandered to the most debased popular taste rather than trying to educate the public. As a result, he wrote, "the more refined class of society" had stopped going to the theater, abandoning it to "those who relish 'Tom and Jerry' better than Shakespeare or Sheridan." Dunlap concluded that the only way to escape the degrading dominance of mass taste would be the establishment of a state-supported theater. Only a subsidized theater could ignore box office and make the drama "truly a school of morality, of patriotism, and every virtue; the glory of the fine arts, and the delight of the wise and the good."[49]

German and Scottish romanticism taught intellectuals to appreciate the folk tale or song as a genuine expression of national culture. In the modern world, however, the bards of the people were the writers of melodramas or the journalists who wrote for the sensational newspapers beginning to emerge in the 1820s. Mass taste for this commercial culture presented a problem with which American culture leaders and intellectuals have continued to struggle as they have sought to find for themselves and for the values and activities they espouse a place within democratic society.

seven

The Spirit of Improvement

Other nations boast of what they are or have been, but the true citizen of the United States exalts his head to the skies in the contemplation of the future grandeur of his country. . . . Others appeal to history; an American to prophecy. . . . This appeal to the future is his never-failing resource.

—*New Monthly Magazine and Literary Journal* (London), 1821

The spirit of improvement is abroad upon the earth.

—John Quincy Adams, inaugural address, 1825

The War of 1812 is sometimes called the Second War for American Independence. By the same token, it was not until the 1820s that the eighteenth-century world of the founding fathers expired completely, to be replaced by the nineteenth-century world of democracy, individualism, and capitalist development. With the world at peace, Americans were less distracted by foreign issues and could devote themselves wholeheartedly to economic development and settlement of the continent. The pace of economic change quickened as states turned to the development of transportation networks and proliferated their grants of corporate power. Power was passing to a new generation of political leaders. Men like Henry Clay, John C. Calhoun, Daniel Webster, and John Quincy Adams had been boys during the Revolution or not yet born; the hopes and memories they brought to political life were quite different from those of the previous generation. President James Monroe, the last of the Virginia dynasty, with his powdered hair and knee breeches, was an anachronistic figure in a world in which Martin Van Buren had begun to work the levers of party politics. Increasingly old republican fears about the corrupting power of avarice and the perils of prosperity subsided, to be replaced by worries about the social problems attendant on modern economies: pauperism and the existence of an underclass, crime and punishment.

Portents of Future Problems

The 1820s opened with two dark portents: the great panic of 1819 and the Missouri crisis. The panic was due to a slump in exports and fall in commodity prices as Europe, now at peace, rebuilt its own agriculture. The overextension of credit after the war, which the new Bank of the United States had done nothing to modify, now imploded. State banks failed and dragged down with them merchants, businessmen, and farmers who were deeply in debt. The panic hit particularly hard in some areas of the South, and its effects lingered well into the decade. Here was dramatic warning of the boom-and-bust cycle to which modern economies were subject and an unnerving demonstration of the extent to which the country was part of an international economy whose problems it could not escape.

The debates over admitting Missouri to the Union brought the terrible problem of slavery back into national politics. The opening of new territory in the West affected the interests of all Americans, and some northerners were convinced that states that allowed slavery were effectively barred to the emigration of free white farmers. From December 1819 to 20 March 1820, Congress was deadlocked on debates over the extension of slavery, as men voted purely on sectional lines. To younger politicians like Henry Clay, however, the Union was the overriding concern. He put together a deal, a pragmatic solution, involving a "fair" division of space: Missouri was admitted with no restriction on slavery, but its admittance was balanced by that of Maine, a free state. After that slavery would be barred in the Louisiana Purchase north of latitude 36′30° but allowed to expand south of it. The survivors of the Revolutionary generation on both sides were uneasy with the compromise, but the generation that was taking charge of American politics wanted to move on to the more important business of developing the resources of the continent. The compromise avoided any decision on the future or morality of slavery itself. It left as a legacy a new feature defining the geography of the continent: a clear line of latitude dividing slavery and freedom.[1]

The debates over Missouri revealed fundamentally divergent attitudes toward the nature of the federal union and, indeed, about the meaning of freedom and equality. In the Senate, the old Federalist Rufus King horrified many people by shifting from constitutional arguments against the extension of slavery to invoking natural law arguments against the institution itself. In the House, some northern congressmen invoked the Declaration of Independence as a national covenant, enshrining the liberty and equality of all as the essence of the republic. Southerners were quick to reply that the Declaration was an "abstraction," not meant to be taken literally as applying to everyone. "All communities stand upon an equality," explained Richard Johnson of Kentucky. The words of the Declaration were not meant to imply an equality "in relation to every human being." Senator James Barbour of Virginia anticipated the argument of Chief Justice Roger Taney in the *Dred Scott* case. What did the Declaration have to do with slavery? he demanded. "Who were the parties—the slaves? No. . . . Did it enter into any human mind that it had the least reference to this species of population?" Though the immediate crisis passed, thoughtful observers realized that an abyss had momentarily opened. Reflecting on the Missouri crisis in his diary, John Quincy Adams commented: "The seeds of the Declaration of Independence are yet maturing. The harvest will be what West, the painter, calls the terrible and sublime."[2]

It was clear from the debates that southern representatives envisaged the United States as a confederacy of equal self-governing communities, each entitled to define its institutions and character. For Congress to legislate slavery out of Missouri would be a kind of colonialism, denying the new state total self-government. From this viewpoint, leaving the West open to slavery was an affirmation of freedom: the freedom of white males to shape their communities without restraint from outside authorities. Restrictionists, according to a Georgia senator, were guilty of the undemocratic "doctrine of saving the people from their worst enemy, themselves."[3]

For many southerners, the attempt to bar slavery from new states, coinciding with John Marshall's assertion of federal power in *McCullough* v. *Maryland* (1819), revived republican fears about "consolidation." To Jefferson, in retirement, the move to restrict slavery in Missouri was a cynical plot by Federalists trying to revive their party and to destroy southern interests. Increasingly suspicious of northern motives, he was appalled by the growing power of the federal judiciary, by the charter of the Second Bank of the United States, and the plans of up-and-coming Republican politicians like Henry Clay for a centrally funded plan of internal improvements. He was impressed by John Taylor's *Construction Construed* (1820), fired off to demonstrate that the tariff, the Bank, *McCullough* v. *Maryland*, and the Missouri question all smacked of an impulse toward centralization that could be traced to Alexander Hamilton. In his old age, Jefferson retreated more and more into a fervent belief in states' rights as the bastion of true republican principles. Federalism had not been finally defeated in 1800; it had merely gone underground, to reemerge in Marshall's Supreme Court and even in the bosom of the Republican party. Conflict between states' rights and consolidation became his version of the perennial battle between virtue and corruption.[4]

In the South, generalized fears of consolidation fused with the particular need to protect slavery. The vulnerability of the institution was confirmed again by the Denmark Vesey conspiracy of 1822. Vesey, a free black carpenter in Charleston, organized a plot of free blacks and slaves to take the city, apparently partly inspired by the hope that the Missouri debates heralded a wholesale northern attack on slavery. The plot was betrayed, the conspirators arrested, and thirty-five were hanged. The crisis left the South nervous about any signs of incipient abolitionism. Would the "Holy Alliance in and out of Congress" decide to give slaves "freedom and a dagger?" Jefferson demanded of John Adams.[5]

Progress

By the mid-1820s, however, as the problem of slavery receded from national debate and the after-effects of the panic of 1819 dissipated, the United States experienced an upsurge of optimism. A number of significant anniversaries offered occasions to assess the state of the republic. In 1824, for the fiftieth anniversary of the beginning of the Revolution, the marquis de Lafayette was brought back to America for a triumphal tour. Both Jefferson and Adams died on the same day, 4 July 1826, the fiftieth anniversary of the Declaration of Independence. The symbolism of this double death was not lost on contemporaries, who saw it as a special sign that the epoch marked by the Revolution was over and a new era beginning. Americans congratulated themselves that the experiment in republican government had endured and that the Union was still intact. But the confidence of these years was associated less with republican institutions than with material progress.

The visible signs of progress were all around them for the tallying. "Progress" was not part of the traditional republican philosophy, in which republics either maintained "first principles" or decayed. But faith in progress, especially when measured in terms of material growth, opened up limitless vistas of change for the better. Americans in the early nineteenth century were becoming increasingly fascinated with quantifiable "facts." When the Pennsylvania physician Adam Seybert published his *Statistical Annals* (1818) with data on commerce, population, the post office, and the military, he provided an easily grasped, and apparently objective, record of growth, something to fling back at foreign critics of the republic. "We have only to refer them to the census," declared Alexander Everett, "for a complete mathematical demonstration of the folly and falsehood of their assertions."[6]

When Lafayette made his grand peregrination around the United States to tumultuous and emotional welcoming crowds, Americans had in the old hero who had been a favorite of Washington a particularly poignant reminder of heroic days of old. They felt a need to justify themselves to him, to demonstrate that they had not wasted their patrimony. Orators addressed Lafayette in the vocabulary of virtue, but he was invariably asked to assess their stewardship in terms of the material progress made since the Revolution. The old general was constantly reminded to look around him at the transformation of wilderness into villages and towns, the abundant agriculture, the busy wharves, the rivers teeming with ships, the thriving cities. His hosts were convinced that this prosperity was the "result of our free institutions."[7]

As material abundance surged to the forefront of the American consciousness, the meaning of America shifted from past to future. Even as Americans celebrated it, the Revolution was becoming less central to their imagination. Conservatives spoke of it as less a revolution than a natural evolution out of the substantial amount of self-government in the colonies. Certainly it was quite unlike the French Revolution, and probably unique; it could not be emulated by other peoples. While there was sympathy for the Latin American rebellions against Spain in the early 1820s, there was also doubt that a people so unschooled to orderly liberty in their colonial state would be able to make the transition to freedom. The Revolution remained the great founding event, but increasingly imaginative identification turned to the ongoing process of subduing and peopling the continent. In his poem "The Ages" (1821), which he always placed at the beginning of successive editions of his works, Bryant personified America as a "young giant" and asked rhetorically, "and who shall place / A limit to the giant's unchained strength / Or curb his swiftness in the forward race!" Tocqueville observed that the American nation was mesmerized by the spectacle of "its own march" across the continent.[8]

Moralists still warned against avarice and the perils of prosperity. The new vocabulary of progress and improvement did not so much replace as overlay the older vocabulary of virtue and corruption. Material advances implied moral ideals: progress, buoyed by millennial thinking, suggested obedience to divine mandate, and "improvement" connoted earnest effort, hard work, and civic concern. Improvement, moreover, provided the post-revolutionary generation with a specific role in the world. At Bunker Hill in 1825, Daniel Webster noted the generational shift of responsibility. As the last members of the Revolutionary generation died off, "the great trust" of the republic "now descends to new hands." This was an onerous responsibility, but was the new generation to be mere caretakers? "We can win no laurels in a war for independence," acknowledged Webster. "Earlier and worthier hands have gathered them all." What remained, however, was not only the duty of preservation but also "a noble pursuit to which the spirit of the times strongly invites us. Our proper business is improvement."[9]

At the state level, governments gave considerable aid to economic development. The federal government expanded harbors and port facilities and provided army engineers to survey routes and lend expertise to the construction of roads and canals. Americans had few inhibitions about demanding governmental aid in special circumstances, which were numerous. But ad hoc adjustments by specific interests to specific circumstances hardly jolted the general assumption that economic decisions were best made by individuals.

The Law and the Economy

At the same time, the legal system was laying down a basic groundwork of rules, providing some uniformity across the Union, and facilitating economic growth. The law protected private property and encouraged enterprise and corporate ventures. Judges assumed a competent and busy populace and leaned toward releasing rather than restraining its economic energies. When property rights clashed—for example, when mill owners dammed streams to provide power—judges tended to favor the more dynamic and enterprising use of resources, even against the interests of prior landowners.

Contract law became increasingly important as society became more thoroughly commercial. While Blackstone's classic *Commentaries on the Laws of England* (1769) had devoted fewer than fifty pages to contracts, by the time Chancellor Kent produced his *Commentaries on American Law* in 1830, it was necessary to devote one whole volume of his four to the subject. By that time judges were replacing the old notion of an equitable contract, in which the validity of a negotiation depended to some extent on its fit with community standards of justice and fairness, with the so-called will doctrine, in which the court asked only if a contract had been properly executed by people acting of their own free will. The courts were backing away from paternalism and assuming the competence of autonomous individuals to look out for their own interests. They were assuming also that the state had only a police interest in enforcing agreements freely made; it was not concerned with the substantive fairness of those agreements.[10]

Two important Supreme Court decisions reveal Chief Justice Marshall's recognition that commercial development depended on a high degree of regularity and certainty. *Fletcher* v. *Peck* (1810) was a classic case of public corruption. A bribed Georgia legislature had handed over huge grants of public land to a private company, which then sold it in lots to people all over the country. An outraged populace elected a new legislature, which cancelled the grants, and the validity of all these sales was called into question. To Marshall what was at stake was neither the venality of the legislature nor the public's capacity to undo wrong but the predictable working of commercial life, which depended on the sanctity of contract. He upheld the original grant on the grounds that a grant was a contract, and a contract was sacred. Similar thinking lay behind his famous decision in the *Dartmouth College* case (1819), in which Daniel Webster created a sensation with his emotional defense of the college. This case involved the attempt of the Republican government of New Hampshire to bring Dartmouth College under state control. Ruling in favor of the college corporation, Marshall declared that a grant of corporate powers must be regarded as a contract, which once given could not be altered. This decision effectively freed from state control a number of existing largely religious colleges and other kinds of corporations as well. It did not mean a wholesale abandonment of state powers to the corporation, since new grants could always include provisions for state intervention, but it did mean that such intervention could not be retroactive.[11]

The New Science of Economics

Many Americans were now thinking about the economy less in the old republican terms of virtue, independence, and corruption and more in the technical vocabulary provided by the new science of economics taking shape in Britain. When Americans themselves began to write theoretically about the economy they began with Adam Smith, with the addition of Thomas Malthus and, after about 1817, of David Ricardo. Probably the most widely read economic exposition by an American in this period was *Outlines of Political Economy* (1825) by John McVickar, professor of moral philosophy at Columbia University. This was a heavily annotated edition of an English article in the *Encyclopaedia Britannica*. McVickar was suspicious of any governmental intervention in the economy, including protective tariffs. Like Adam Smith he assumed that a society in which all are left free to follow their own self-interest was the most natural and the happiest.

A tireless popularizer, McVickar even produced a text on political economy for children because he felt that the "truths" of the science were "a source of safety for existing institutions" and exemplified "the necessary connections that subsist between national virtue, national interest and national happiness." McVickar still used the language of virtue, but he saw no antagonism between it and acquisitiveness because he had narrowed the meaning of virtue down to sober bourgeois habits of industry and law abidingness. He asserted that as a matter of observation, acquisitiveness, far from destroying virtue, in fact led to it: "Where do you find the sober, industrious, moral part of our community?" he asked in a public lecture in 1830. Where but in the pursuit of wealth?

Where do you find domestic order and peaceful subordination, and a careful training of youth in the paths of virtue? Where but among those engaged in this stigmatized pursuit? And where, on the other hand, do you find the crimes and vices of society? Where do you find the turbulent agitator . . . the candidates for prisons and penitentiaries? Where, but among such as have never engaged in the steady pursuit of wealth . . . men reckless of the morrow, and caring for nothing but the gratification of the passing hour? . . . When does such an one begin to reform? Is it not so soon as he begins to accumulate, or rather to desire [wealth]?[12]

A less influential, but in many ways more interesting, and opposed, approach to economic policy came from a Baltimore lawyer, Daniel Raymond, usually considered America's first theoretical economist. Against both Adam Smith and the main trends of educated opinion in the United States, Raymond saw government as a powerful moral force for good in the economy, a necessary discipline against individual greed and selfishness. In his *Thoughts on Political Economy* (1820), expanded in 1823 into *Elements of Political Economy*, Raymond started from the same fundamental question as Adam Smith— what constitutes the wealth of nations?—but came up with quite different answers. His most important insight was that the wealth of the community is something distinct from the aggregate of individual wealth. Indeed, "individual interests are perpetually at variance with national interests." While it might be in the interest of individuals to buy as cheaply as they could, for example, it was in the interest of the nation to do its own manufacturing, even though this meant that goods would be more expensive. A nation was a community, not a mere collection of individuals, and so government had the right to take from some and give to others (as in protective tariffs) so long as the protected activity was for the long-term general benefit. The ideal was that everyone in the nation should be fully employed; consumers should be prepared to pay whatever costs were necessary to ensure this because they benefited indirectly by living in a country of stable employment and developing skills. For Raymond, the individual was always secondary to the public good and was expected, in good republican fashion, to submit his or her own desires to it.

Yet there was a decidedly unrepublican side to Raymond's thinking. He believed that what produced wealth was a steadily increasing demand for goods, the pressure of ever-rising human wants. Consumption was the key to economic well-being. Thus he supported government expenditure for public works that stimulated economic activity and facilitated exchange, and he was not horrified by a public debt. The insatiability of human desires had traditionally been thought to undermine virtue. To Raymond, however, the consumer society was necessary to ensure constant employment; work itself was the primary moral educator.[13]

Much as they disagreed over issues of governmental interference in the economy, American economic thinkers were generally hopeful about economic prospects in America. Jacob Cardozo, an editor and economic theorist in Charleston, disagreed entirely with Raymond on the subject of the tariff but joined him in the conviction that there was an infinite market for goods and thus no limit to growth. American optimism contrasted with the pessimism of English writers like Malthus and Ricardo, whose gloomy predictions about the pressure of increasing population on means of subsistence and on wages seemed to have little meaning in a new world of abundant land.[14]

The Factory and the Republic

Although Americans grew less concerned about the corrupting power of prosperity, they were still wary of the effects of economic development on republican equality and the independence of citizens. Their model of a fully developed modern economy was Britain. To what extent would America replicate the pattern of British experience? The United States was distinct from Britain in its republican institutions, its general "equality," and its vast supply of land relative to population. How far could these differences be expected to modify the "universal laws" put forward by the British masters like Smith, Malthus, and Ricardo? Would they enable the United States to develop its commerce and industry while escaping the terrible social problems attendant on economic development in the Old World?

Although Malthusian fears of overpopulation seemed foolish, Madison, in his retirement, worried about the day when the United States would be as densely populated as Europe and more and more people would be without hope of gaining property in land. In addition, to the end of his long life, he was perturbed by the productivity of American agriculture. Supply was bound to outrun demand eventually, and then people would no longer be able to make a living on the land. Increased manufacturing might take up the human surplus but with the inevitable result that "the people will be formed into the same great classes here as elsewhere." In 1821 he predicted that eventually the United States would be divided between "wealthy capitalists" and "indigent labourers" and characterized by "a dependence of an increasing number on the wealth of a few." Would it then still be a republic?[15]

The specter of armies of dependent workers marshaled by the will of their employer at the polls was still useful ammunition for defenders of traditional property qualifications for the franchise. In the Massachusetts Constitutional Convention of 1820, conservatives unwilling to remove the last barriers to universal manhood suffrage warned that eventually there would be great manufacturing establishments in the state. An unrestricted franchise allowing factory operatives to vote would mean hundreds of votes of propertyless men dictated by one great capitalist. The spirit of the Massachusetts Constitution, declared Josiah Quincy, "is a spirit of limited liberty . . . not of abstract liberty. The theory of our constitution is that extreme poverty—i.e., pauperism is inconsistent with independence."[16]

Advocates of manufacturing knew that they had to show not only that manufacturing was good for the independence of the American economy but that it was compatible with American political institutions. This meant, above all, finessing the problem of dependence. The solution was to blur the distinction between independence of status and economic well-being. The American factory worker, they insisted, was not like his degraded counterpart in Europe because he was well paid: he could afford decent housing, he could save, he was literate, he was a voter. The democratic forces arguing for the removal of the remaining, though quite low, property qualifications in Massachusetts concurred with the industrial spokesmen in revising the basis of virtue. Laboring men might not have property perhaps, but they supported their families and were "respectable." Respectability was a personal characteristic, which depended not on the objective condition of economic independence but on "institutions, laws, habits and associations" and on "education, and the diffusion of intelligence." There was no real distinction between the respectable operative and the self-employed artisan, or indeed, anyone else in the country, where everyone worked for a living. By the late 1820s the political argument was gaining familiarity that everyone was a workingman in America where very few could live off inherited wealth. The work ethic threw a cover of equal respect over all classes, and workers' self-esteem came increasingly to rest not on their independent status but on their high standard of living.[17]

The factory town of Lowell presented one solution to the problem of labor in a republic. Conceived of by a group of young Boston merchants who had studied industrial conditions in Britain, Lowell was intended to be a model community, free of the degradations of Manchester. The first Lowell factory was opened in 1823, and others soon followed. They employed mainly young farm women who would not become a permanent proletariat but work only until they married. The young women were housed in supervised boardinghouses and supplied with churches and strict moral as well as industrial discipline. Since it was run on water power, the town remained clean. The result was a new kind of industrial environment. Lowell became an important stopping-off place for serious tourists in America. It captured the imagination because it seemed to have solved the problem of modern industrial labor: the work force was both docile and respectable, and the factory ran with clockwork precision. Indeed, the factory, with each mechanical and human part carrying out its allotted task, seemed an epitome of social discipline. "The moral spectacle here presented," exclaimed an awed visitor in 1836, "is in itself beautiful and sublime."[18]

In an 1830 Fourth of July speech in Lowell, Edward Everett managed to link the Lowell complex with the bounty of God and nature (waterpower), with the spirit of a free country (which produced technical innovation), and with the "home-bred virtues of the parental roof" still preserved by the operatives. He described Lowell as the realization of a "Holy Alliance" between capital and labor. It incorporated the only kind of "socialism" compatible with "the primary instincts of our nature": without disrupting property rights, it brought capital and muscle power into mutual benefit.[19]

Not everyone thought that the problems of industrial society could be solved by waterpower, religion, and elite benevolence. In the late 1820s radical visions of a new social organization of society were being promoted by two British reformers, Robert Owen, who had founded a much publicized, but short-lived, utopian community at New Harmony, Indiana, and Frances Wright, who lectured publicly on free thought, women's rights, and universal systems of egalitarian education. Most Americans rejected these reformers' radical ideas on sex and religion, but for a brief period at the end of the 1820s, Wright and Owen's son, Robert Dale Owen, were at the center of a subculture of radicals in New York City and played significant roles in the creation of the short-lived Workingmen's party.

The Workingmen's party continued the tradition of artisan resistance to the development of a modern capitalist economy. They protested corporate monopolies, banks, and increasing economic inequality and proclaimed themselves the "legitimate children of '76." One of the leaders of the party, Thomas Skidmore, in his *Rights of Man to Property* (1829), offered a very American solution to the problem of inequality. His ideal was a society in which every individual—including women and children—owned property, receiving at birth an equal share of the nation's wealth. This property was theirs to use as they pleased during their lifetime; whatever they owned at death would revert to the common stock. One corollary was that no adult would then have any claim on the society for support or charity. Here was an effort to enshrine individualism and private property while avoiding the inequality that that combination inevitably produced. The Workingmen's party soon disassociated itself from radicals like Skidmore and settled for moderate demands like a mechanic's lien law and free public schooling.[20]

The Problem of the Poor

Wealth was clearly becoming more uneven in its distribution, and the dislocations of an urban commercial economy hit hard at those at the bottom of the economic ladder. In the nation's growing cities, civic leaders were made increasingly aware of the existence of intractable poverty and an underclass. Modern urban life demanded a great deal from people in terms of self-discipline. It required that individuals withstand the psychic and social stresses of proximity and economic anxiety so as not to lash out in anger and violence and that they be able to support themselves. An urban commercial economy in a free society worked only if most people were self-sustaining and self-regulating. The growing numbers of people incapable of or unwilling to be either could no longer be absorbed by the traditional village social supports or punishments. In 1816 more than seven thousand European immigrants arrived in New York City. Few had skills, and most sought public assistance during the early winter of 1817. An ad hoc committee formed in February 1817 to gather contributions for the poor estimated that fifteen thousand people (about one-seventh of the population of the city) were dependent on public and private charity that winter.[21]

City governments and civic elites turned serious attention to the problem of poor relief in the 1820s. Both Boston and New York commissioned comprehensive reports with recommendations for new relief policies. "Poverty, vice, and crime," the Boston report acknowledged, "in our day, are, in fact, in some measure the necessary consequences of the social state." This did not imply that nothing could be done, however. Both reports toyed with the idea that the state should get out of poor relief altogether and leave it to private charity but opted instead for regularization of relief. Since the United States was "exempt from all the acknowledged causes of vagrancy and beggary in Europe," indigence in the New World must be due to "the enactments and artificial arrangements of the society." The existing system of outdoor relief was objectionable because it encouraged sponging by the able-bodied but lazy. The poor started to look on relief "as a right," and "the just pride of independence, so honorable to a man, in every condition" was "corrupted by the certainty of public provision." The solution was Houses of Industry in which the indigent would be housed and fed in return for labor. This was not only cheaper for the city but would give the poor the kind of moral education in good habits that might eventually enable them to become self-supporting members of society.[22]

Voluntary citizen groups took over much of the work of distributing aid and studying problems of indigency and crime. In New York, for example, the Society for the Prevention of Pauperism started a savings bank for the poor in order to inspire economy and "inculcate a spirit of enterprise and industry, and self-respect, among the laboring classes of the community." Most of the available modern literature on social problems was British, and American reformers approached their task with categories and outlook shaped by their reading in British reform works and government reports. New York reformer Thomas Eddy corresponded regularly with the influential British writer on poverty problems, Patrick Colquhoun, who kept him supplied with pamphlets and information. After undertaking an investigation into the causes of poverty in New York, the society was convinced that almost all cases of want proceeded "directly or indirectly from the want of correct moral principle" and that this was often the result of bad family upbringing. Those who succumbed to the temptations surrounding them in the city were people who had not acquired good habits as children. What was needed were institutions that would overcome the defects of inadequate families. The society then reformed itself into the Society for the Reformation of Juvenile Delinquents and sponsored the House of Refuge, the first American reform school. [23]

Societies such as these were run by men of the professional and mercantile elite who were also active in educational and prison reform and in founding cultural institutions. John Pintard, for example, the chief officer of New York's first savings bank, besides organizing the Society for the Prevention of Pauperism, also founded the Mechanics and Apprentices Library, was active in the Free School Society and the American Bible Society, helped to organize the New-York Historical Society, and laid the foundation of its fine library. All these endeavors were part of the same spirit of civic improvement. Pintard was a man of deep religious faith, but in his organizational work this was subsumed in the belief that education of various kinds, permeating the social structure from top to bottom, would solve all social ills. [24]

The American Penitentiary

Belief that the answer to social problems lay in the reform of individual character through specialized institutions was behind the movement for prison reform. Most states had revised their penal codes after the Revolution, reducing the number of capital offenses and abolishing harsh physical punishments. This left the prison as the central method of punishing and deterring crime. By the 1820s, however, crime rates were rising, and reformers were turning their attentions to prisons not merely as means of punishment but as a way of reforming offenders. Two rival systems were developed. In New York, in the Auburn prison (1817) and Sing Sing (1829), prison discipline was based on labor, a military lockstep precision in moving from one place to another, and strict silence at all times. The prisoners were "to move and act like machines." In the Pennsylvania system, on the other hand, inmates were kept in solitary confinement, sometimes in total idleness. The object of the New York Auburn system was to teach habits of regular industry, for work itself was seen as reformatory, and virtue might be routinized as good habits. In the Pennsylvania system, which owed much to Quaker influence, the stress was on conscience; solitary confinement was designed to force the inmate into introspection in the confidence that it was "scarcely possible that the guilty prisoner can long inhabit a cell where darkness and silence reign . . . without . . . some real penitence of heart."[25]

Initially the penitentiaries were based on an extraordinary optimism that an engineered environment might produce individual reformation. Several people prominent in prison reform were also active in improving treatment of the mentally ill. Among them were the New York Quaker Thomas Eddy and Benjamin Rush, who had pioneered in the use of controlled environment for the "moral" treatment of the insane. In the prison as in the asylum, the old-fashioned physical harshness was replaced by a new discipline of regularity, vigilance, and moral control. Prison officials were instructed to study the criminal as well as try to reform him. In the 1820s rudimentary analyses of the backgrounds of prisoners emphasized lack of family discipline and intemperance as keys to their criminal behavior. The causes of crime, in short, were personal deficiencies.[26]

By the 1830s, nine of the most populous states had penitentiaries of either the New York or Pennsylvania type. Two new penitentiaries built at Pittsburgh and Philadelphia in the 1820s were the largest public works undertaken by the government of Pennsylvania to that time. Prisons were undoubtedly expensive, especially those that provided for solitary confinement on a large scale. They were, however, statements of the community's willingness to take measures for public order that were also designed to bring the erring back to virtue by teaching them the habits of civilized life. Recognizing the importance of the visual statement made by the new penitentiaries, Philadelphia's city fathers launched a competition for the best design for the new Eastern prison. They chose one by John Haviland, who in a striking departure from the standard neoclassical style of American public buildings produced one of the first buildings in the United States in the gothic style, hitherto used only for a few churches. According to one commentator in 1829, the effect that the "grave, severe, and awful character" of the structure produced on the imagination was "peculiarly impressive, solemn and instructive." "The Penitentiary," he concluded, "is the only edifice in this country which is calculated to convey to our citizens the external appearance of those magnificent castles of the Middle Ages, which contribute so eminently to embellish the scenery of Europe."[27]

The combination of the architecture and the system made Eastern one of the most famous prisons in the world, and the serious tourist might take in Auburn or Eastern along with Lowell as characteristic institutions of the country. As the United States became a world leader in the human and architectural technology of prison discipline, the new penitentiaries became objects of great pride. Their governing principles might even be applicable outside the walls. The Prison Discipline Society of Boston certainly thought so, advocating in its 1829 report the system of Sing Sing, which exemplified "a principle of very extensive application to families, schools, academies, colleges, factories, mechanics' shops: i.e. the importance of unceasing vigilance."[28]

Renewed Concern for Mass Education

Urban problems of poverty and crime reinvigorated the old republican concern for systems of public education. Arguments that the people needed education to understand their rights and appreciate their relation to the republic merged with a newer emphasis on teaching the people to understand their duties and internalize values of industry, regularity, and obedience to law. The number of children enrolled in some kind of school for at least part of the year had in fact been rising from the turn of the century, especially among girls. There were no comprehensive systems of free education, however. In the first quarter of the century, cities began to develop charity schooling for the poor, run by private organizations aided by government grants, like the Free School Society of New York.

There was virtual consensus among American civic elites on the desirability of educating the children of the poor. Even conservatives did not think that the security of government in a republic could rest on the ignorance of the lower classes. In fact, they saw intellectual awakening as tied to moral feeling. Jared Sparks, editor of the *North American Review* and later president of Harvard, argued that "all branches of intellectual improvement will lead to moral goodness." Daniel Webster in 1820 celebrated public provision for schooling as "a wise and liberal system of police, by which property, and life, and the peace of society are secured." "We seek to prevent," he told his audience, "in some measure, the extension of the penal code, by inspiring a salutary and conservative principle of virtue and of knowledge in an early age. . . . We hope to continue, and to prolong the time, when, in the villages and farm houses of New England, there may be undisturbed sleep, within unbarred doors." Similarly, the governor of Tennessee, urging a system of public schools in 1827, pointed out that a large number of the inmates of the penitentiaries had had no education, whereas the experience of New York and Scotland demonstrated that the poor who had received some schooling were less likely to commit crimes.[29]

Other social groups believed that education would enhance their own self-respect and foster greater social equality. Free blacks sometimes set up their own schools, often with the aid of white philanthropists. By the 1820s mechanics' organizations were running their own free schools for the children of working people in the major northern cities. Public schooling without the stigma of pauperism was a major plank in all workingmen's parties. Artisans wanted an education that would bridge the gap between head and hand work, not denigrate the latter. When the workingmen of Philadelphia addressed the legislature on the topic of common schooling in 1830, they singled out an experimental school at Hofwyl in Switzerland as a model. This school mixed manual labor with advanced pedagogy with the intention of blurring the distinction between manual and mind work, as well as helping to pay for the school.

In the 1820s elite reformers not only stepped up their campaigns to ensure that the children of the poor received some instruction but also began to argue for statewide systems of education, open free to all classes. As in the case of prisons and poverty, many of the arguments that have continued to be the staples of educational debate were laid out in this period. Reformers deplored the poor quality of teachers, who were either ill educated themselves or did not understand how to communicate what they did know, and worried about how good people could be attracted to the profession when it was so miserably paid and of low status. There was a growing interest in the individual psychology of children and in improving techniques of instruction. They insisted that instruction should be interesting because children would not learn what was deadly dull, and they attacked mere rote learning as not answering the real purpose of education, which was to call out all the powers of the mind.

The educational reform work of James G. Carter in Massachusetts stimulated a good deal of discussion about schooling in the major reviews. Carter deplored the fact that because of the low quality of the public schools of Massachusetts, middle-class parents sent their children to private schools, depriving public education of the interest and concern of the most active citizens, with the result that its standards declined even further. Separate schooling reinforced and widened growing class distinctions so that "the pure republican nature of the free school is . . . wholly destroyed." The fissures of class became an important argument for universal public elementary schooling. From its beginnings, the public school was expected to take on a major share of the burden of creating both republican solidarity and republican equality, now defined as a superficial ease among the social classes and "equality of opportunity" at the beginning of the race.[30]

Penitentiaries, asylums, schools for the deaf or blind, poor houses, houses of refuge, and free elementary schools for the poor—all stemmed from the same impulse. Their creators assumed that once a stable hierarchy was no longer possible, social order depended on a community of values centered on the work ethic and self-restraint. Everyone must be brought within this community of values. Some, like the handicapped, had been outside it through no fault of their own; some, like criminals, had deliberately stepped outside it. Still others, like delinquent children, the poor, or the insane, fell somewhere in between in degrees of blameworthiness. Most, if not all, could be brought back inside: with effort and the correct design of institutions, they could be trained to good habits. While the Enlightenment's environmentalism faded in respect to race, there was no shortage of faith in the educative power of institutions for white people, especially the young. It was one more strand in the commitment to improvement.

"In Assuming Her Station among the Civilized Nations of the Earth"

An effort to entrench a national commitment to systematic improvement marked the unhappy presidency of John Quincy Adams. Adams was a highly cultivated man, with wide interests in the sciences, and none of the traditional republican fears of governmental power. He did, however, have a strong measure of the conservative republican belief in the leadership of a natural aristocracy of the wise and good. His philosophy of government and ideals for the unfolding of American civilization, however, stepped way beyond the republican paradigm. "The great object of the institution of civil government," he told Congress in his first annual message, "is the improvement of the condition of those who are parties to the social compact." Going beyond Henry Clay's American system of coordinated economic development that had dominated political debate for some fifteen years, Adams proposed that the federal government should commit itself to programs for "the improvement of agriculture, commerce and manufactures, the cultivation and encouragement of the mechanic and of the elegant arts, the advancement of literature, and the progress of the sciences, ornamental and profound." In practical terms that meant a host of projects from canals to a national university, surveys of natural resources to a national observatory, an expanded navy to scientific exploring expeditions to the West. The Constitution, he assured Congress, already gave the government ample powers to accomplish all this.

Adams could not resist placing everything in the widest possible context. Three years earlier while preparing a report on a uniform standard of weights and measures for Congress, he had embedded the discussion in an extended disquisition on the nature of man and civil society. Now he placed his call for an ambitious plan of national improvements in the context of the quickening of intellect and enterprise all over Europe and called for America to join this international march of mind: "In assuming her station among the civilized nations of the earth, it would seem that our country had contracted the engagement to contribute her share of mind, of labor, and of expense to the improvement of those parts of knowledge which lie beyond the reach of individual acquisition." Adams was in effect calling for a public commitment to the idea of the United States as an integral, if junior, member of the international "republic of letters," even if that meant learning some lessons from corrupt Old World governments. "While foreign nations less blessed with that freedom which is power than ourselves are advancing with gigantic strides in the career of public improvement," he asked, was the Congress and government of the United States going to "fold up our arms and proclaim to the world that we are palsied by the will of our constituents?"[31]

When Adams showed the message to his cabinet before delivering it, they were aghast—not because they disapproved of its particular recommendations but because they knew the political repercussions of such a sweeping program. Clay thought that by now projects for a national university were "entirely hopeless." William Wirt, the attorney general, feared that people would think "we wanted a great, magnificent government," and reference to foreign scientific achievements would be "cried down as a partiality for monarchies." All these predictions proved correct. Adams activated new prejudices and old. Jefferson denounced his plans as moving toward "a single and splendid government of an aristocracy, founded on banking institutions, and moneyed incorporations . . . riding and ruling over the plundered ploughman and beggared yeomanry." Adams's flowery phrase for observatories—"light houses of the skies"—became the subject of much ridicule. His patrician disregard for the opinions of constituents reflected an ideal of the representatives as acting for the good of the people but not as their direct agent, no longer tenable in an age of spreading democracy.[32]

Adams's ambitious program would entail increased power for the national bank and restriction on easy popular access to public lands, which instead would help to fund development. Further, the vision of the nation that Adams championed, a vision of a rather complex society led by the elite, sometimes requiring the sacrifice of present interests for future benefit, appealed mainly to men of Adams's own class and own region. His belief in the educative and civilizing role of government flew in the face of what had clearly become the most widespread American sense of what government was for: to clear the way for individual self-determination.[33]

The Sovereignty of the People

In the 1828 presidential campaign, old republican battles of local autonomy against centralization, of virtue against corruption, were refought. In rejecting Adams and electing Andrew Jackson, the American people responded not so much to specific programs as to their perception of what the two men stood for: a complex society disciplined by a national elite, or the unabridged sovereignty of the people. Personal image became all-important. The Jacksonian depiction of Adams as a Europeanized "luxurious" aristocrat was effective; the Adams supporters' depiction of Jackson as a barbarian fell flat. In the popular mind, Jackson's lack of education did him no harm, and

Adams's erudition did him no good. In the neat summing up of one election slogan, there was no contest between "John Quincy Adams who can write / And Andrew Jackson who can fight!"[34]

At Jackson's inauguration in 1829, a mob, frantic to get a glimpse of "their" president, stormed the white house, smashing furniture and china in the melee. The incident immediately became notorious. To Jackson's conservative opponents, it confirmed all their worst fears about the new age. One Washington observer, Margaret Bayard Smith, gave a more balanced assessment, one that might stand as emblematic of the unexpected way in which the world of the founding fathers had been transformed and of the mixture of self-restraint and abandon that would characterize democracy. First, she described the orderly crowds at the oath taking: "It was sublime! . . . Even Europeans must have acknowledged that a free people collected in their might, silent and tranquil, restrained solely by a moral power, without a shadow around of military force, was majesty rising to sublimity." Then she described how the mob had surged over the White House: "This concourse had not been anticipated and therefore not provided against. Ladies and gentlemen, only had been expected at this Levee, not the people en masse. But it was the People's day, and the People's President and the People would rule."[35]

When James Monroe was elected unopposed in 1816, Jefferson had proclaimed triumphantly: "The four and twenty years, which he will accomplish, of administration in *republican forms and principles*, will so consecrate them in the eyes of the people as to secure them against the danger of change." The republican paradigm was stretched to its limits, however, by the economic, social, and demographic transformations of the early nineteenth century. By 1830 the republican equality of citizens had been extended far beyond anything envisaged by the founding generation into a triumphant assertion of democracy, and liberty was increasingly conceived in individualist terms as a potential for unlimited individual expansion or, alternatively, in its most basic, and precivic form, as the right to be left alone. By the end of Jackson's presidency, the very term *republicanism* had been almost entirely supplanted by *democracy* in political discourse. Jacksonianism was less the beginning of a new movement, however, than a triumphant culmination of the developments of the past thirty years. Jefferson thought Jackson a "dangerous man" unfit for the presidency, but Jackson rightly saw himself in the Jeffersonian tradition. Jefferson had set a pattern of national commitment to continental expansion, coupled with a determination that government at the center should be both minimal and cheap. The Jeffersonian republicans had championed popular participation in politics and the basic equality and dignity of all white males while being indifferent or hostile to racial equality. Under Jackson this translated into Indian removal, easier access to public lands, and the general removal of any impediments to de-centralized private enterprise. Jefferson's last public statement, declaring the "palpable truth, that the mass of mankind has not been born with saddles on their backs, nor a favored few booted and spurred, ready to ride them legitimately, by the Grace of God," might stand both as his vision of the meaning of America and as the essence of Jacksonian democracy.[36]

Although Republican principles had not been secured against change, neither were they entirely abandoned. As a way of viewing the world, republicanism proved extremely tenacious. It remained embedded in American thought patterns in certain fundamental ways and gave a particular slant to American democracy. It persisted in a suspicion of concentrations of private or governmental power, in resistance to being governed or taxed too much, in hatred of special privilege, and a constant preoccupation with corruption.

The liberal individualism that wss coming to pervade conscious values as well as economic behavior undermined much of the social solidarity and social discipline implicit in republicanism, but it also possessed moral and intellectual possibilities that republicanism did not. Republicanism had never offered much to those outside the constituent people: women, blacks, Indians, the poor. Nor had republicanism provided a hospitable environment for cultural creativity; it was too parsimonious and suspicious of pleasure; it subordinated the individual too firmly to the collectivity.

And what of virtue? This concept was the other, and more positive, legacy of republicanism. The term was still sometimes used in its public and political sense in the 1830s, but increasingly it lost its rich penumbra of republican connotations and its association with male strength and integrity. By the mid-nineteenth century its meaning had become narrowed down to the primary sense it had always had in connection with women: sexual restraint. In a society that was letting the individual loose from so many other restraints, the internalization of sexual repression and a social imposition of prudery came to stand for the essence of civilized self-control.

Yet the old concept of virtue still slumbered in the republican depths of American thought, from which it could sometimes be roused. For all their avid pursuit of the economic main chance, Americans would never quite be able to abandon the belief that there was a common good to which the individual must defer; that the economic arrangements of society had moral as well as material implications; that the health of the republic depended on the character of its citizens. Emerson recounts an anecdote about a sermon he preached as a young man in 1828 in which he had used the term *virtue* in its republican sense. "Dr. Ripley remarked on the frequent occurrence of the word *Virtue* in it, and said his people would not understand it, for the largest part of them, when Virtue was spoken of, understood *Chastity*." "I do not imagine, however," commented Emerson to his journal, "that the people thought any such thing."[37]

Chronology

1800   Thomas Jefferson elected president. Mason Weem's *Life of Washington*. Library of Congress founded.

1801   Revival meeting at Cane Ridge, Kentucky, signals beginning of Second Great Awakening. *Port Folio* founded. Charles Willson Peale reconstructs the mammoth.

1802   American Academy of Fine Arts (New York) established.

1803   The Louisiana Purchase. Lewis and Clark expedition.

1804   Samuel Miller, *A Brief Retrospect of the Eighteenth Century*. New-York Historical Society founded.

1805   Pennsylvania Academy of the Fine Arts founded. Mercy Warren, *History of the American Revolution*.

1807   The embargo. Joel Barlow, *The Columbiad*. Washington Irving and James Kirke Paulding, *Salmagundi*. First run of Robert Fulton's *Claremont*. Boston Athenaeum founded.

1808   James Madison elected president. Alexander Wilson, *American Ornithology*.

1809   Washington Irving, *Knickerbocker's History of New York*.

1810   Samuel Stanhope Smith, *Essay on the Causes of the Variety of Complexion and Figure in the Human Species* (2d ed.).

1812   American Antiquarian Society founded. War with Britain. Benjamin Rush, *Observations upon the Diseases of the Mind*.

1814   Francis Scott Key, "Star Spangled Banner." John Taylor, *An Inquiry into the Principles and Policy of the Government of the United States.*

1815   Battle of New Orleans. End of war with Britain. End of Napoleonic wars. *North American Review* founded.

1816   James Monroe elected president.

1817   William Cullen Bryant, "Thanatopsis." Lyceum of Natural History, New York, founded. American Colonization Society founded.

1818   *American Journal of Science* founded.

1819   *Dartmouth College* Case. *McCullough* v. *Maryland.* Washington Irving, *The Sketchbook.*

1820   The Missouri Compromise. Major Long's expedition. Edward Hicks, first *Peaceable Kingdom.*

1821   James Fenimore Cooper, *The Spy.* New York Constitutional Convention held. Timothy Dwight, *Travels in New England and New York.*

1822   Denmark Vesey slave plot.

1823   The Monroe Doctrine. Charles J. Ingersoll, "The Influence of America on the Mind." Daniel Raymond, *Elements of Political Economy.*

1824   William Strickland, Second Bank of the United States building.

1825   John Quincy Adams elected president. Erie Canal opened. University of Virginia opened. Dedication of Bunker Hill monument. Marquis de Lafayette tours United States.

1826   John Adams and Thomas Jefferson die 4 July. James Fenimore Cooper, *The Last of the Mohicans.*

1828   Andrew Jackson elected president. Noah Webster, *American Dictionary of the English Language.* The Yale Report.

1829   Jacob Bigelow, *Elements of Technology.* James Marsh's edition of Coleridge's *Aids to Reflection.* David Walker, *An Appeal to the Colored Citizens of the World.* Pennsylvania's Eastern Penitentiary opened.

1830   *Book of Mormon.*

Notes and References

Chapter One

1. Quoted in Arthur H. Shaffer, *The Politics of History: Writing the History of the American Revolution, 1783–1815* (Chicago: Precedent Publishing, 1975), 26.

2. Robert H. Wiebe, *The Opening of American Society* (New York: Alfred A. Knopf 1984), 132; Russel Blaine Nye, *The Cultural Life of the New Nation, 1776–1830* (New York: Harper & Row, 1960), 118–9.

3. Gordon S. Wood, "The Significance of the Early Republic," *Journal of the Early Republic* 8 (Spring, 1988):1–20, and his Introduction to *The Rising Glory of America, 1760–1820* (New York: George Braziller, 1971), 1–22; Noble E. Cunningham, Jr., *The United States in 1800: Henry Adams Revisited* (Charlottesville: University of Virginia Press, 1988).

4. Robert E. Shalhope, "Republicanism and Early American Historiography," *William and Mary Quarterly* 39 (April 1982):334–56.

5. Lance Banning, "Jeffersonian Ideology Revisited: Liberal and Classical Ideas in the New American Republic," *William and Mary Quarterly* 43 (January 1986):3–19.

6. Daniel Sisson, *The American Revolution of 1800* (New York: Alfred A. Knopf, 1974).

7. Jefferson, "First Inaugural Address, March 4, 1801," in Noble E. Cunningham, Jr., ed., *The Early Republic, 1789–1828* (New York: Harper & Row, 1968), 73; Jefferson to John Taylor, 26 May 1816, in Adrienne Koch, ed., *The American Enlightenment* (New York: George Braziller, 1965), 363–64.

8. Cunningham, *United States in 1800*, 54–56. King is quoted in David Hackett Fischer, *The Revolution of American Conservatism: The Federalist Party in the Era of Jeffersonian Democracy* (New York: Harper & Row, 1965), 303.

9. Quoted in Ralph Ketcham, *From Colony to Country: The Revolution in American Thought, 1750–1820* (New York: Macmillan, 1974), 177.

10. Lewis Perry, *Intellectual Life in America* (New York: Franklin Watts, 1984), 175–77; J. R. Pole, *The Pursuit of Equality in American History* (Cambridge: Cambridge University Press, 1978), 40–42; Gordon Wood, "Ideology and the Origins of Liberal America," *William and Mary Quarterly* 44 (July 1987):628–40.

11. Nye, *Cultural Life of the New Nation*, 106–9, 133–37; Jack Larkin, *The Reshaping of Everyday Life, 1790–1840* (New York: Harper & Row, 1988), 182–91.

12. Jefferson to Adams, 28 October 1813, in Lester J. Cappon, ed., *The Adams-Jefferson Letters* (Chapel Hill: University of North Carolina Press, 1959), 2:388.

13. Gordon S. Wood, "The Democratization of Mind in the American Revolution," in *The Moral Foundations of the Republic*, ed. Robert H. Horowitz (Charlottesville: University of Virginia Press, 1979), 102–28; Ronald P. Formisano, "Deferential-Participant Politics: The Early Republic's Political Culture: 1789–1840," *American Political Science Review* 68 (1974):473–87; Latrobe quoted in Gordon Wood, "Interests and Disinterestedness in the Making of the Constitution," in Richard Beeman, Stephen Botein, and Edward C. Carter II, eds., *Beyond Confederation: Origins of the Constitution and American National Identity* (Chapel Hill: University of North Carolina Press, 1987), 102.

14. Albert J. Von Frank, *The Sacred Game: Provincialism and Frontier Consciousness in American Literature, 1630–1860* (Cambridge: Cambridge University Press, 1985), 44–48; Lewis P. Simpson, *The Brazen Face of History: Studies in the Literary Consciousness in America* (Baton Rouge: Louisiana State University Press, 1980), 35.

15. Peter M. Briggs, "Timothy Dwight 'Composes' a Landscape for New England," *American Quarterly* 40 (September 1988):359–77.

16. Benjamin Rush to John Adams, 13 June 1803, in *The Spur of Fame: Dialogues of John Adams and Benjamin Rush, 1805–1813*, ed. John A. Schutz and Douglass Adair (San Marino, Calif.: Huntington Library, 1966), 108–9; Steven Watts, "Masks, Morals, and the Market: American Literature and Early Capitalist Culture, 1790–1820," *Journal of the Early Republic* 6 (Summer 1986):127–49.

17. William Wirt, *Letters of the British Spy* (New York: Harper & Brothers, 1832), 191–92.

18. Ralph Ketcham, *Presidents above Party: The First American Presidency, 1789–1829* (Chapel Hill: University of North Carolina Press, 1984), 176–81; Michael Kammen, *A Season of Youth: The American Revolution and the Historical Imagination* (New York: Oxford University Press, 1980), 96–99; Adams to Jefferson, 21 December 1819, in Cappon, *Adams-Jefferson Letters*, 2:551.

19. Drew R. McCoy, "Political Economy," in Merrill D. Peterson, ed., *Thomas Jefferson: A Reference Biography* (New York: Scribners, 1986), 101–18; Jefferson quoted in Joyce Appleby, "Republicanism in Old and New Contexts," *William and Mary Quarterly* 43 (January 1986):23.

20. Drew R. McCoy, *Elusive Republic: Political Economy in Jeffersonian America* (New York: W. W. Norton & Co., 1982), 196–99, 211–23.

21. Ibid., 209–23; John Mayfield, *The New Nation, 1800–1845*, rev. ed. (New York: Hill & Wang, 1982), 27–29; David E. Shi. *The Simple Life: Plain Living and High Thinking in American Culture* (New York: Oxford University Press, 1985), 88.

22. Jefferson quoted in Charles A. Miller, *Jefferson and Nature: An Interpretation* (Baltimore: Johns Hopkins University Press, 1988), 214. See also John R. Nelson,

Jr., *Liberty and Property: Political Economy and Policymaking in the New Nation, 1789–1812* (Baltimore: Johns Hopkins University Press, 1987), 150–62.

23. John M. Murrin, "The Great Inversion, or Court versus Country," in J. G. A. Pocock, ed., *Three British Revolutions: 1641, 1688, 1776* (Princeton: Princeton University Press 1980), 368–453; Adams to Rush, December 27, 1810, in *Spur of Fame*, 174.

24. Duncan Macleod, "The Political Economy of John Taylor of Caroline," *Journal of American Studies* 14 (December 1980):387–405; Robert E. Shalhope, *John Taylor of Caroline: Pastoral Republican* (Chapel Hill: University of North Carolina Press, 1980); Paul K. Conkin, *Prophets of Prosperity: America's First Political Economists* (Bloomington: Indiana University Press, 1980), 43–76.

25. Sean Wilentz, *Chants Democratic: New York City and the Rise of the American Working Class, 1788–1850* (New York: Oxford University Press, 1984), 23–145; Howard B. Rock, *Artisans of the New Republic: The Tradesmen of New York City in the Age of Jefferson.* (New York: New York University Press, 1984), 264–323.

26. Wilentz, *Chants Democratic*, 282.

27. Richard J. Twomey, "Jacobins and Jeffersonians: Anglo-American Radical Ideology, 1790–1810," in *The Origins of Anglo-American Radicalism*, ed. Margaret Jacob and James Jacob (London: George Allen & Unwin 1984); Jamil Zainaldin, *Law in Antebellum Society: Legal Change and Economic Expansion* (New York: Knopf, 1983): 125–33.

28. Charles J. Ingersoll, *Inchiquin, the Jesuit's Letters* (New York: I. Riley 1810), 110, 123; Niles quoted in Wilentz, *Chants Democratic*, 101.

29. Steven Watts, *The Republic Reborn: War and the Making of Liberal America, 1790–1820* (Baltimore: Johns Hopkins University Press, 1987), 86–107, 242–50.

30. Richard E. Ellis, "The Persistence of Antifederalism after 1789," in Beeman, Botein, and Carter, *Beyond Confederation*, 294–314.

31. Gallatin is quoted in John Mayfield, *The New Nation, 1800–1845* (New York: Hill and Wang, 1982), 41.

32. *The Works of Joel Barlow* (Gainesville, Fla.: Scholars' Facsimiles and Reprints, 1970), 1:529–33; Joseph H. Harrison, Jr., *"Sic et Non:* Thomas Jefferson and Internal Improvements," *Journal of the Early Republic* 7 (Winter 1987):341.

33. Rush Welter, Introduction to *Popular Education and Democratic Thought in America* (New York: Columbia Press, 1962); Andrew R. Clayton, *The Frontier Republic: Ideology and Politics in the Ohio Country, 1780–1825* (Kent, Ohio: Kent State University Press, 1986), 142–44.

34. Nye, *Cultural Life of the New Nation*, 155–56.

35. David P. Peeler, "Thomas Jefferson's Nursery of Republican Patriots: The University of Virginia," *Journal of Church and State* 28 (Winter 1986):79–93; Joseph F. Kett, "Education," in *Thomas Jefferson: A Reference Biography*, 248.

36. Alan Gowans, *Images of American Living: Four Centuries of Architecture and Furniture as Cultural Expression* (Philadelphia: J. B. Lippincott, 1964), 238–67; Neil Harris, *The Artist in American Society: The Formative Years, 1790–1860* (Chicago: University of Chicago Press, 1982), 41–47; Nye, *Cultural Life of the New Nation*, 271–73; Wayne Andrews, *Architecture, Ambition and Americans: A Social History of American Architecture* (Glencoe, Ill.: Free Press, 1964), 76–78, 137–38.

37. Kammen, *Season of Youth*, 80, 106–7; Harris, *Artist in American Society*, 39–41; Jefferson and Crockett quoted in John S. Crawford, "The Classical Tradition in American Sculpture," *American Art Journal* 11 (July 1979):41–42.

38. Meyer Reinhold, *Classica Americana: The Greek and Roman Heritage in the United States* (Detroit: Wayne State University Press 1984), 190–94; *New England Quarterly Magazine* quoted in Linda K. Kerber, *Federalists in Dissent: Imagery and Ideology in Jeffersonian America* (Ithaca: Cornell University Press, 1980), 118.

39. Mercy Warren, *History of the Rise, Progress, and Termination of the American Revolution* (1805), in Edwin H. Cady, ed., *Literature of the Early Republic* (New York: Holt, Rinehart & Winston, 1965), 57–63; Lester H. Cohen, "Explaining the Revolution: Ideology and Ethics in Mercy Otis Warren's Historical Theory," *William and Mary Quarterly* 37 (April 1980):200–218.

40. Lawrence J. Friedman, *Inventors of the Promised Land* (New York: Alfred A. Knopf, 1975), 44–78.

41. Mason L. Weems, *The Life of Washington*, ed. Marcus Cunliffe (Cambridge: Belknap Press of Harvard University Press, 1962), ix–lxii, 209–13.

42. Harris, *Artist in American Society*, 194; Kammen, *Season of Youth*, 35, 243.

43. Quoted in Maxwell Bloomfield, *American Lawyers in a Changing Society, 1776–1876* (Cambridge: Harvard University Press 1976), 166.

44. George Dargo, *Law in the New Republic: Private Law and the Public Estate* (New York: Alfred A. Knopf, 1983), 49–59; Lawrence M. Friedman, *A History of American Law* (New York: Simon and Schuster 1973), 276–81; Bloomfield, *American Lawyers*, 173–76; Wirt quoted in Robert A. Ferguson, *Law and Letters in American Culture* (Cambridge: Harvard University Press 1984), 12; Perry Miller, *The Life of the Mind in America: From the Revolution to the Civil War* (New York: Harcourt, Brace & World, 1965), 109–116.

45. Richard E. Ellis, *The Jeffersonian Crisis: Courts and Politics in the Young Republic* (New York: W. W. Norton & Co., 1971), 250–62.

46. Miller, *Life of the Mind*, 239–65; Friedman, *History of American Law*, 282–92; A. J. Beitzinger, *A History of American Political Thought* (New York: Dodd, Mead, 1972), 357–61; Alexis de Tocqueville, *Democracy in America*, ed. J. P. Meyer (Garden City, N.Y.: Doubleday, 1966), 263–70.

47. G. Edward White, *The American Judicial Tradition* (New York: Oxford University Press, 1976), 7–34; R. Kent Newmyer, *The Supreme Court under Marshall and Taney* (Arlington Heights, Ill.: Harlan Davidson, 1968), 24–55; William M. Wiecek, *Liberty under Law: The Supreme Court in American Life* (Baltimore: Johns Hopkins University Press, 1988), 32–55.

48. Story quoted in Beitzinger, *American Political Thought*, 358; Tocqueville, *Democracy in America*, 270; Lincoln in *The Happy Republic*, ed. George E. Probst (New York: Harper & Brothers, 1962), 386–87.

Chapter Two

1. For the "moderate Enlightenment," see Henry F. May, *The Enlightenment in America* (New York: Oxford University Press, 1976), 3–101.

2. Gordon S. Wood, *The Rising Glory of America, 1760–1820* (New York: George Braziller, 1971), 14.

3. John B. Boles, *The Great Revival, 1787–1805* (Lexington: University Press of Kentucky, 1972), 12–18; Steven J. Novak, *The Rights of Youth: American Colleges and Student Revolt, 1798–1815* (Cambridge: Harvard University Press, 1977), 16–71; Timothy Dwight, "Discourse on Some Events of the Last Century," in H. Shelton Smith, Robert T. Handy, and Lefferts A. Loetscher, *American Christianity: An Historical Interpretation with Representative Documents* (New York: Charles Scribner's Sons, 1963), 1:530–38.

4. Gary B. Nash, "American Clergy and the French Revolution," *William and Mary Quarterly* 22 (July 1965):392–412; Novak, *The Rights of Youth*, 60–61; Dwight, "Some Events of the Last Century."

5. William Gribbin, "Republican Religion and the American Churches in the Early National Period," *Historian* 35 (November 1972):61–74; Novak, *Rights of Youth*, 61–69.

6. Charles F. O'Brien, "The Religious Issue in the Presidential Campaign of 1800," *Essex Institute Historical Collections* 109 (1971):82–93; Constance B. Schulz, "'Of Bigotry in Politics and Religion': Jefferson's Religion, the Federalist Press, and the Syllabus," *Virginia Magazine of History and Biography* 91 (1983):73–91; Adolph Koch, *Republican Religion: The American Revolution and the Cult of Reason* (New York: Henry Holt & Co., 1933), 184.

7. Henry F. May, *Ideas, Faiths and Feelings: Essays in American Intellectual and Religious History* (New York: Oxford University Press, 1983), 110–29; Donald G. Mathews, *Religion in the Old South* (Chicago: University of Chicago Press, 1977), 13–19; T. Scott Miyakawa, *Protestants and Pioneers: Individualism and Conformity on the American Frontier* (Chicago: University of Chicago Press, 1964), esp. 213–40.

8. William G. McLoughlin, *Revivals, Awakenings, and Reform* (Chicago: University of Chicago Press, 1978), 98–140; Joseph F. Kett, *Rights of Passage: Adolescence in America, 1790 to the Present* (New York: Basic Books, 1979), 64–79; Richard D. Shiels, "The Feminization of American Congregationalism, 1730–1835," *American Quarterly* 33 (Spring 1981):46–62.

9. May, *Enlightenment in America*, 329–31; Paul Goodman, *Towards a Christian Republic: Antimasonry and the Great Transition in New England, 1826–1836*, (New York: Oxford University Press, 1988), 30–31; Richard M. Rollins, *The Long Journey of Noah Webster* (Philadelphia: University of Pennsylvania Press, 1980), 109, 113, 119.

10. Timothy L. Smith, *Revivalism and Social Reform* (New York: Abingdon Press, 1958), 22.

11. Cartwright quoted in McLoughlin, *Revivals, Awakenings, and Reform*, 135; Nathan O. Hatch, *The Democratization of American Christianity* (New Haven: Yale University Press, 1989), 3–16, 133–61, 102–13, 68–81.

12. Boles, *The Great Revival*, 186–88; Donald G. Mathews, "The Second Great Awakening as an Organizing Process, 1780–1830: An Hypothesis," *American Quarterly* 21 (Spring 1969):23–43.

13. Daniel Walker Howe, *The Unitarian Conscience: Harvard Moral Philosophy, 1805–61* (Cambridge: Harvard University Press, 1970), 215–16; Joseph Haroutunian, *Piety versus Moralism: The Passing of New England Theology* (New York: Henry Holt & Co., 1932), 183–219.

14. Conrad Cherry, *Nature and Religious Imagination: From Edwards to Bushnell* (Philadelphia: Fortress Press, 1980), 139–40; Jared Sparks in Sidney E. Ahlstrom and Jonathan S. Carey eds., *An American Reformation: A Documentary History of Unitarian Christianity* (Middletown, Conn.: Wesleyan University Press, 1985), 337.

15. Woods quoted in Haroutunian, *Piety versus Moralism*, 215.

16. *The Autobiography of Lyman Beecher*, ed. Barbara M. Cross (Cambridge: Belknap, Harvard University Press, 1961), 2:81–82; Howe, *Unitarian Conscience*, 220–21, 172–73, 355 n. 75.

17. Howe, *Unitarian Conscience*, 152–57; Joanna Bowen Gillespie, "'The Clear Leadings of Providence': Pious Memoirs and the Problems of Self-Realization for Women in the Early Nineteenth Century," *Journal of the Early Republic* 5 (Summer 1985):214.

18. Sidney E. Mead, *Nathaniel William Taylor, 1786–1858: A Connecticut Liberal* (Chicago: University of Chicago Press, 1942), 125–27; Cherry, *Nature and Religious Imagination*, 66–69.

19. Stephen E. Berk, *Calvinism versus Democracy: Timothy Dwight and the Origins of American Evangelical Orthodoxy* (Hamden, Conn.: Archon Books, 1974), 74–105.

20. Mead, *Taylor*, 100–127; Bruce Kuklick, *Churchmen and Philosophers: From Jonathan Edwards to John Dewey* (New Haven: Yale University Press, 1985), 94–105; Nathaniel William Taylor, "Concio ad Clerum" (1828), in Sidney E. Ahlstrom, ed., *Theology in America: The Major Protestant Voices from Puritanism to Neo-Orthodoxy* (Indianapolis: Bobbs-Merrill, 1967), 217, 219, 229, 241.

21. Leonard Woods, quoted in Haroutunian, *Piety versus Moralism*, 271; McLoughlin, *Revivals, Awakenings, and Reform*, 113–22.

22. Conrad Cherry, "Nature and the Republic: The New Haven Theology," *New England Quarterly* 51 (December 1978):509–26; Mead, *Taylor*, 158–62.

23. *Quarterly Register and Journal of American Education Society* 1 (April 1829):212–13; Gordon S. Wood, "Evangelical America and Early Mormonism," *New York History* 61 (1980):380.

24. Andrews Norton, *Tracts Concerning Christianity* (Cambridge, Mass.: John Bartlett, 1852), 69.

25. E. S. Gaustad, "Religion," in Merrill D. Peterson ed., *Thomas Jefferson: A Reference Biography* (New York: Scribners, 1986), 277–93; Eugene R. Sheridan, Introduction to Dickinson W. Adams, ed., *Jefferson's Extracts from the Gospels* (Princeton: Princeton University Press, 1983), 3–42.

26. Moses Stuart, *Miscellanies* (Andover 1846), 10–11, 76–79, 183–7; Jerry Wayne Brown, *The Rise of Biblical Criticism in America, 1800–1870* (Middleton, Conn.: Wesleyan University Press, 1969).

27. May, *Enlightenment in America*, 342–50.

28. Mark A. Noll, "Common Sense Traditions and American Evangelical Thought," *American Quarterly* 37 (Summer 1985):216–238; Douglas Sloan, *The Scottish Enlightenment and the American College Ideal* (New York: Teachers College Press, 1971), 153–56; Merle Curti, *Human Nature in American Thought: A History* (Madison: University of Wisconsin Press, 1980), 129–41; [Samuel Gilman], "Cause and Effect," *North American Review* 12 (April 1821):423.

29. May, *Enlightenment in America*, 342–50; Sloan, *Scottish Enlightenment*, 225–30; Josef Brozek, "The Origins of American Academic Psychology," in *Explorations in*

the History of Psychology in the United States (Lewisburg, Penn.: Bucknell University Press, 1984), 37.

30. Cappon, ed., *Adams-Jefferson Letters*, 2:492.

31. Elwyn A. Smith, *The Religion of the Republic* (Philadelphia: Fortress Press, 1971), 154–82; Miller, *Life of the Mind*, 59–66.

32. Donald M. Scott, *From Office to Profession: The New England Ministry, 1750–1850* (Philadelphia: University of Pennsylvania Press 1978), 55–57; Hatch, *Democratization of American Christianity*, 141–46. Beecher quoted in Peter Dobkin Hall, *The Organization of American Culture, 1700–1900* (New York: New York University Press, 1984), 88.

33. Charles I. Foster, *An Errand of Mercy: The Evangelical United Front, 1790–1837* (Chapel Hill: University of North Carolina Press, 1960), 105–8, 121, 156–78, 187–88, 224; Clifford S. Griffin, *Their Brothers' Keepers: Moral Stewardship in the United States* (New Brunswick, N.J.: Rutgers University Press, 1960), 8–9, 27–39, 65. Beecher quoted in Sidney E. Mead, *The Old Religion in the Brave New World* (Berkeley: University of California Press, 1977), 177.

34. Paul Boyer, *Urban Masses and Moral Order in America, 1820–1920* (Cambridge: Harvard University Press, 1978) 5–16, 61–64; Gregory H. Singleton, "Protestant Voluntary Organizations and the Shaping of Victorian America," *American Quarterly* 27 (1975):549–60, esp. 552–53.

35. Daniel Walker Howe, "Victorian Culture in America," in Howe, ed., *Victorian America* (Philadelphia: University of Pennsylvania Press, 1976), 3–28.

36. John G. Palfrey, "Discourses on Intemperance," reviewed in *United States Review and Literary Gazette* 2 (June 1827):184–200. Adams to Rush, February 2, 1807, in *Spur of Fame*, 75–76; Scott, *From Office*, 40–42.

37. Clement Eaton, *The Freedom of Thought Struggle in the Old South* (New York: Harper & Row, 1964), 302–9; Niels Henry Sonne, *Liberal Kentucky, 1780–1828* (New York: Columbia University Press, 1939), 188–250.

38. Miyakawa, *Protestants and Pioneers*, 130–44; Lawrence Buell, *Literary Transcendentalism: Style and Vision in the American Renaissance* (Ithaca: Cornell University Press, 1973), 27–30; Boles, *Great Revival*, 190; Tocqueville, *Democracy in America*, 1:292.

39. Winthrop S. Hudson, *Religion in America* (New York: Scribner, 1965), 129; Mathews, "Second Great Awakening," 39–43.

40. Kathleen Smith Kutolowski, "Freemasonry and Community in the Early Republic: The Case for Antimasonic Anxieties," *American Quarterly* 34 (Winter 1982):543–61; Dorothy Ann Lipson, *Freemasonry in Federalist Connecticut* (Princeton: Princeton University Press, 1977), 116–27, 140–45, 188–200, 228–66; Goodman, *Towards a Christian Republic*, 12–17, 34–53.

41. William Warren Sweet, *The Story of Religion in America* (New York: Harper & Row, 1950):257; Bertram Wyatt-Brown, "The Antimission Movement in the Jacksonian South: A Study in Regional Folk Culture," *Journal of Southern History* 36 (November 1970):501–29; Ezra Stiles Ely, "The Duty of Christian Freemen to Elect Christian Rulers" (1828), in Joseph L. Blau, ed., *American Philosophic Addresses, 1700–1900* (New York: Columbia University Press, 1946), 558, 562.

42. Bertram Wyatt-Brown, "Prelude to Abolitionism: Sabbatarian Politics and the Rise of the Second Party System," *Journal of American History* 58 (September

1971):316–41; James R. Rohrer, "Sunday Mails and the Church-State Theme in Jacksonian America," *Journal of the Early Republic* 7 (Spring 1987):53–74.

43. H. Frank Way, "Death of the Christian Nation: The Judiciary and Church-State Relations," *Journal of Church and State* 29 (Autumn 1987):509–29.

44. Fred J. Hood, *Reformed America: The Middle and Southern States, 1783–1837* (University: University of Alabama Press, 1980), 68–86; J. F. Maclear, "The Republic and the Millennium," in Smith, ed., *Religion of the Republic*, 183–20.

45. Maclear, "Republic and the Millennium," 198–200. Beecher quoted in David Morse, *American Romanticism* (New York: Macmillan, 1987), 1:23.

46. Hood, *Reformed America*, 73; William R. Hutchison, *Errand to the World: American Protestant Thought and Foreign Missions* (Chicago: University of Chicago Press, 1987), 43–61.

Chapter Three

I have used the word *culture* in this chapter in a way that is both old-fashioned and anachronistic—old-fashioned in that I use it to designate "high" culture, what Matthew Arnold in the nineteenth century called "the best that has been thought and said in the world"; anachronistic because the term was not current in the early nineteenth century. It does, however, serve as a convenient shorthand for a complex of intellectual and artistic activities that people saw as crucial to high civilization.

1. Charles Brockden Brown, Preface to *The American Review and Literary Journal* (1801), in Robert E. Spiller, ed., *The American Literary Revolution, 1783–1837* (Garden City, N.Y.: Doubleday, 1967), 34; Von Frank, *The Sacred Game*, 4.

2. Benjamin T. Spencer, *The Quest for Nationality: An American Literary Campaign* (Syracuse: Syracuse University Press, 1957), 22–24.

3. Thomas Bender, *New York Intellect: A History of Intellectual Life in New York City from 1750 to the Beginnings of Our Own Time* (New York: Alfred A. Knopf, 1987), 42–45.

4. Samuel Miller, *A Brief Retrospect of the Eighteenth Century . . .* (New York: Burt Franklin, 1970), 2:409; Ralph Waldo Emerson, *The Journals and Miscellaneous Notebooks*, ed. William H. Gilman et al. (Cambridge: Harvard University Press, 1960–82), 13:115; William Cullen Bryant, in Richard Rutland ed., *The Native Muse: Theories of American Literature* (New York: Dutton, 1972), 1:148–49.

5. Martin Green, "The God That Neglected to Come: American Literature 1780–1820," in Marcus Cunliffe, ed., *History of Literature in the English Language*, vol. 8: *American Literature to 1900* (London: Barrie and Jenkins, 1973), 72–104.

6. Wood, "The Democratization of Mind," 121; Merle Curti, *The Growth of American Thought* (New York: Harper & Row, 1964), 217; Cunningham, *United States in 1800*, 19–21; Miller, *Brief Retrospect*, 2:252.

7. William J. Gilmore, "Elementary Literacy in Rural New England," *American Antiquarian Society Proceedings* 92, pt. 1 (1982):87–178; Joseph F. Kett and Patricia A. McClung, "Book Culture in Post-Revolutionary Virginia," *American Antiquarian Society Proceedings* 94 (1984):97–200. Richard Beale Davis, *Intellectual Life in Jefferson's Virginia, 1790–1830* (Knoxville: University of Tennessee Press, 1972), 84–118.

8. Curti, *Growth of American Thought*, 258–62; Ralph Leslie Rusk, *The Literature of the Middle Western Frontier* (New York: Columbia University Press, 1925), 1:72.

9. William Charvat, *The Profession of Authorship in America, 1800–1870*, ed. Matthew J. Bruccoli (Columbus: Ohio State University Press, 1968).

10. Richard B. Kielbnowicz, "The Press, Post Office, and Flow of News in the Early Republic," *Journal of the Early Republic* 3 (Fall 1983):255–80.

11. Terence Martin, *The Instructed Vision: Scottish Common Sense Philosophy and the Origins of American Fiction* (Bloomington: Indiana University Press, 1961), 60–103; Cathy Davidson, *Revolution and the Word: The Rise of the Novel in America* (New York: Oxford University Press, 1986), and "Ideology and Genre: The Rise of the Novel in America," *Proceedings, American Antiquarian Society* 96, pt. 2 (October 1986):295–321.

12. Van Wyck Brooks, *The World of Washington Irving* (London: J. M. Dent & Sons, 1947), chaps. 1–4; William Charvat, *The Origins of American Critical Thought, 1810–1835* (New York: A. S. Barnes & Co., 1961), 5; Curti, *Growth of American Thought*, 213–32; Samuel Goodrich, *Recollections of a Lifetime* (New York: Miller, Orton and Mulligan, 1856), 2:100; Davis, *Intellectual Life*, 73–118; David Lundberg and Henry May, "The Enlightened Reader in America," *American Quarterly* 28 (Summer 1976):262–71.

13. Ferguson, *Law and Letters in American Culture*, 5; Bender, *New York Intellect*, 9–78.

14. M. F. Heiser, "Decline of Neoclassicism 1801–48," in Harry Hayden Clark, ed., *Transitions in American Literary History* (Durham, N.C.: Duke University Press, 1953), 94–98.

15. Emory Elliott, *Revolutionary Writers: Literature and Authority in the New Republic, 1725–1810* (New York: Oxford University Press, 1982), 112–13; Cecelia Tichi, *New World, New Earth: Environmental Reform in American Literature from the Puritans through Whitman* (New Haven: Yale University Press, 1979), 150.

16. "Edinburgh Review" (1809) in Rutland, *Native Muse*, 72–73.

17. Washington Irving, *A History of New York* (1809), (Library of America edition, 1983), 535–56; Ferguson, *Law and Letters*, 150–69.

18. Brackenridge, *Modern Chivalry*, pt. II, vol. 1 (1804), 401; John C. Greene, *American Science in the Age of Jefferson* (Ames: Iowa State University Press, 1984), 8–9, 21; George H. Daniels, *Science in American Society: A Social History* (New York. Alfred A. Knopf, 1971), 129–30.

19. Brackenridge, *Modern Chivalry*, 447.

20. William B. Cairns, *British Criticisms of American Writings, 1783–1815* (Madison: University of Wisconsin, 1918), 36, 71; Smith quoted in Cairns, *British Criticism of American Writings, 1815–1833* (Madison: University of Wisconsin, 1922), 11.

21. Larry J. Reynolds, *James Kirke Paulding* (Boston: Twayne Publishers, 1984), 41–46; John C. Greene, "American Science Comes of Age," *Journal of American History* 55 (June 1968):22–41.

22. Representative arguments can be found in: Miller, *Brief Retrospect*, 2:404–9; John Bristed, *America and Her Resources* (1818) (New York: Research Reprints, 1970), 310–21; Joseph Dennie in the *Portfolio* (1807) in Edwin H. Cady, *Literature of the Early Republic* (New York: Holt, Rinehart and Winston, 1965), 482; and Joseph Hopkinson, in Wood, *Rising Glory of America*, 318–34.

23. Tudor (1810) quoted in Lewis P. Simpson, *The Man of Letters in New England and the South* (Baton Rouge: Louisiana State University Press 1973), 55; [Edward Everett] "University Education," *North American Review* (January 1820):133, 137.

24. Martin Green, *The Problem of Boston* (New York: W. W. Norton & Co., 1966), 60–66; Lillian Miller, *Patrons and Patriotism: The Encouragement of the Fine Arts n the United States, 1790–1860* (Chicago: University of Chicago Press, 1966), 145–55; Simon Baatz, "Philadelphia Patronage: The Institutional Structure of Natural History in the New Republic, 1800–1833," *Journal of the Early Republic* 8 (Summer 1988):111–38; Washington Irving, *Miscellaneous Writings, 1803–1859*, ed. Wayne R. Kime (Boston: Twayne Publishers, 1981), 52.

25. J. T. Kirkland, "Literary Institutions," *North American Review* 8 (December 1818), 197; Benjamin Latrobe: "Oration to the Society of Artists," Philadelphia, 8 May 1811, inserted in *Port Folio* 5, n.s. between issues for June and July 1811, p. 5; Howard Mumford Jones, *Ideas in America* (New York: Russell & Russell, 1965), 282.

26. Adams is quoted in Robert Spiller et al., *Literary History of the United States* (New York: Macmillan, 1948), 1:150; Joseph J. Ellis, *After the Revolution: Profiles of Early American Culture* (New York: W. W. Norton and Co., 1979), 29–38.

27. Richard Hofstadter, *Anti-intellectualism in American Life* (New York: Alfred A. Knopf 1963), 147–51, 154–61.

28. James Gilbreath, "American Book Distribution," *American Antiquarian Society Proceedings* 95 (October 1985):531–32.

29. Arthur Bestor, "Thomas Jefferson and the Freedom of Books," in *Three Presidents and Their Books* (Urbana: University of Illinois Press 1955), 2–3; Augustus John Foster, *Jeffersonian America* (San Marino, Calif.: Huntington Library, 1954), 156–57.

30. Ferguson, *Law and Letters*, 94.

31. Richard D. Brown, *Knowledge Is Power: The Diffusion of Information in Early America: 1700–1865* (New York: Oxford University Press, 1989), 197–217.

32. Ferguson, *Law and Letters*, 87–95; John Quincy Adams quoted in Benjamin T. Spencer, *The Quest for Nationality: An American Literary Campaign* (Syracuse, N.Y.: Syracuse University Press 1957), 65; St. George Tucker in Robert Colin McLean, *George Tucker, Moral Philosopher and Man of Letters* (Chapel Hill: University of North Carolina Press, 1961), 72.

33. Buckminster, in Lewis P. Simpson, ed., *The Federalist Literary Mind: Selections from the "Monthly Anthology and Boston Review," 1803–1811* (Baton Rouge: Louisiana State University Press 1962), 99, 101.

34. J. Meredith Neill, *Toward a National Taste: America's Quest for Aesthetic Independence* (Honolulu: University Press of Hawaii, 1975), 82; Miller, *Patrons and Patriotism*, 14, 18; Ronald Story, "Class and Culture in Boston: The Athenaeum, 1807–1860," *American Quarterly* 27 (May 1975):190; Ralph Leslie Rusk, *Literature of the Middle Western Frontier* (New York: Columbia University Press 1925), 2:434.

35. Bender, *New York Intellect*, 46–78.

36. Curti, *Growth of American Thought*, 250–81; Louis B. Wright, *Culture on the Moving Frontier* (Bloomington: Indiana University Press, 1955), 64–72, 116–17; John C. Greene, *American Science in the Age of Jefferson* (Ames: Iowa State University Press, 1984), 115–20.

37. Paul Goodman, "Ethics and Enterprise: The Values of a Boston Elite, 1800–1860," *American Quarterly* 18 (Fall 1966):437–52; Walter Muir Whitehill, "Early Learned Societies in Boston and Vicinity," in Alexandra Oleson and Sanborn C.

Brown, eds., *The Pursuit of Knowledge in the Early American Republic* (Baltimore: Johns Hopkins University Press 1976), 1:151–173.

38. Greene, *American Science in the Age of Jefferson*, 61, 112; Parke Godwin, ed., *Prose Writings of William Cullen Bryant* (New York: D. Appleton & Co., 1889), 1:45–46 (1818), and 305 note (1825).

39. Frank Luther Mott, *A History of American Magazines* (New York: D. Appleton & Co., 1930), 200, 223–46; Randolph C. Randall, "Joseph Dennie's literary Attitudes in the *Port Folio*, 1801–1812," in James Woodress, ed., *Essays Mostly on Periodical Publishing in America* (Durham, N.C.: Duke University Press 1973), 66.

40. Edward E. Chielens, *American Literary Magazines: The 18th and 19th Centuries* (Westport, Conn.: Greenwood Press, 1986), 289–300.

41. Charvat, *Origins of American Critical Thought*, 7–26; Lewis P. Simpson, "Federalism and the Crisis of Literary Order," *American Literature* 32 (November 1960):253, 260, 263; [Tudor], *North American Review* 3 (September 1816):355.

42. Daniel J. Boorstin, *The Americans*, vol. 2: *The National Experience* (New York: Random House, 1965), 281–89.

43. Dennis E. Baron, *Grammar and Good Taste: Reforming the American Language* (New Haven: Yale University Press, 1982), 101–12.

44. Baron, *Grammar and Good Taste*, 35, 42–53.

45. David Simpson, *The Politics of American English, 1776–1850* (New York: Oxford University Press 1986), 42; *The General Repository and Review* 4 (July 1813):174; "Marsh's Address," *North American Review* 24 (April 1827):473.

46. Baron, *Grammar and Good Taste*, 54–55; Richard M. Rollins, *The Long Journey of Noah Webster* (Philadelphia: University of Pennsylvania Press 1980), 125–38.

47. Jeffrey quoted in Jeffrey Rubin-Dorsky, "A Crisis of Identity: *The Sketch Book* and Nineteenth-Century American Culture," in Jack Salzman, ed., *Prospects* (Cambridge: Cambridge University Press, 1987), 12:255; Niles is quoted in James D. Wallace, *Early Cooper and His Audience* (New York: Columbia University Press, 1986), 174.

48. Charvat, *Profession of Authorship in America*, 68–83.

49. George H. Daniels, *American Science in the Age of Jackson* (New York: Columbia University Press, 1966), 13–15, 32–33.

50. John C. Greene, "Science, Learning, and Utility: Patterns of Organization in the Early American Republic," in Oleson and Brown, *Pursuit of Knowledge*, 19; Bender, *New York Intellect*, 75; A. Hunter Dupree, "The National Pattern of American Learned Societies, 1769–1863," in Oleson, *Pursuit of Knowledge*, 21–32.

Chapter Four

1. Daniel N. Robinson, *Towards a Science of Human Nature* (New York: Columbia University Press, 1982), 5–30.

2. Curti, *Human Nature*, 89–91; Benjamin Rush, "The Progress of Medicine" (1801), in Dagobert D. Runes, ed., *Selected Writings of Benjamin Rush* (New York: Philosophical Library, 1947), 236–37; Rush to Adams, November 4, 1812, in L. H. Butterfield, ed., *Letters of Benjamin Rush* (Princeton: Princeton University Press, 1951), 2:1164.

3. Mary Ann Jimenez, *The Medical Face of Madness* (Hanover, N.H.: University Press of New England, 1987), 73.

4. Eric T. Carlson, Jeffrey L. Wollock, and Patricia S. Noel, eds., *Benjamin Rush's Lectures on the Mind* (Philadelphia: American Philosophical Society, 1981), 419.

5. Joseph Buchanan, *The Philosophy of Human Nature* (1812) (Gainesville, Fla.: Scholars' Facsimiles and Reprints, 1969), 3, 6, 20; Cappon, ed., *Adams-Jefferson Letters*, 2:515–17; Sonne, *Liberal Kentucky*, 78–107.

6. Jefferson to Adams, 8 January 1825, 15 August 1820, in Cappon, *Adams-Jefferson Letters*, 2:605–6, 568–69.

7. Edwin G. Boring, *A History of Experimental Psychology*, 2d ed. (New York: Appleton-Century-Crofts, 1950), 50–60.

8. Ralph W. Emerson, "Life and Letters in New England," in *Complete Works* (Boston: Houghton Mifflin, 1904), 10:325–26.

9. Nye, *Cultural Life of the New Nation*, 6–9, 248; Curti, *Human Nature*, 148–53. Howard Mumford Jones, *Ideas in America* (New York: Russell & Russell, 1965).

10. Peter Gregg Slater, *Children in the New England Mind in Death and in Life* (Hamden, Conn.: Archon Books, 1977), esp. 73, 111, 162–65; Jan Lewis, *The Pursuit of Happiness: Family and Values in Jefferson's Virginia* (Cambridge: Cambridge University Press, 1983), 210–17; "One's Self" (anon.) *Monthly Anthology* 4 (October 1807):543; James Hoopes, *Consciousness in New England* (Baltimore: Johns Hopkins University Press, 1989), 164–65.

11. Curti, *Human Nature*, 71–72, 148–51.

12. James Marsh, "Preliminary Essay" (1829) to Coleridge's *Aids to Reflection* (reprint ed., New York: Chelsea House, 1983), liii.

13. John William Ward, *Andrew Jackson: Symbol for an Age* (London: Oxford University Press, 1980), 153–85.

14. John Todd, *The Story of His Life: Told Mainly by Himself*, comp. and ed. John E. Todd (New York: Harper & Brothers, 1876), 113.

15. Ward, *Andrew Jackson*, 170; Kett, *Rites of Passage*, 105–8; Lewis, *Pursuit of Happiness*, 153.

16. Cass quoted in Robert E. Bieder, *Science Encounters the Indian, 1820–1880: The Early Years of American Ethnology* (Norman: University of Oklahoma Press, 1986), 152. This remark occurs in a discussion of the Indians, whose problem was that they did not operate in this way.

17. Miller, *Brief Retrospect*, 2:280, 179–91; May, *Enlightenment in America*, 225; Lawrence J. Friedman, *Inventors of the Promised Land* (New York: Alfred A. Knopf, 1975), 107–44.

18. Linda Kerber, *Women of the Republic: Intellect and Ideology in Revolutionary America* (Chapel Hill: University of North Carolina Press, 1980), 193; Miller, *Brief Retrospect*, 2:280; Brown and Adams quoted in Janet Wilson James, *Changing Ideas about Women in the United States, 1776–1825* (New York: Garland, 1981), 206, 271.

19. Theodore Dwight, Jr., *President's Dwight's Decisions of Questions Discussed by the Senior Class in Yale College in 1813 and 1814* (New York: West & Trow, 1833), 41–43; Carl F. Kaestle, *Pillars of the Republic: Common Schools and American Society, 1780–1860* (New York: Hill & Wang, 1983), 27–28; Emma Willard, in Charles L. Sanford, ed., *Quest for America, 1810–1824* (Garden City, N.Y.: Anchor Books, 1964), 290.

20. Ruth H. Bloch, "American Feminine Ideals in Transition: The Rise of the Moral Mother, 1785–1815," *Feminist Studies* 4 (1978):101–26, and "The Gendered Meanings of Virtue in Revolutionary America," *Signs* 13 (Autumn 1987):37–58; Jan

Lewis, "The Republican Wife: Virtue and Seduction in the Early Republic," *William and Mary Quarterly* 44 (October 1987):689–721.

21. Nancy F. Cott, *The Bonds of Womanhood: "Woman's Sphere" in New England, 1780–1835* (New Haven: Yale University Press, 1977), 99; Tocqueville, *Democracy in America*, 600–603.

22. Richard H. Popkin, "Pre-Adamism in 19th Century American Thought: 'Speculative Biology' and Racism," *Philosophia* 8 (November 1978):212–14.

23. Charles A. Miller, *Jefferson and Nature: An Interpretation* (Baltimore: Johns Hopkins University Press, 1988), 66–75, quotations from Jefferson's *Notes*, p. 72; Winthrop D. Jordan, *White over Black, American Attitudes toward the Negro, 1550–1812* New York: W. W. Norton & Co., 1977, 429–81; John P. Diggins, "Slavery, Race, and Equality: Jefferson and the Pathos of the Enlightenment," *American Quarterly* 28 (Summer 1976):206–28.

24. Samuel Stanhope Smith, *An Essay on the Causes of the Variety of Complexion and Figure in the Human Species* (1810), (Cambridge, Mass.: Belknap Press of Harvard University Press, 1965), 163–64.

25. Jordan, *White over Black*, 518–25.

26. Greene, *American Science in the Age of Jefferson*, 320–342; William Stanton, *The Leopard's Spots: Scientific Attitudes towards Race in America, 1815–59* (Chicago: University of Chicago Press, 1960), 1–23; Herbert Hovenkamp, *Science and Religion in America, 1800–1860* (Philadelphia: University of Pennsylvania Press, 1978), 166–68.

27. Archibald Alexander (1829) in Mark A. Noll, ed., *The Princeton Theology, 1812–1921* (Grand Rapids, Mich.: Baker Book House, 1983), 102; Jordan, *White over Black*, 509.

28. Ruth Miller Elson, *Guardians of Tradition: American Schoolbooks of the Nineteenth Century* (Lincoln: University of Nebraska Press, 1964), 88–92; William J. Mahar, "Black English in Early Blackface Minstrelsy: A New Interpretation of the Sources of Minstrel Show Dialect," *American Quarterly* 37 (Summer 1985):260–85.

29. Richard Hofstadter, *The American Political Tradition* (New York: Alfred A. Knopf, 1949), 25–26; Jack P. Greene, *All Men Are Created Equal* (Oxford: Clarendon Press 1976), esp. 30–33.

30. David Brion Davis, *The Problem of Slavery in the Age of Revolution* (Ithaca: Cornell University Press, 1975), 336.

31. Larry E. Tise, *Proslavery: A History of the Defense of Slavery in America, 1701–1840* (Athens: University of Georgia Press 1987), 43–50.

32. Jordan, *White over Black*, 574–82; Leonard P. Curry, *The Free Black in Urban America, 1800–1850* (Chicago: University of Chicago Press, 1981), 174–81.

33. Charles H. Wesley, "Negro Suffrage in the Period of Constitution-Making, 1787–1865," *Journal of Negro History* 32 (April 1947):143–68; Merrill D. Peterson, ed., *Democracy, Liberty, and Property: The State Constitutional Conventions of the 1820s* (Indianapolis: Bobbs-Merrill, 1966), 226–29; Robert Walsh, Jr., *An Appeal from the Judgments of Great Britain Respecting the United States of America*, 2d ed. (1819) (New York: Negro Universities Press, 1969), 392.

34. Jared Sparks, *North American Review* 18 (January 1824):59–60.

35. Marie Tyler McGraw, "Richmond Free Blacks and African Colonization, 1816–1832," *Journal of American Studies* 21 (August 1987):207–24; Lawrence J. Friedman, *Inventors of the Promised Land* (New York: Alfred A. Knopf, 1975), 180–254.

'36. "Protest from Black Philadelphia" (1817) in David Brion Davis, *Antebellum American Culture* (Lexington, Mass.: D. C. Heath, 1979), 284; Gary B. Nash, *Forging Freedom: The Formation of Philadelphia's Black Community, 1720–1840* (Cambridge: Harvard University Press, 1988), 180–83.

37. David Walker, *An Appeal to the Colored Citizens of the World* (1829), in Herbert Aptheker, *"One Continual Cry"* (New York: Humanities Press, 1965), 54, 90–91, 143.

38. Madison quoted in Richard Drinnon, *Facing West: The Metaphysics of Indian Hating and Empire Building* (Minneapolis: University of Minnesota Press, 1980), 182.

39. Smith quoted in Greene, *American Science in the Age of Jefferson*, 323–24; Roy Harvey Pearce, *The Savages of America*, rev. ed. (Baltimore: Johns Hopkins Press, 1965), 106–13; James P. Rhonda, "Lewis and Clark and Enlightenment Ethnography," in William F. Willingham and Leonore S. Ingraham, *Enlightenment Science in the Pacific North West* (Portland, Ore.: Lewis and Clark College, 1984), 5–17.

40. Greene, *American Science in the Age of Jefferson*, 343–75.

41. Bernard W. Sheehan, *Seeds of Extinction: Jeffersonian Philanthropy and the American Indian* (Chapel Hill: University of North Carolina Press, 1973), 45–65; Greene, *American Science in the Age of Jefferson*, 376–408.

42. Sheehan, *Seeds of Extinction*, 137–39; William G. McLoughlin, *Cherokee Renascence in the New Republic* (Princeton: Princeton University Press, 1987), 351.

43. Gary B. Nash, "The Image of the Indian in the Southern Colonial Mind," in *Race, Class, and Politics: Essays on American Colonial and Revolutionary Society* (Urbana: University of Illinois Press, 1986), 55–57; Jordan, *White over Black*, 475–81 (Jefferson quoted on p. 479).

44. Miller, *Jefferson and Nature*, 65; Crawford is quoted in McLoughlin, *Cherokee Renascence*, 213; Annette Kolodny, *The Land before Her: Fantasy and Experience of the American Frontiers, 1630–1860* (Chapel Hill: University of North Carolina Press, 1984), 70–81.

45. Pearce, *Savages of America*, 82–91.

46. Sheehan, *Seeds of Extinction*, 1–12; Adams in Drinnon, *Facing West*, 113.

47. *North American Review* (1823) quoted in Sheehan, *Seeds of Extinction*, 177–78.

48. William G. McLoughlin and Walter H. Conser, Jr., "'The First Man Was Red'—Cherokee Responses to the Debate over Indian Origins, 1760–1860," *American Quarterly* 41 (June 1989):258.

49. Sheehan, *Seeds of Extinction*, 243–75.

50. Joseph Story, *Miscellaneous Writings* (Boston: James Munroe and Co. 1835), 34–87.

51. Ruth Miller Elson, *Guardians of Tradition*, 79; William Cullen Bryant, "The Disinterred Warrior," *United States Review and Literary Gazette* 2 (August 1827): 386–87.

52. G. Harrison Orians, "The Romance Ferment after Waverley," *American Literature* 3 (January 1932):418; Werner Sollors, *Beyond Ethnicity: Consent and Descent in American Culture* (New York: Oxford University Press, 1986), 104–29.

53. Richard Slotkin, *The Fatal Environment: The Myth of the Frontier in the Age of Industrialization, 1800–1890* (Middletown, Conn.: Wesleyan University Press, 1985), 81–106.

54. George Sand in George Dekker and John P. McWilliams, *Fenimore Cooper: The Critical Heritage* (London and Boston: Routledge & Kegan Paul, 1973) 267–68.

55. James Fenimore Cooper, *The Last of the Mohicans* (New York: New American Library, 1962), 36.

56. Catlin quoted in Lee Clark Mitchell, *Witnesses to a Vanishing America: The Nineteenth Century Response* (Princeton: Princeton University Press, 1981), 98.

57. De Witt Clinton, in William C. Campbell, ed., *The Life and Writings of De Witt Clinton* (New York, 1849), 252; Andrew Jackson, "Second Annual Message," 6 December 1830, in James D. Richardson, *A Compilation of the Messages and Papers of the Presidents* (New York: Bureau of National Literature, n.d.), 3:1082–85.

Chapter Five

1. Edward Everett, "Long's Expedition," *North American Review* 16 (April 1823):268.

2. Jefferson quoted in Gerald Holton, "Jefferson, Science, and National Destiny," in Leslie Berlowitz, ed., *America in Theory* (New York: Oxford University Press, 1989), 155.

3. John Logan Allen, *Passage through the Garden: Lewis and Clark and the Image of the American Northwest* (Urbana: University of Illinois Press, 1975), 375–94 (Barlow quoted on 370); Wayne Franklin, *Discoverers, Explorers, Settlers: The Diligent Writers of Early America* (Chicago: University of Chicago Press, 1979), 71.

4. Robert Lawson-Peebles, *Landscape and Written Expression in Revolutionary America: The World Turned Upside Down* (Cambridge: Cambridge University Press, 1988), 206, Lewis quoted on 214.

5. Greene, *American Science in the Age of Jefferson*, 195–217. For Lewis's inner conflicts and probable suicide, see Howard Kushner, "The Suicide of Meriwether Lewis: A Psychoanalytic Inquiry," *William and Mary Quarterly* 38 (July 1981):464–81.

6. Lawson-Peebles, *Landscape and Written Expression*, 223–26; Greene, *American Science*, 213–15; William Goetzmann, *New Lands, New Men: America and the Second Great Age of Discovery* (New York: Viking Penguin, 1986), 119–124; Arrell Morgan Gibson, "The West as Region," *Journal of American Culture* 3 (Summer 1980):285–301; Jacob Bigelow, "Nuttall's Journal," *North American Review* 16 (January 1823):59.

7. Myra Jehlen, *American Incarnation: The Individual, the Nation and the Continent* (Cambridge: Harvard University Press, 1986), 50–57; Lawrence J. Friedman and Arthur H. Shaffer, "History, Politics, and Health in Early American Thought: The Case of David Ramsay," *Journal of American Studies* 13 (April 1979):35–56; Frank N. Egerton, "Ecological Studies and Observations before 1900," in Benjamin J. Taylor and Thurman J. White, eds., *Issues and Ideas in America* (Norman: University of Oklahoma Press, 1976), 328.

8. Egerton, "Ecological Studies," 331; *The Portico*, in Nathan Reingold, ed., *Science in Nineteenth Century America* (New York: Hill and Wang, 1964), 29–30.

9. Greene, *American Science*, 253–76, Elliott quoted 271–72.

10. Charlotte M. Porter, *The Eagle's Nest: Natural History and American Ideas* (University: University of Alabama Press, 1986), 48; Greene, *American Science in the Age of Jefferson*, 301–5.

11. Sidney Hart, "'To encrease the comforts of Life': Charles Willson Peale and the Mechanical Arts," *Pennsylvania Magazine of History and Biography* 110 (1986):323–57; Charles Coleman Sellers, *Mr. Peale's Museum: Charles Willson Peale and the First*

Popular Museum of Natural Science and Art (New York: W. W. Norton & Co., 1980), 148; Ellis, *After the Revolution:* 41–71.

12. Marcus B. Simpson, Jr., and Donald Steven McAllister, "Alexander Wilson's Southern Tour of 1809," *North Carolina Historical Review* 63 (October 1986): 421–476.

13. Alexander Wilson, "Proposals for American Ornithology," quoted in ibid., 433.

14. Ibid., 533; S. Willard, "Philosophy of Natural History," *North American Review* 19 (October 1824):405.

15. Timothy Dwight, *Travels in New England and New York*, ed. Barbara M. Solomon (Cambridge: Belknap Press of Harvard University Press, 1969), 2:300–301; Channing, *Memoir of William Ellery Channing and Extracts from his Correspondence and Manuscripts* (Boston: William Crosly and H. P. Nichols, 1848), 205.

16. Greene, *American Science in the Age of Jefferson*, 282–91.

17. Daniel Boorstin, *The Lost World of Thomas Jefferson* (Chicago: University of Chicago Press, 1981), 36; Miller, *Jefferson and Nature*, 55; Barton quoted in Greene, *American Science in the Age of Jefferson*, 288.

18. Daniels, *Science in American Society*, 208–9; Miller, *Jefferson and Nature*, 46–50.

19. Albert Furtwangler, *American Silhouettes: Rhetorical Identities of the Founders* (New Haven: Yale University Press 1987), 117 ("Jefferson's Trinity"); Theodore Dwight Bozeman, *Protestants in an Age of Science: The Baconian Ideal and Antebellum American Religious Thought* (Chapel Hill: University of North Carolina Press 1977), 3–62, Barlow quoted on 24; Chandos Michael Brown, *Benjamin Silliman: A Life in the Young Republic* (New Jersey: Princeton University Press, 1989), 203; Daniels, *American Science in the Age of Jackson*, 66.

20. Nathan Reingold, *Science in Nineteenth Century America*. (New York: Hill and Wang, 1964), 4; Hovenkamp, *Science and Religion*, 119–29; Conrad Wright, "The Religion of Geology," in Wilson Smith ed., *Essays in American Intellectual History* (Hinsdale, Ill.: Dryden Press, 1975), 253–63.

21. Hovenkamp, *Science and Religion*, 132–40; James Fenimore Cooper, *The Prairie* (Albany: State University of New York Press, 1985), 3–4.

22. Channing quoted in Andrew DelBanco, *William Ellery Channing: an essay on the Liberal Spirit in America* (Cambridge: Harvard University Press, 1981), 36; Hovenkamp, *Science and Religion*, 144–45.

23. Donald A. Ringe, *The Pictorial Mode: Space and Time in the Art of Bryant, Irving and Cooper* (Lexington: University Press of Kentucky, 1971), 6–8; Elizabeth McKinsey, *Niagara Falls: Icon of the American Sublime* (Cambridge: Cambridge University Press, 1985), 32–33, 57–61.

24. [Walter Channing], "American Medical Botany," *North American Review* 6 (March 1818):345; Richard Ray (1825), quoted in Howard S. Merritt, Introduction to catalog, *Thomas Cole, 1801–1848* (Rochester: University of Rochester, 1969), 11.

25. McKinsey, *Niagara Falls*, 64–85.

26. Matthew Baigell, *Thomas Cole* (New York: Watson-Guptill Publications, 1981), 10; Miller, *Patrons and Patriotism*, 150–51; Cole quoted in Ringe, *Pictorial Mode*, 14; Bryan Jay Wolf, *Romantic Re-Vision: Culture and Consciousness in Nineteenth-Century American Painting and Literature* (Chicago: University of Chicago Press, 1982), 244–45.

27. Nye, *Cultural Life of the New Nation*, 7–17; Ringe, *Pictorial Mode*, 222–23;

Bryant, preface to *The American Landscape* (1830), quoted in Merritt, *Thomas Cole*, 14.

28. Bryant, "Lectures on Poetry" (1825) in *Prose Writings of William Cullen Bryant*, ed. Parke Godwin (New York: Russell and Russell, 1964), I: 19.; Albert F. McLean, Jr., *William Cullen Bryant* (New York: Twayne Publishers, 1964), 28–31, 56–60; William Cullen Bryant, *Poems* (New York: D. Appleton & Co., 1871), 28, 26, 30, 88.

29. Henry Nash Smith, *Virgin Land: The American West as Symbol and Myth* (New York: Vintage Books, 1957), 56–63; Richard Slotkin, *Regeneration through Violence: The Mythology of the American Frontier, 1600–1860* (Middletown, Conn.: Wesleyan University Press, 1973), 348–53.

30. Smith, *Virgin Land*, 64–69.

31. John William Ward, *Andrew Jackson: Symbol for an Age* (London: Oxford University Press, 1955), 13–79.

32. H. Whiting, "M'Kenney's Tour to Lake Superior," *North American Review* 25 (October 1827):334; Hans Huth, *Nature and the American* (Berkeley: University of California Press, 1957), 77–79; McKinsey, *Niagara Falls*, 127, 148.

33. John F. Sears, "Timothy Dwight and the American Landscape: The Composing Eye in Dwight's *Travels in New England and New York*," *Early American Literature* 11 (Winter 1976):311–21; Peter M. Briggs, "Timothy Dwight 'Composes' a Landscape for New England," *American Quarterly* 40 (September 1988):359–77, quotation from Dwight's *Travels*, vol. 2, 372.

34. James T. Flexner, *The Light of Distant Skies* (New York: Dover, 1969, 221–25; Charlotte M. Porter, *The Eagle's Nest: Natural History and American Ideas* (University: University of Alabama Press, 1986), 159–76.

35. Timothy Flint, *A Condensed Geography and History of the Western States, or the Mississippi Valley* (1828) (Gainesville, Fla.: Scholars' Facsimiles & Reprints, 1970), ix–xii, 10–11.

36. Jeffrey Rubin-Dorsky, "A Crisis of Identity: *The Sketch Book* and Nineteenth-Century American Culture," in *Prospects*, ed. Jack Salzman. (Cambridge: Cambridge University Press, 1987), 12:273; John R. Stilgoe, *The Common Landscape of America, 1580–1845* (New Haven: Yale University Press, 1982), 104; Hendrik Hartog, *Public Property and Private Power: The Corporation of the City of New York in American Law, 1730–1870* (Chapel Hill: University of North Carolina Press, 1983), 159–67.

37. Emory Washburn, address to the Worcester Agricultural Society, quoted in *North American Review* 24 (April 1827):483; Jehlen, *American Incarnation*, 66–68; Shalhope, *John Taylor of Caroline*, 108–10, 136–42.

38. Timothy Flint, *Recollections of the Last Ten Years in the Valley of the Mississippi* (1826); Carbondale: Southern Illinois University Press, 1968), 41.

39. Wilson is quoted in Egerton, "Ecological Studies", 334; *The Pioneers*, 247–49, 231–39; *The Prairie*, 79; Donald A. Ringe, "Man and Nature in Cooper's *The Prairie*," *Nineteenth Century Fiction*, 15 (March 1961):313–23.

40. "Woodman Spare That Tree" is in Charles L. Sanford, ed., *Quest for America, 1810–1824* (Garden City, N.Y.: Doubleday, 1964), 460–68.

41. M. R. Audubon and Elliott Coues, *Audubon and His Journals*, vol. 1 (London, 1898), 182; William Cullen Bryant, "An Indian at the burial-Place of his Fathers" (1823), in *Poems*, 66.

42. Philip Freneau, "On the Uniformity and Perfection of Nature," in *A Freneau Sampler*, ed. Philip M. Marsh (New York: Scarecrow Press, 1963), 123.

Chapter Six

1. Everett quoted in Fred Lewis Pattee, *The First Century of American Literature, 1770–1870* (New York: Cooper Square Publishers, 1966), 171.

2. Joy S. Kasson, *Artistic Voyagers: Europe and the American Imagination in the Works of Irving, Allston, Cole, Cooper, and Hawthorne* (Westport, Conn.: Greenwood Press, 1982), 187–90; Washington Irving, *The Sketchbook* (1819) (New York: Library of America, 1983), 744.

3. Bryant quoted in Kasson, *Artistic Voyagers*, 94–95; John Griscom, *A Year in Europe* (New York, 1823), 251; Jared B. Flagg, ed., *The Life and Letters of Washington Allston* (New York: Benjamin Blom, 1969), 55.

4. Harold E. Dickson, *Arts of the Young Republic: The Age of William Dunlap* (Chapel Hill: University of North Carolina Press, 1968), 24–37.

5. Wayne Craven, "The Grand Manner in Early Nineteenth-Century American Painting: Borrowings from Antiquity, the Renaissance, and the Baroque," *American Art Journal* 11 (April 1979):5–43; Mark Thistlethwaite, "The Most Important Themes: Historical Painting and Its Place in American Art," in William H. Gerdts and Mark Thistlethwaite, *Grand Illusions: History Painting in America* (Fort Worth, Texas: Amon Carter Museum, 1988), 21.

6. James I. Flexner, *The Light of Distant Skies: American Painting, 1760–1835* (New York: Dover Publications, 1969), 143–53, 170–82.

7. Dickson, *Arts of the Young Republic*, 54; Flexner, *Light of Distant Skies;* William H. Gerdts, "On Elevated Heights: American Historical Painting and Its Critics," in Gerdts and Thistlethwaite, *Grand Illusions*, 61–123.

8. Carl Diehl, *Americans and German Scholarship, 1770–1870* (New Haven: Yale University Press, 1978), 49–100; Orie William Long, *Literary Pioneers: Early American Explorers of European Culture* (New York: Russell and Russell 1963 [1935], 12–13; Reinhold, *Classica Americana*, 207.

9. Long, *Literary Pioneers*, 19–20, 122; Diehl, *Americans and German Scholarship*, 89; Lilian Handlin, *George Bancroft: The Intellectual as Democrat* (New York: Harper & Row, 1986), 62–63.

10. Reinhold, *Classica Americana*, 204–11; Diehl, *Americans and German Scholarship*, 1–5.

11. Frederick Rudolph, *The American College and University: A History* (New York: Alfred A. Knopf, 1962), 112–43; Novak, *Rights of Youth*, 164–67.

12. Spencer, *Quest for Nationality*, 90–91; Charvat, *Origins of American Critical Thought*, 60–65.

13. For the campaign for literary nationalism see Spencer, *The Quest for Nationality*, and the essays by Tudor (1815), Knapp (1818), and Palfrey (1821) in Rutland, ed., *The Native Muse*, 1:93–113, 132, 160–64.

14. Charvat, *Profession of Authorship in America, 1800–1870*, 30–39; Frank Luther Mott, *Golden Multitudes: The Story of Best Sellers in the United States* (New York: R. R. Bowker & Co. 1947), 67–69; Ralph Leslie Rusk, *The Literature of the Middle Western Frontier* (New York: Columbia University Press 1925), 1:12–13.

15. Cooper is quoted in John P. McWilliams, "Red Satan: Cooper and the American Indian Epic," in Robert Clarke, ed., *James Fenimore Cooper: New Critical Essays* (Totowa, N.J.: Barnes & Noble, 1985), 149; Spencer, *Quest for Nationality*, 96.

16. James D. Wallace, *Early Cooper and His Audience* (New York: Columbia University Press 1986), 118–23.

17. Cooper, in Robert E. Spiller, *The American Literary Revolution, 1783–1837* (Garden City, N.Y.: Anchor Books, 1967), 400.

18. G. Harrison Orians, "The Romance Ferment after *Waverley*," *American Literature* 3 (January 1932):424; Henry James, *Hawthorne* (London: Macmillan, 1967), 55; Howard Mumford Jones, *O Strange New World: American Culture: The Formative Years* (New York: Viking Press, 1964), 349–350.

19. Goodrich, *Recollections of a Lifetime*, 2:103–7; Charvat, *Origins of American Critical Thought, 1810–1835*, 23–26; Marsh is quoted in Lewis S. Feuer, "James Marsh and the Conservative Transcendentalist Philosophy: A Political Interpretation," *New England Quarterly* 31 (March 1958): 11.

20. Edward Tyrrell Channing, in Spiller, ed., *American Literary Revolution*, 154–62.

21. Bryant, in ibid., 203; Neal quoted in Spencer, *Quest for Nationality*, 131.

22. Doreen M. Hunter, *Richard Henry Dana, Sr.* (Boston: Twayne Publishers, 1987), 20–25, 30–39.

23. William Ellery Channing, "Remarks on the Character and Writings of John Milton," in *The Works of William E. Channing* (Boston: American Unitarian Association, 1877), 498–99, 497, 503.

24. Charvat, *Origins of American Critical Thought, 1810–1835*, 14–26; *North American Review* quoted on p. 25; Hunter, *Richard Henry Dana*, 40; Doreen Hunter, "America's First Romantics: Richard Henry Dana, Sr., and Washington Allston," *New England Quarterly* 45 (March 1972):3–30.

25. Andrew Delbanco, *William Ellery Channing: An Essay on the Liberal Spirit in America* (Cambridge: Harvard University Press, 1981), 173–79; Handlin, *George Bancroft*, 105. Bancroft quoted in G. Harrison Orians, "The Rise of Romanticism 1805–1855," in Clark, *Transitions*, 172, and Bryant in Ferguson, *Law and Letters*, 182.

26. Larry J. Reynolds, *James Kirke Paulding* (Boston: Twayne Publishers, 1984), 31.

27. J. G. Palfrey, *North American Review* 10 (January 1820):204.

28. Ferguson, *Law and Letters*, 79; Adams quoted in Boorstin, *The Americans: The National Experience*, 310, 313.

29. [Edward Everett], "Phi Beta Kappa Orations," *North American Review* 24 (January 1827):131–32.

30. Washington Irving, "Salmagundi," paper no. 7 (New York: Library of America Edition, 1983), 144.

31. "Intellectual Economy," *Atlantic Magazine* 2 (February 1825):278.

32. Charles Jared Ingersoll, "A Discourse Concerning the Influence of America on the Mind," in Spiller, *American Literary Revolution*, 244, 253, 255–56.

33. John F. Kasson, *Civilizing the Machine: Technology and Republican Values in America, 1776–1900* (Harmondsworth, England: Penguin Books Ltd. 1977), 146–47; Brooke Hindle, "The Underside of the Learned Society in New York, 1754–1854," In Oleson and Brown, *Pursuit of Knowledge*, 101; Jacob Bigelow, in Wood, ed., *Rising Glory of America*, 251; second Bigelow quotation in *North American Review* 30 (April 1830):342.

34. Kasson, *Civilizing the Machine*, 23–24, 154–58; Sanford, *Quest for America*,

98; Joseph Gurn, *Charles Carroll of Carrollton, 1737–1832* (New York: P. J. Kenedy & Sons, 1932), 256–57.

35. Miller, *Life of the Mind in America*, 297.

36. "The Meeting of the Waters," in Sanford, *Quest for America*, 332–35.

37. Hugh S. Legaré in ibid., 18.

38. Edward Everett, "Oration on the Peculiar Motives to Intellectual Exertion in America," in Spiller, *American Literary Revolution*, 284–318, quotations 311, 303, 317, 294. This speech is often printed with the title: "The Circumstances Favorable to the Progress of Literature in America."

39. Daniels, *American Science in the Age of Jackson*, 34–35, 106; John C. Greene, "Science and the Public in the Age of Jefferson," in Brooke Hindle, ed., *Early American Science* (New York: Science History Publications, 1976), 201–13; [Ware] review of "Gorham's Chemistry," *North American Review* 9 (1819):114, 134–35.

40. Greene, *American Science in the Age of Jefferson*, 277–319; Daniels, *American Science*, 38–39.

41. Daniels, *American Science*, 36, 60–61; Porter, *Eagle's Nest*, 147.

42. Bruce Sinclair, "Science, Technology, and the Franklin Institute," in Oleson and Brown, eds., *Pursuit of Knowledge*, 194–207.

43. "Historical Overview" in *Transactions of the New York Academy of Sciences*, ser. 2, vol. 37 (1975); Bender, *New York Intellect*, 70–75; Patsy A. Gerstner, "The Academy of Natural Sciences of Philadelphia, 1812–1850," in Oleson and Brown, eds., *Pursuit of Knowledge*, 174–93.

44. Miller, *Patrons and Patriotism*, 101–2, 110; Bender, *New York Intellect*, 126–30.

45. David S. Reynolds, *Beneath the American Renaissance* (New York: Knopf, 1988), 59–61, 170–76, 449; Arthur F. Moore, *The Frontier Mind* (Lexington: University of Kentucky Press, 1957), 127. See also Constance Rourke, *American Humor* (New York: Harcourt, Brace & Co., 1931), chap. 6.

46. Paul Johnson, "'Art' and the Language of Progress in Early Industrial Paterson: Sam Patch at Clinton Bridge," *American Quarterly* 40 (December 1988):433–49; Susan G. Davis, *Parades and Power: Street Theater in Nineteenth Century Philadelphia* (Philadelphia: Temple University Press, 1986), 78–85.

47. Joseph J. Ellis, *After the Revolution: Profiles of Early American Culture* (New York: W. W. Norton & Co., 1979), 130–34; David Grimsted, *Melodrama Unveiled: American Theater and Culture 1800–1850* (Berkeley: University of California Press, 1987 [1968]), 31–32.

48. Lawrence W. Levine, *Highbrow/Lowbrow: The Emergence of Cultural Hierarchy in America* (Cambridge: Harvard University Press, 1988), 12–81, minimizes the degree of cultural separation; Grimsted, *Melodrama Unveiled*, 115–17, 171–231, 78–83.

49. Ellis, *After the Revolution*, 113–58; Paulding quoted in Reynolds, *James Kirke Paulding*, 83.

Chapter Seven

1. Robert Wiebe, *The Opening of American Society* (New York: Alfred A. Knopf 1984) 202–3, 215–16.

2. Philip F. Detweiler, "Congressional Debate on Slavery and the Declaration

of Independence, 1819–1821," *American Historical Review* 63 (April 1958):598–616; Major L. Wilson, *Space, Time and Freedom: The Quest for Nationality and the Irrepressible Conflict* (Westport, Conn.: Greenwood Press, 1974), 22–48.

3. Wilson, *Space, Time and Freedom*, 32–35.

4. Robert E. Shalhope, "Thomas Jefferson's Republicanism and Antebellum Southern Thought," *Journal of Southern History* 42 (November 1976):529–556; Kathryn R. Malone, "The Fate of Revolutionary Republicanism in Early National Virginia," *Journal of the Early Republic* 7 (Spring 1987):27–51; Wilson, *Space, Time and Freedom*, 33–34.

5. Shalhope, "Thomas Jefferson's Republicanism," 552.

6. Patricia Cline Cohen, *A Calculating People: The Spread of Numeracy in Early America* (Chicago: University of Chicago Press, 1982), 150–74; Kammen, *Season of Youth;* Fred Somkin, *Unquiet Eagle: Memory and Desire in the Idea of American Freedom, 1815–1860* (Ithaca: Cornell University Press 1967), 68.

7. Somkin, *Unquiet Eagle*, 131–74.

8. Kammen, *Season of Youth*, 43–49; Bryant is quoted in Somkin, *Unquiet Eagle*, 54.

9. Daniel Webster, "The Bunker Hill Monument" (1825), in *Select American Classics* (New York: American Book Company, 1896), 42; George B. Forgie, *Patricide in the House Divided: A Psychological Interpretation of Lincoln and His Age* (New York: W. W. Norton & Co., 1979), 50–53.

10. Morton J. Horwitz, *The Transformation of American Law, 1780–1860* (Cambridge: Harvard University Press, 1977), 63–109, 160–211.

11. R. Kent Newmyer, *The Supreme Court under Marshall and Taney* (Arlington Heights, Ill.: Harlan Davidson, 1968) 56–89; William B. Scott, *In Pursuit of Happiness* (Bloomington: Indiana University Press, 1977), 114–32.

12. Conkin, *Prophets of Prosperity*, McVickar quoted in Joseph Dorfman and R. G. Tugwell, *Early American Policy: Six Columbia Contributors* (Plainview, N. Y.: Books for Libraries Press, 1972), 132.

13. Daniel Raymond, *The Elements of Political Economy* (Baltimore, 1823), 2: 26, 225.

14. Conkin, *Prophets of Prosperity*, 76–107.

15. McCoy, *Elusive Republic*, 255–56.

16. Merrill D. Peterson, *Democracy, Liberty, and Property: The State Constitutional Conventions of the 1820s* (Indianapolis: Bobbs-Merrill, 1966), 64–65.

17. Ibid., 67; Scott, *In Pursuit of Happiness*, 75–79, 102–4; Carl Siracusa, *A Mechanical People: Perceptions of the Industrial Order in Massachusetts 1815–1880* (Middletown, Conn.: Wesleyan University Press, 1979), 82–115.

18. Kasson, *Civilizing the Machine*, 80.

19. Edward Everett, in Michael Brewster Folsom and Steven D. Lubar, eds., *The Philosophy of Manufactures: Early Debates over Industrialization in the United States* (Cambridge: MIT Press, 1982), 281–94.

20. Scott, *In Pursuit of Happiness*, 80–89; Wilentz, *Chants Democratic*, 176–216; Kamen, *Season of Youth*, 45.

21. Raymond A. Mohl, *Poverty in New York, 1783–1825* (New York: Oxford University Press, 1971), 116.

22. The Boston Report, written by Josiah Quincy (1822), quoted in Michael S. Hindus, *Prison and Plantation: Crime, Justice and Authority in Massachusetts and South Carolina, 1767–1878* (Chapel Hill: University of North Carolina Press 1980), 234; David Rothman, *The Discovery of the Asylum* (Boston: Little, Brown, 1971), 165–7; Michael B. Katz, *In the Shadow of the Poorhouse: A Social History of Welfare in America* (New York: Basic Books, 1986), 17–24.

23. Ibid., M. J. Heale, "From City Fathers to Social Critics: Humanitarianism and Government in New York, 1790–1860," *Journal of American History* 63 (June 1976):21–41, and "Humanitarianism in the Early Republic: The Moral Reformers of New York, 1776–1825," *Journal of American Studies* 2 (October 1968):161–75.

24. Larry E. Sullivan, "Books, Power, and the Development of Libraries in the New Republic: The Prison and Other Journals of John Pintard of New York," *Journal of Library History* 21 (Spring 1986):407–24.

25. Hindus, *Prison and Plantation*, 166; Myra C. Glenn, *Campaigns against Corporal Punishment* (Albany: State University of New York Press, 1984), 141–42.

26. Thomas L. Dumm, *Democracy and Punishment: Disciplinary Origins of the United States* (Madison: University of Wisconsin Press, 1987), 87–112.

27. Ibid., 106–7; Negley K. Teeters, *They Were in Prison* (Chicago: John C. Winston Co., 1937), 178.

28. Rothman, *Discovery of the Asylum*, 64–69; Prison Discipline Society (Boston) Fourth Annual Report (1829), in David Brion Davis, *AnteBellum American Culture: An Interpretive Anthology* (Lexington, Mass.: D.C. Heath, 1979), 32.

29. Karl F. Kaestle, *Pillars of the Republic: Common Schools and American Society, 1780–1860* (New York: Hill & Wang, 1983); [Sparks], *North American Review* 13 (October 1821):336–37. Webster quoted in George Ticknor, "Free Schools of New England," *North American Review* 19 (October 1824):451–52; Carroll is in Rush Welter, ed., *American Writings on Popular Education* (Indianapolis: Bobbs-Merrill, 1971), 31–32.

30. See, for example, the reviews of Carter's *Essays* in the *North American Review* 24 (January 1827), by Orville Dewey, 156–68; by George Ticknor, ibid. 19 (October 1824):448–57; *United States Literary Gazette* 1 (1824), 185–88, and ibid., December 1, 1825, 170–79; and *United States Review and Literary Gazette* 1 (February 1827):346–68.

31. Ketcham, *Presidents above Party*, 136.

32. A. Hunter Dupree, *Science in the Federal Government* (Cambridge: Harvard University Press, 1957), 41; Ketcham, *Presidents above Party*, 138.

33. Ketcham, *Presidents above Party*, 137–38.

34. Hofstadter, *Anti-intellectualism in American Life*, 159.

35. Frank Otto Gatell and John M. McFaul, *Jacksonian America, 1815–1840* (Englewood Cliffs, N.J.: Prentice-Hall, 1970), 116–20.

36. Jefferson to Lafayette, 14 May 1817, quoted in Sisson, *American Revolution of 1800*, 63; Ketcham, *Presidents above Party*, 150–54; Robert V. Remini, *The Legacy of Andrew Jackson* (Baton Rouge: Louisiana State University Press, 1988), 8; Jefferson in *The Portable Thomas Jefferson*, ed. Merrill D. Peterson (New York: Viking Penguin Inc., 1977), 585.

37. Quoted in Ralph Waldo Emerson, *Young Emerson Speaks: Unpublished Discourses on Many Subjects*, ed. Arthur Cushman McGiffert, Jr. (New York: Houghton Mifflin, 1938), 217, note.

Bibliographic Essay

A good selection of documents is in Chales L. Sanford, ed., *Quest for America, 1810–1824* (Garden City, N.Y.: Doubleday & Co., 1964), and in Robert E. Spiller, *The American Literary Revolution, 1783–1837* (Garden City, N.Y.: Doubleday & Co., 1967). A more recent collection is *The Rising Glory of America, 1760–1820*, with a brilliant introduction by Gordon Wood (New York: George Braziller, 1971). Other useful collections are: Perry Miller, *The Legal Mind in America. From Independence to the Civil War* (Garden City, N.Y.: Doubleday & Co., 1962); Merrill D. Peterson, ed., *Democracy, Liberty and Property: The State Constitutional Conventions of the 1820s* (Indianapolis: Bobbs-Merrill, 1966); and Rush Welter, ed., *American Writings on Popular Education* (Indianapolis: Bobbs-Merrill, 1971).

Jefferson is a key figure for this period. The literature on him is vast, but a good place to begin is Merrill D. Peterson, ed., *Thomas Jefferson: A Reference Biography* (New York: Scribners, 1986). A useful brief selection from his writings is in *The Portable Thomas Jefferson*, ed. Merrill D. Peterson (New York: Viking Penguin Inc., 1977). A fascinating introduction to his mind is his correspondence with John Adams, available in Lester J. Cappon, ed., *The Adams-Jefferson Letters* (Chapel Hill: University of North Carolina Press, 1959), 2 vols. Charles A. Miller, *Jefferson and Nature* (Baltimore: Johns Hopkins University Press, 1988), shows the centrality of nature for Jefferson's thought. The letters of Benjamin Rush are also interesting, especially his correspondence with John Adams, in *The Spur of Fame: Dialogues of John Adams and Benjamin Rush, 1805–1813*, eds. John A. Schutz and Douglass Adair (San Marino, Calif.: Huntington Library, 1966). The *Autobiography of Lyman Beecher*, ed. Barbara M. Cross (Cambridge: Belknap Press of Harvard University Press, 1961), put together by his children, is unexpectedly lively reading.

A good selection of extracts from the major reviews of the period is Richard Rutland, ed., *The Native Muse. Theories of American Literature* (New York: Dutton, 1972), and also Lewis P. Simpson, *The Federalist Literary Mind: Selections from the*

"Monthly Anthology and Boston Review," 1803–1811 (Baton Rouge: Louisiana State University Press, 1962). Finally, Alexis de Tocqueville's *Democracy in America* (ed. J. P. Meyer [Garden City, N.Y.: Doubleday, 1966]) remains a penetrating exploration of American society in the early 1830s.

Any overview of this period should begin with Henry Adams's classic surveys of the American mind in 1800 and in 1817 in his *The History of the United States of America during the Administrations of Jefferson and Madison*, conveniently abridged by Ernest Samuels (Chicago: University of Chicago Press, 1967). His picture of the somnolent nature of American life in 1800 is corrected by Noble E. Cunningham in *The United States in 1800: Henry Adams Revisited* (Charlottesville: University of Virginia Press, 1988), and by Gordon S. Wood, "The Significance of the Early Republic," *Journal of the Early Republic* 8 (Spring 1988), an important interpretation.

The most thorough modern survey of intellectual life is Russel Blaine Nye, *The Cultural Life of the New Nation, 1776–1830* (New York: Harper & Row, 1960), which has a good bibliography of books published to 1960, and Thomas P. Slaughter, "The Historian's Quest for Early American Culture(s), c. 1750–1825," *American Studies International* 24 (April 1986): 29–59, is an excellent review of some important recent literature. Perry Miller's brilliant *The Life of the Mind in America: From the Revolution to the Civil War* (New York: Harcourt, Brace and World, 1965) is particularly good on legal thinking, and Daniel Boorstin, *The Americans: The National Experience* (New York: Random House, 1965), is crammed with interesting information and insights. Richard D. Brown, *Knowledge Is Power: The Diffusion of Information in Early America: 1700–1865* (New York: Oxford University Press, 1989), is an innovative approach to intellectual history.

Henry F. May, *The Enlightenment in America* (New York: Oxford University Press, 1976), is crucial to understanding the ways in which the Enlightenment was assimilated and transformed in the early nineteenth century. Ralph Ketcham's two excellent books, *From Colony to Country: The Revolution in American Thought, 1750–1820* (New York, 1974), and *Presidents above Party: The First American Presidency, 1789–1829* (Chapel Hill: University of North Carolina Press, 1984), and Robert H. Wiebe, *The Opening of American Society* (New York: Alfred A. Knopf, 1984), are important interpretations. Steven Watts, *The Republic Reborn: War and the Making of Liberal America, 1790–1820* (Baltimore: Johns Hopkins University Press, 1987), is a fascinating intellectual and psychological interpretation of the cultural tensions leading up to the War of 1812.

Lawrence J. Friedman, *Inventors of the Promised Land* (New York: Alfred A. Knopf, 1975), is particularly good on early nineteenth-century attitudes toward blacks and women. Jan Lewis, *The Pursuit of Happiness: Family and Values in Jefferson's Virginia* (Cambridge: Cambridge University Press, 1983), is a contribution to the new "history of feeling." Thomas Bender, *New York Intellect: A History of Intellectual Life in New York City from 1750 to the Beginnings of Our Own Time* (New York: Alfred A. Knopf 1987), and Richard Beale Davis, *Intellectual Life in Jefferson's Virginia, 1790–1830* (Knoxville: University of Tennessee Press, 1972), cover intellectual life in local context. Meyer Reinhold, *Classica Americana: The Greek and Roman Heritage in the United States* (Detroit: Wayne State University Press, 1984), is the most comprehensive work on the role of the classics in cultural life. A good introduction to Scots Common Sense philosophy can be found in Douglas Sloan, *The Scottish Enlightenment and the American College Ideal*

(New York: Teachers College Press, 1971), and Mark A. Noll, "Common Sense Traditions and American Evangelical Thought," *American Quarterly* 37 (Summer 1985):216–38. Carl Diehl, *Americans and German Scholarship, 1770–1870* (New Haven, Yale University Press, 1978), is an excellent work on the experience of American scholars in Germany. Richard M. Rollins, *The Long Journey of Noah Webster* (Philadelphia: University of Pennsylvania Press, 1980), is a useful intellectual biography, and Joseph J. Ellis, *After the Revolution: Profiles of Early American Culture* (New York. W. W. Norton & Co., 1979), discusses a number of significant individuals, including Noah Webster and William Dunlap.

The special issue "Republicanism in the History and Historiography of the United States," *American Quarterly* 37 (Fall 1985), covers many aspects of republicanism as an ideology. The most recent summary of the debate over republicanism and liberalism is Lance Banning, "Jeffersonian Ideology Revisited: Liberal and Classical Ideas in the New American Republic," *William and Mary Quarterly* 43 (January 1986):3–19. The most important historians interpreting Jeffersonian America in terms of republican ideas are Lance Banning, *The Jeffersonian Persuasion: Evolution of a Party Ideology* (Lawrence: University of Kansas Press, 1978); Drew R. McCoy, *The Elusive Republic: Political Economy in Jeffersonian America* (Chapel Hill: University of North Carolina Press, 1980); and Robert E. Shalhope, *John Taylor of Caroline: Pastoral Republican* (Columbia, S.C.: University of South Carolina Press, 1980). For the Jeffersonians as liberals, see Joyce Appleby, "Republicanism in Old and New Contexts," *William and Mary Quarterly* 43 (January 1986): 20–34; "What Is Still American in the Political Philosophy of Thomas Jefferson?" *William and Mary Quarterly* 39 (April 1982):287–309; and *Capitalism and a New Social Order: The Republican Vision of the 1790s* (New York: Oxford University Press, 1984). John P. Diggins, in his provocative *The Lost Soul of American Politics* (New York: Basic Books, 1984), plays down the influence of republicanism and insists that liberalism has always been the central American ideology. See also John M. Murrin, "Gordon S. Wood and the Search for Liberal America," *William and Mary Quarterly* 44 (July 1987):597–601, and Gordon Wood, "Ideology and the Origins of Liberal America," in the same issue, 628–40. James T. Kloppenberg, "The Virtues of Liberalism: Christianity, Republicanism, and Ethics in Early American Political Discourse," *Journal of American History* 74 (June 1987):9–33, reminds us of the importance of Christian values in the early republic as well as the moral dimension of liberalism. For artisan republicanism, see Sean Wilentz, *Chants Democratic: New York City and the Rise of the American Working Class, 1788–1850* (New York: Oxford University Press, 1984).

Linda Kerber, *Federalists in Dissent* (Ithaca: Cornell University Press, 1980), is excellent on the Federalist "mind." Andrew R. Clayton, *The Frontier Republic: Ideology and Politics in the Ohio Country, 1780–1825* (Kent: Kent State University Press, 1986), deals very well with the tensions between those men with projects of various kinds and those who merely wished to be let alone in a frontier context. Major L. Wilson, *Space, Time and Freedom: The Quest for Nationality and the Irrepressible Conflict* (Westport, Conn.: Greenwood Press, 1974), posits a basic philosophical division between those believing in centrifugal geographical expansion and those wishing to plan for development over time. John William Ward, *Andrew Jackson: Symbol for an Age* (London: Oxford University Press, 1980), remains the classic exposition of the meaning of the Jackson phenomenon.

The literature on American religion in this period is extensive. A good overview of the Second Great Awakening is in William G. McLouglin, *Revivals, Awakenings, and Reform* (Chicago: University of Chicago Press, 1978), and Donald G. Mathews, *Religion in the Old South* (Chicago: University of Chicago Press, 1977) and his important article, "The Second Great Awakening as an Organizing Process, 1780–1830: An Hypothesis," *American Quarterly* 21 (Spring 1969):23–43. The standard work on the Unitarians, which is also informative on the cultural ambience of New England, is Daniel Walker Howe, *The Unitarian Conscience: Harvard Moral Philosophy, 1805–61* (Cambridge: Harvard University Press, 1970). On Channing see also Andrew DelBanco, *William Ellery Channing* (Cambridge: Harvard University Press, 1981). Donald M. Scott, *From Office to Profession: The New England Ministry, 1750–1850* (Philadelphia: University of Pennsylvania Press, 1978), is an important book on changes in the status and function of the minister in New England. Nathan O. Hatch, *The Democratization of American Christianity* (New Haven: Yale University Press, 1989), is an important book on the popular aspects of the revivals. For the extensive networks of evangelical reform organizations, see Charles I. Foster, *An Errand of Mercy: The Evangelical United Front, 1790–1837* (Chapel Hill: University of North Carolina Press, 1960), and Clifford S. Griffin, *Their Brothers' Keepers: Moral Stewardship in the United States* (New Brunswick, N.J.: Rutgers University Press, 1960).

The standard account of literary nationalism is Benjamin T. Spencer, *The Quest for Nationality: An American Literary Campaign* (Syracuse: Syracuse University Press, 1957). William Charvat, *The Profession of Authorship in America, 1800–1870*, ed. Matthew J. Bruccoli (Columbus: Ohio State University Press, 1968), and his *The Origins of American Critical Thought, 1810–1835* (New York: A. S. Barnes & Co., 1961), are standard works. Cathy Davidson, *Revolution and the Word: The Rise of the Novel in America* (New York: Oxford University Press, 1986), pays attention to the popular novels of the period. Terence Martin, *The Instructed Vision: Scottish Common Sense Philosophy and the Origins of American Fiction* (Bloomington: Indiana University Press, 1961), is good on the philosophical background to the antinovel feeling in the early republic.

Robert A. Ferguson, *Law and Letters in American Culture* (Cambridge: Harvard University Press, 1984), is a superb piece of intellectual history, as well as a sensitive reading of Jefferson, Irving, Bryant, and others. Also illuminating for intellectual history is Emory Elliott, *Revolutionary Writers: Literature and Authority in the New Republic, 1725–1810* (New York: Oxford University Press, 1982). Van Wyck Brooks, *The World of Washington Irving* (London: J. M. Dent 1947), is a charming book. Two important recent books on language are Dennis E. Baron, *Grammar and Good Taste: Reforming the American Language* (New Haven: Yale University Press, 1982), and David Simpson, *The Politics of American English, 1776–1850* (New York: Oxford University Press, 1986). For the connection between literature and art, see Donald A. Ringe, *The Pictorial Mode* (Lexington: University Press of Kentucky, 1971). For the theater, see David Grimsted, *Melodrama Unveiled: American Theater and Culture, 1800–1850* (Berkeley: University of California Press, 1987). There is a huge literature on Cooper; one of the best of the recent works for the historian is James D. Wallace, *Early Cooper and His Audience* (New York: Columbia University Press, 1986).

On the arts, Neil Harris, *The Artist in American Society: The Formative Years, 1790–1860* (Chicago: University of Chicago Press, 1982), is the best introduction.

James T. Flexner, *The Light of Distant Skies: American Painting, 1760–1835* (New York: Dover Publications, 1969), is a standard work, and Harold E. Dickson, *Arts of the Young Republic: The Age of William Dunlap* (Chapel Hill: University of North Carolina Press, 1968), gives a thorough discussion of a great variety of artistic expression. Alan Gowans, *Images of American Living: Four Centuries of Architecture and Furniture as Cultural Expression* (Philadelphia: J. B. Lippincott Co., 1964) is particularly good on the didactic function of neoclassicism. Lillian B. Miller, *Patrons and Patriotism: The Encouragement of the Fine Arts in the United States, 1790–1860* (Chicago: University of Chicago Press, 1966), is excellent on institutional developments in the art world and on individual art patrons. Also useful and interesting are J. Meredith Neill, *Toward a National Taste: America's Quest for Aesthetic Independence* (Honolulu: University Press of Hawaii, 1975), and Joy S. Kasson, *Artistic Voyagers: Europe and the American Imagination in the Works of Irving, Allston, Cole, Cooper, and Hawthorne* (Westport, Conn.: Greenwood Press, 1982).

An explosion of good legal history in recent years links legal development to crucial changes in the economy and society. Among the most important works are Richard E. Ellis, *The Jeffersonian Crisis: Courts and Politics in the Young Republic* (New York: W. W. Norton & Co., 1971), and R. Kent Newmyer, *The Supreme Court under Marshall and Taney* (Arlington Heights, Ill.: Harlan Davidson, 1968). Two very useful books, whch contain brief explanatory essays and a number of important legal documents, are George Dargo, *Law in the New Republic: Private Law and the Public Estate* (New York: Alfred A. Knopf, 1983), and Jamil Zainaldin, *Law in Antebellum Society: Legal Change and Economic Expansion* (New York: Knopf, 1983). An extremely important and controversial work is Morton J. Horwitz, *The Transformation of American Law, 1780–1860* (Cambridge: Harvard University Press, 1977).

The two major books for the history of science in this period are John C. Greene, *American Science in the Age of Jefferson* (Ames: Iowa State University Press, 1984), and George H. Daniels, *Science in American Society: A Social History* (New York: Alfred A. Knopf, 1971). See also Daniels, *American Science in the Age of Jackson* (New York: Columbia University Press, 1966). Alexandra Oleson and Sanborn C. Brown, eds., *The Pursuit of Knowledge in the Early American Republic* (Baltimore: Johns Hopkins University Press, 1976), covers the organization of various learned societies. Herbert Hovenkamp, *Science and Religion in America, 1800–1860* (Philadelphia: University of Pennsylvania Press, 1978), deals with the accommodation between the two in this period. Charles Coleman Sellers, *Mr. Peale's Museum: Charles Willson Peale and the First Popular Museum of Natural Science and Art* (New York: W. W. Norton & Co., 1980), is the most thorough account of this fascinating and important phenomenon. Charlotte M. Porter, *The Eagle's Nest: Natural History and American Ideas, 1812–1842* (University: University of Alabama Press, 1986), is a full account of developments in American natural history.

Winthrop D. Jordan, *White over Black: American Attitudes towards the Negro, 1550–1812* (New York: W. W. Norton & Co., 1977), is brilliant and comprehensive. William Stanton, *The Leopard's Spots: Scientific Attitudes towards Race in America, 1815–1859* (Chicago: University of Chicago Press, 1960), takes up the story where Jordan ends. David Brion Davis, *The Problem of Slavery in the Age of Revolution, 1770–1823* (Ithaca: Cornell University Press 1975), places ideas about slavery in an international context.

The best recent works on the attitudes and policy of Jeffersonian America toward Indians are Bernard W. Sheehan, *Seeds of Extinction: Jeffersonian Philanthropy and the American Indian* (Chapel Hill: University of North Carolina Press, 1973), and Robert E. Beider, *Science Encounters the Indian, 1820–1880: The Early Years of American Ethnology* (Norman: University of Oklahoma Press, 1986), which is good on research into Indian languages. Richard Slotkin, *The Fatal Environment: The Myth of the Frontier in the Age of Industrialization, 1800–1890* (Middleton, Conn.: Wesleyan University Press, 1985), and his *Regeneration through Violence: The Mythology of the American Frontier, 1600–1860* (Middleton, Conn.: Wesleyan University Press, 1973), deal with white American fantasies about violence and Indians. For attitudes toward women, the most comprehensive work is Janet Wilson James, *Changing Ideas about Women in the United States 1776–1825* (New York: Garland, 1981), and for women's experience, see Nancy F. Cott, *The Bonds of Womanhood: "Woman's Sphere" in New England, 1780–1835* (New Haven: Yale University Press, 1977).

John F. Kasson, *Civilizing the Machine: Technology and Republican Values in America, 1776–1900* (Harmondsworth, England: Penguin Books, Ltd., 1977 [1976]), is fascinating. For economic thought in this period, see Paul K. Conkin, *Prophets of Prosperity: America's First Political Economists* (Bloomington: Indiana University Press, 1980). John R. Nelson, Jr., *Liberty and Property: Political Economy and Policymaking in the New Nation, 1789–1812* (Baltimore: Johns Hopkins University Press, 1987), is an interesting new interpretation of Jeffersonian political economy, stressing the centrality of economic development.

Index

Academy of Natural Sciences, 58, 99, 129

Adams, John, 8, 11, 72, 73, 78; on the arts, 59; on banking, 14; death of, 136; on oratory, 124; and sexual morality, 42

Adams, John Quincy, 56, 59, 61, 89, 96, 107, 133, 135; and Andrew Jackson, 150–51; on oratory, 123–24; philosophy of government, 149–50

Alexander, Archibald, 82

Allston, Washington, 58, 114–15

American Academy of Fine Arts, 63, 104

American Colonization Society, 84–85

American Journal of Science, 64, 103, 118, 129

American Philosophical Society, 49–50, 95, 101

Architecture, gothic, 146; neo-classical, 19–20

Audubon, John James, 99, 110

Bacon, Francis, cult of, 102

Bancroft, George, 116, 122–23

Barlow, Joel, on education, 18–19; on Francis Bacon, 102; and Lewis and Clark, 95; on liberty, 3; and Tom Paine, 29; *The Columbiad*, 54

Barton, Benjamin Smith, 98, 101

Beecher, Lyman, 44, 45; and Calvinism, 34–35; and Christian influence, 40

Bentley, William, 61

Bigelow, Jacob, 97, 125–26

Boone, Daniel, 106

Boston Athenaeum, 62, 63–64

Botany, 98, 128

Brackenridge, Hugh Henry, 23, 55, 56; *Modern Chivalry*, 9

British Critics, 56

Brown, Charles Brockden, 47, 49, 77–78, 97

Bryan, Daniel: *The Mountain Muse*, 106

Bryant, William Cullen, 49, 53, 114, 121; and nature, 105–6; on poetry, 123; "The Ages," 137

Buchanan, Joseph: *The Philosophy of Human Nature*, 73

Buckminster, Joseph Stevens, 61–62, 65, 123

Buffon, Georges Louis Leclerc, comte de, 97

Byron, Lord George Gordon, 121

Caldwell, Charles, 74, 81

Calhoun, John C., 16, 89, 133

Cardozo, Jacob, 141

Carey, Mathew, 50, 51, 119

Carroll, Charles, 126

Carter, James G., 148

Cartwright, Peter, 31

The Author

Jean Matthews was educated at the University of London, Smith College, and Harvard University. She is now an associate professor at the University of Western Ontario in Canada, where she teaches American and women's history. She is the author of *Rufus Choate: The Law and Civic Virtue* (Temple University Press, 1980), and is also the book review editor of the *Canadian Review of American Studies*.